THE
Fishing
HANDBOOK

WAYNE THOMAS

Published by SILVERDALE BOOKS
An imprint of Bookmart Ltd
Registered number 2372865
Trading as Bookmart Ltd
Blaby Road
Wigston
Leicester LE18 4SE

© 2004 D&S Books Ltd

D&S Books Ltd
Kerswell,
Parkham Ash, Bideford
Devon, England
EX39 5PR

e-mail us at:-
enquiries@dsbooks.fsnet.co.uk

ISBN 1-856058-80-8

DS0111 Fishing Handbook

Creative Director: Sarah King
Editor: Clare Haworth-Maden
Project Editor: Anna Southgate
Designer: Axis Design Editions

fonts: lapidary333, linotype didot

Printed in Hong Kong

1 3 5 7 9 10 8 6 4 2

Contents

INTRODUCTION 7

1 GETTING STARTED 10
Angling environments 14
Tackle 38
Knots and rigs 108
Bait 122
Lure-fishing 172
Fly-fishing 183
Casting 202

2 CATCHING FISH 214
A trout stream 220
A small still water 232
A large still water 240
Tempting predators with lures 258
Tempting predators with live and dead baits 272
Catching still-water trout 278
Salmon fishing 302
A river 314
Shore fishing 332
Saltwater boat-fishing 374
Hooking and landing fish 401

3 NATURAL FACTORS 414
The weather 418
The lunar cycle 427
Tides 428
Migrations 429
Spawning 431
Light values and time of day 433
An abundance of natural food 437
Geographical features 438

4 THE ROVING ROD 442
Angling holidays 446
Opportunistic angling 454
Match fishing 458

5 SAFETY 466
Fishing in deep water 469
Wading 470
Boat-angling 471
Fish hooks 473
Lines 474
Casting 475
Dangerous fish 476
Miscellaneous advice 478

6 ANGLING PHOTOGRAPHY 480
Choosing a camera 484
Taking photographs 487

7 CLUBS & ORGANISATIONS 490
Angling clubs 494
National & international angling bodies 496

8 THE FUTURE 498

A FINAL MESSAGE 506

INDEX 508
Credits and acknowledgements 512

Introduction

Fishing has been a big part of my life for the last thirty years or so. I started as a small boy, dangling worms into a brook, and progressed to catching sharks weighing more than 100lb (45.4kg). I am what is generally termed an all-rounder, casting my bait here and there for whatever catches my attention at the time.

Non-anglers often ask me what the attraction of fishing is, and I do not believe that there is a straight answer to this question. There are many obvious advantages, including taking you out into the open air, closer to nature. It can also be a very relaxing pastime; on the other hand, it can be demanding, too. I suppose that it all depends on the individual and on why one decides to take up the hobby. Many anglers enjoy wetting a line to relax and get away from school, the office or the pressures of life. Some become totally obsessed with the sport and devote every waking minute to it. Most of us fall somewhere in-between.

LEFT No angler can cross a bridge without peering into the waters beneath.

This book is an introduction to the wide world of angling. Note that most of what I have written in these pages is a matter of personal opinion, and that fishing is a sport in which right and wrong methods are difficult to define. It is certainly not all about catching fish. I look upon angling as a jigsaw puzzle, the fun being in slotting the pieces together. And while the final outcome is pleasing, the pleasure lasts for only for a short time because we immediately start on another puzzle.

There are many techniques that today's anglers use in their pursuit of fish, not least because each angling situation demands careful consideration on how it should be tackled. Many non-anglers fail to understand the need for different rods and reels, and certainly fail to comprehend why some anglers struggle along a bank or shore loaded down like sherpas on a Himalayan expedition. Don't let me give you the impression that you need a vast array of gear when you first start angling. At its simplest, fishing demands no more than a rod, line,

ABOVE A salmon is a fine reward for a day's fishing.

hook and bait. Indeed, a young angler can have plenty of fun with tackle that costs only a couple of weeks' pocket money. If you become hooked on the sport, however, you will probably build up a vast array of tackle. It is important to understand that each bit of kit is designed for a particular purpose: to put it simply, each rod or reel is a tool that performs a specific task. Some anglers branch out into collecting antique tackle or books, while others collect lures or tie artificial flies with which to tempt the fish that they seek.

Fishing can come to occupy more of your life than simply the time spent at the water's edge casting a line. Over the years, I have made many friends through my love of angling. I have become the secretary of my local angling club, which involves much correspondence and, at times, far too much hassle. I also write an angling column for my local newspaper and currently find myself writing a book. And because all of these angling-related activities have to be fitted around life's priorities, namely my family and work, I now have less time to go fishing. I have nevertheless always found time to go fishing and, I hope, always will. My enthusiasm for the sport has never deserted me, although I have seen many anglers lose interest over the years. One of the great things about angling is its ability to break down social barriers: a shared fascination with fish and fishing leads to people of vastly different backgrounds, cultures and religions coming together to debate or tell tales of the whopper that got away (or perhaps didn't).

If you take up angling, you should be rewarded by many hours of pleasure. You will, however, find it difficult to cross a bridge without peering into the stream or river below and wondering what lurks beneath. As you sit on a beach, you will probably find yourself looking out to sea and wondering what swims beneath that rippling blue sheet of water. When at work or at school, your mind may wander to the water's edge to plan your next trip or relive the last. I can assure you that if you become an angler, your life will become richer, but you will first have to cast out your line and see if you become hooked.

I will now take you through the basic principles of angling and will advise you on the equipment that you will need, where to go and how to tempt different species of fish in various environments in all seasons. Most importantly, I hope to help you to enjoy fishing.

Chapter 1

Getting started

The world of angling is wide and varied, so deciding where to start is not as easy as many would think. Your decision will be influenced to a large extent by your proximity to fisheries. And if you have friends who go fishing, they are an obvious starting point, so have a chat to them and try to join them on the bank to see what it's all about. Check local tackle shops or bookshops to see whether they sell any local angling guides that will give you some idea of the angling opportunities on your doorstep. Another source of information is the Internet, which is awash with angling websites.

BELOW Match anglers on a small still water.

Before I progress any further, I should probably discuss the different branches of angling and the various environments that you will encounter. There are three major categories within angling: coarse, sea and game. To make matters even more complicated, there is a vast range of differing modes of angling within these categories: within coarse angling, for example, there are what are termed 'pleasure anglers', 'match anglers' and 'specialist anglers', and sea and game fishing have similar subcategories.

If you are wondering about the difference between coarse, sea and game fish, I believe that a game fish is defined as having an adipose fin (a posterior dorsal fin). Game fish are basically members of the salmon family, although the grayling, which seems to fit within both the game and coarse categories, is an exception. Coarse fish are freshwater fish that do not have an adipose fin, such as carp and roach. Sea fish are fish that live in salt water. Yet the boundaries are often blurred between these definitions: the freshwater eel, for example, lives in fresh water for most of its life, but returns to the sea to spawn somewhere in the mid-Atlantic, which is why it is often caught in estuaries.

ABOVE A specimen bream is carefully returned.

I will explain the methods used for catching the species of fish within these groups in detail later in the book. At this point, however, it will probably be more helpful to explore the various environments in which you can fish, and the species of fish that you can expect to find within each.

Angling environments

I mentioned in the introduction how I used to fish in a brook as a child, and I was fortunate that there was a small stream flowing through the garden when I was growing up. This stream taught me much about watercraft and the basic principles of angling. I learned, for example, that in order to catch a fish, you must present a bait, or something that the fish believes to be edible, without scaring it. Much of what you see in a tiny brook is mirrored in a mighty river, which is why it is perhaps the ideal place for a beginner to start an angling journey.

Brooks and streams

Small fish weighing just a few ounces, or grams, generally inhabit small watercourses like brooks and streams. In the streams of my home county of Devon, brown trout are the predominant species. These are the fish that I tempted as a child by dangling a worm into the water. As an adult, I still enjoy tempting the same fish with an

RIGHT Small streams chatter merrily on their way.

BELOW The tranquil waters of a bridge pool.

artificial fly (as anglers mature, their approach may become more refined, and they may choose fishing methods for their aesthetic nature rather than their outright effectiveness).

Small streams are fascinating places to spend time beside as they chatter merrily along their way. Some streams contain such coarse fish as dace. Eels may also live here, but will not generally be of a size worth catching, and will often tangle the line into a horrible, slimy mess. I can remember as a child watching with bated breath as an eel sinuously approached my bait; there seemed to be something slightly creepy about it, I suppose because it was so snake-like. A young fisher will be happy to catch anything from minnows and sticklebacks through newts to insects. Indeed, many anglers are created when they first dip a net into a pond or stream.

Sadly, many brooks and streams have become polluted over the years, or have dried up as a result of overabstraction. Many still remain as charming as ever, however, and are perfect places for a young person to visit.

Rivers

As brooks and streams grow in size, they eventually become rivers. There is an extremely wide variety of river types, each with its own, distinctive character. Some rivers flow through varied landscapes, leading to several zones within a river system. The make-up of the land through which the river flows determines the nature of the environment, which in turn determines the species that live within the river.

ABOVE Fishing in sparkling waters.

RIGHT Each river has its own character.

NEXT PAGE The clear waters of a chalk stream.

ABOVE Each river is unique.

Let's follow an imaginary river from its source to the sea, exploring the different zones. Remember, however, that many rivers do not share the following characteristics. The chalk streams of southern England, for example, are crystal clear and rich in weeds and water life. Some rivers meander slowly from their source to the sea. Each river is unique, and part of the joy of angling is exploring, and becoming acquainted with, their peculiarities.

The upper reaches

The upper reaches tend to be fast-flowing, shallow and clear. Brown trout are abundant throughout this section of a river, and can provide exciting sport for the fly-fisherman during the spring

ABOVE Fly-fishing for brown trout.

and summer. During the winter months, salmon travel high up the upper reaches, to what are termed 'redds' (gravel beds), to spawn. The salmon are protected from anglers at this vulnerable time to safeguard future stocks.

The surrounding area is typically moorland or mountain, and there is limited food for the fish, which is why they are often small. The pH of the water is liable to be slightly acidic.

The middle reaches

Grayling and a few coarse fish, such as dace, join the brown trout in the middle reaches, which are fast-flowing and quite deep in parts. Salmon are also to be found, especially after spates (sudden floods), which encourage them to forge upstream.

Farm- and woodland dominate the landscape around the middle reaches. Food becomes more abundant for the species within the river, and the trout are potentially bigger. Herons, kingfishers and otters may hunt for fish alongside the angler.

BELOW The river landscape framed within autumn foliage.

ABOVE Anglers fish the majestic river Wye in Wales for grayling.

LEFT The river Wye meanders through farm and woodland.

The lower reaches

The fish dominate the wider, slower-moving lower reaches, whose water is usually tinged with colour. Good-sized bream, roach, chub, pike and carp can be caught down to the tidal limit, as well as slightly beyond.

Estuaries

The ebb and flood of the tide dominates the estuarial environment. At low tide, the muddy banks support flocks of wading birds as they feed on marine worms and other creatures. As the tide floods in, flounder, grey mullet and bass

LEFT A fine chub from the lower reaches.

BELOW The upper tidal section.

ABOVE The muddy tidal environment.

LEFT The estuary channels as seen from the air.

BELOW LEFT The tidal zone holds a wide range of food for birds and fish.

swim in in search of food. This tidal zone consists of brackish water, and it is sometimes possible to catch salt- and freshwater fish at the same location.

Estuaries vary greatly in character: some are short, rocky affairs; others are long and shrouded by woods; and still others are flanked by fields and marshes as they run inland for many miles.

Canals

Canals are manmade watercourses that lie somewhere between rivers and still waters in character. They are generally slow-moving waters that predominantly hold coarse-fish species, such as bream, tench and roach, along with the predatory pike and perch.

Canals were generally dug out to provide navigation for boats and ships, and how a canal is used today will significantly affect the fishing. Heavily-used canals will have little weed growth

ABOVE A predatory pike from a canal.

and coloured water as a result of boats or barges continually stirring up sediment from the bottom. Rarely-used canals may contain clear water and have heavy weed growth.

BELOW Water lilies in a perfect tench swim.

Still water

An enormous range of still water is available to the angler, including both natural and manmade lakes, reservoirs, tiny ponds, meres, quarry pits and gravel pits. Each of these types of water has developed its own, complex ecosystem, which the wise angler will try to understand. The location of the water to a large extent determines the life within. In addition, most of such waters in which we fish will have been artificially stocked to a greater or lesser degree.

Note that although I have used the term 'still water' to describe these bodies of water, the water is actually seldom still because it is almost always being moved by currents caused by springs or rivers flowing in and out of them. The wind will also create substantial movement of the water mass, especially on larger expanses.

There follows a brief outline of the different types of still water.

ABOVE Reflections in still waters.

ABOVE This brightly coloured golden orfe came from a small still water.

RIGHT A tree-shrouded lake.

Upland lakes, tarns, lochs and reservoirs

Upland lakes, tarns, lochs and reservoirs are often slightly acidic. Brown trout, rainbow trout and, in some cases, char can be found in them. Coarse fish will not generally be abundant, although a

ABOVE Casting a fly for the trout of an upland reservoir.

LEFT Angling boats at their moorings in Llyn Brenig, North Wales.

BELOW Enjoying the solitude.

LEFT The wild expanse of an upland lake.

few predatory species, such as pike and perch, are often to be found. Migratory fish like salmon and sea trout can be caught in some lakes and lochs through which river systems flow. Such fish as pike can grow to a large size in such

environments. Many reservoirs are heavily stocked with rainbow trout on a put-and-take basis to provide good sport for the fly-fisherman.

ABOVE Rainbow trout provide good sport.

ABOVE Admiring a fine rainbow trout.

Lowland lakes, reservoirs and meres

Numerous species of fish inhabit lowland lakes, reservoirs and meres, including many coarse fish, as well as put-and-take-stocked trout. The depth often determines the nature of these waters, and large, shallow waters generally have the most abundant weed growth and silt deposits, thus providing a rich habitat in which water life can flourish. In the ideal body of water, a food chain will develop that supports a huge range of fish.

Because they have been formed by the damming of a watercourse in a valley, reservoirs are often quite deep. The surrounding features will give clues as to what lies beneath the surface: a stream flowing into the reservoir will often indicate a deeper channel, for instance, while steep banks generally denote deep water close into the shoreline or bank. and a gently sloping bank the opposite. Reading the water is a skill that will be discussed later, under location (see pages 278 to 301).

Gravel pits and quarries

The building of roads and motorways linking our towns and cities has led to the excavation of vast areas of land in the form of gravel pits and quarries. When left alone, these excavations become

RIGHT A lowland lake.

BELOW Gravel pits provide anglers with a wealth of opportunity.

flooded, and are often landscaped and turned into recreation areas. Angling clubs may stock them with fish to provide exciting sport for their members.

These environments have proved to be very productive, in that the fish within them have grown to weights that were previously thought to be unfeasibly large.

Commercial pools

There has been a huge increase in small, heavily stocked waters in recent years.

ABOVE Anglers line the banks of a commercial fishery.

Carp are the fish that are most often stocked because they grow quickly, fight hard when hooked and are relatively hardy. Because the fish are relatively easy to catch and provide almost guaranteed sport, such commercial pools are ideal for the beginner or match angler.

The large amount of angler's bait introduced into these waters ensures good growth rates, despite the frequently small amounts of natural food available.

LEFT My son James cradles a carp from a popular day ticket fishery.

Ponds and pools

Ponds and pools, like brooks, are often the places where people first become anglers. Children will spend many happy hours dipping their nets into the smallest of pools, happy to catch any living creature, be it a tadpole or small fish. From here they may progress to fishing for the hordes of small fish, such as roach and perch, that will eagerly engulf a worm or maggot.

LEFT Displaying a fine golden orfe.

Such ponds produce the occasional big fish: perch that have grown to the extent that they dominate the food chain and devour their own young, for instance. Large eels can sometimes also be found lurking in a pond's lonely recess.

LEFT Father and son enjoy sport on a small pool.

BELOW A Crucian carp is carefully returned.

Saltwater fishing

Saltwater fishing is primarily the pursuit of fish that live within the sea or ocean. Note, however, that there is also a zone that is partway between fresh and salt water, namely estuaries or water systems in which salt and fresh water mix to form brackish water. The Baltic Sea, for instance, contains both fresh- and saltwater species, with large pike (freshwater fish) feeding on herrings (saltwater fish), thereby providing a good example of how a particular food chain can produce big fish.

A huge range of species can be found in the world's seas and oceans. My father used to tell me that the lure of sea angling is the unknown factor: the sea being totally wild, you can never tell what will take the bait (although after years of fishing, you can normally hazard an educated guess).

The biggest influence on the seas and oceans is the tides, which are created by the gravitational pull of the sun and moon. Spring tides occur during full and new moons, when there is the greatest movement of water. Neap tides are smaller, and occur between the spring tides. There are two high tides and two low tides over a twenty-four-hour period in most parts of the world, and before any angler approaches the sea, he or she should invest in a tide table covering the intended fishing area.

The seasons also affect sea angling, to a greater extent than freshwater fishing. Fish travel vast distances through the world's oceans, migrating much like birds as they follow the food and temperature that they require. A

MAIN PICTURE Fishing into the surf.

RIGHT A huge range of species inhabit the world's oceans.

fish's life is dominated by the need for food and the desire to reproduce, and anglers need to know where to intercept the species that they are targeting.

Sea angling tends to be divided into two main sections: boat-fishing and shore fishing, both of which contain an enormous range of subgroups, which is why the following sections have been broken down to cover different environments. The rules governing the freshwater food chain mentioned above apply just as much to salt water, although the species present will be different. In seas and oceans, the shark, rather than the freshwater pike, is near the top of the food chain, while the sardine is near the base, mirroring the freshwater roach's position.

Boat-fishing

Before boarding any boat, it is vital to ensure that all is safe. The skipper should be fully qualified, insured and licensed. If you are venturing out in your own boat, make sure that you are aware of the local tides and check the weather forecast. Ensure that you have

ABOVE Charter boats at rest.

some means of communication, life rafts, flares and so on, and that you are wearing a lifejacket. See also the chapter on safety, pages 466 to 479.

Inshore boat-fishing

Small boats can fish within a couple of miles or kilometres of the shoreline. The waters tend to be shallower here than they are further out, and the fishing areas are influenced by the landmass. Headlands and estuaries affect the way in which the currents flow and how food is distributed, too (remember that the tides have a major influence on the movement and location of fish).

Offshore boat-fishing

Larger boats are needed in order to venture far out to sea in search of large species of fish, and anglers usually hire charter boats housing the latest navigational and fish-finding equipment. Anglers are often taken to shipwrecks many miles from land to target the fish that surround them: in large, barren areas of sea, a wreck is like an oasis in a desert, an environment within which fish can find food and shelter. In the United States' offshore waters, the dumping of chained-together tyres has created artificial reefs. Natural reefs also provide a rich habitat in which fish can thrive.

Offshore boats use a variety of methods with which to target large, predatory species of fish like shark, tuna and sailfish. The species present will depend upon wherever it is in the world that you are lowering your baited hook or lure.

Shore fishing

There is a vast range of shore-fishing locations. Note, however, that the tide will have a great influence on where and when you fish.

ABOVE Sunset on the beach.

Beaches

Beaches vary according to their location and local geographical features, and the tidal flow and prevailing weather conditions also have considerable influence upon them.

Shallow, sandy beaches that are exposed to the wind and tide are often referred to as 'surf beaches' or 'storm beaches'. Although they initially appear to offer little food for fish, careful inspection will often show marine-worm casts and various shellfish. Small fish,

ABOVE A lone angler on a sandy beach.

LEFT Fishing from a steep pebble beach.

BELOW LEFT A steep shelving pebble ridge.

but because they contain a wealth of life, frequently house the largest numbers of fish.

Manmade structures

Piers, breakwaters, bridges and harbour walls give the angler access to deep water and a wide variety of species. In many harbours, waste that has been dumped into the sea acts as an attraction to fish, encouraging them to venture within range of the angler.

such as the sand eel, are also frequently present, and provide food for predatory species like bass.

Steep, shelving beaches are often made up of large pebbles and shingle. These beaches allow anglers to cast their bait beyond the tidal zone. A wider variety of species is likely to be present, too.

Rocky beaches are difficult to fish,

RIGHT This mile-long breakwater in Alderney gives anglers access to deep water.

LEFT Waves surge onto a rocky shoreline.

Rocks

Deep water can frequently be found within a short distance of rocks, and a wide variety of species can be caught from these natural fishing platforms. Indeed, rock fishing is probably the most productive location for shore fishing.

Rocks are, however, among the most hazardous of places to fish. They are often slippery, and anglers can be swept from them by large waves. Always check the times of the tides and ensure that you cannot be cut off. Be aware of the weather conditions, too: some rocks are easy to walk on when dry, but become slick after rain. A section of coast will often have a variety of differing rock

RIGHT Estuaries can provide good sport with flatfish such as this flounder.

types and structures, and it is important always to consider any potential dangers, especially when visiting a rocky area for the first time.

Estuaries

The nature of an estuary is largely determined by the river that flows into it. Estuaries are, however, typically rather muddy environments that have been created by silt deposited by the river over many years. Flatfish, and fish that are tolerant of brackish water, tend to haunt these waters. During rough weather, estuaries can provide anglers with a safe alternative to the open sea.

Tackle

An enormous array of tackle is available to today's angler, and a massive marketing industry is supported by the angler's love of new gear. When you are getting started, you need not spend vast sums of money on equipment, however, although it is important to understand that each item of tackle that you buy is designed with a specific job in mind.

Remember that the basic principles of angling are to present a bait or lure to a fish in order to tempt that fish onto a hook, and then to bring the fish to a bank or boat, after which it will either be released or eaten. The tackle that you use therefore needs to be capable of casting, or placing, the bait where the fish is located. It needs to be strong enough to land the fish, but not so apparent to the fish that it may decline the invitation to take the bait. Getting this balance right is not always easy, and a compromise must often be reached.

Skilful anglers should be able to get the best from their tackle, and a friend of mine used to tell me that fish are lost as a result of bad angling, not bad luck, a statement that is true more often than most anglers are ready to admit.

BELOW A selection of tackle.

Note that the purpose of a rod, reel, line and hook is as follows:

- The rod is used to propel the terminal tackle to its destination.
- The reel stores the line.
- The line connects the angler to the terminal tackle and bait.
- The hook holds the bait and then, it is hoped, the fish.

These points may appear obvious, but it is amazing how many anglers seem to lose sight of these simple truths and spend huge amounts of money on rods and reels, yet economise on lines and hooks. This seems incredible to me because although big fish can be landed using any rod or reel within reason, a breakage is inevitable without a good line and strong hooks. (I am not suggesting that you purchase any old rod and reel, but am just pointing out that there is no room for a weak link between anglers and their quarry.)

To avoid breaking it, your tackle needs to be carefully matched to both the environment and your target fish, and it must also be enjoyable to use (a point that is of vital importance because enjoyment is anglers' prime motivation in going fishing). The tackle that you require should therefore be determined by the species of fish, its location within its environment and the bait that you will use to entice it. I will now explain an angler's tackle and its purpose.

The rod

The rod is often described as an extension of the angler's arm, and in many styles of angling the rod seems as though it were part of the body. Indeed, the pleasure of propelling a bait into the water is part of the joy of angling.

The purpose of the rod is to cast, or place, the terminal tackle and bait. The rod is also used to keep the line clear of obstructions when retrieving the bait or fish. In addition, the tip of the rod is used to detect when a fish takes the bait (referred to as a bite).

In ancient times, rods consisted of thin branches with a length of horsehair tied to the end, but their design was improved, and different materials were used, over the centuries. During the

BELOW A rod – Note how rod tapers from butt to tip.

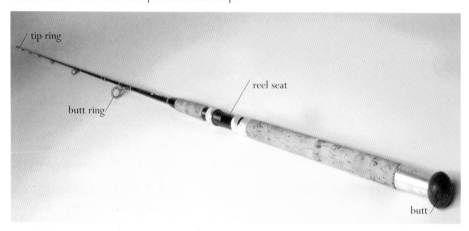

tip ring

reel seat

butt ring

butt

nineteenth century, the forerunners of today's rods were made with split cane. They were strong, yet flexible, and are still used to this day by anglers who prefer the natural feel and characteristics of such rods. (Indeed, vintage tackle has quite a following, and some items fetch considerable sums of money at specialist tackle auctions.)

After World War II, tackle development evolved rapidly, and rods started to be made from new materials. Steel and aluminium were briefly used before the discovery of fibreglass. Solid fibreglass rods were subsequently replaced with hollow fibreglass, which was lighter and stronger than any

material previously used. Carbon fibre and boron have now become the materials used in the manufacture of most rods, being flexible, strong and light, and transmitting the throb of a lure or the pull of a fish to an angler far better than any other material. The big change in rod-making has therefore been the swing from natural to manmade material.

Now let's look at the anatomy of a rod. The butt of a rod is the thick end, to which the reel is attached, the rod's main body then being tapered to its tip. A series of line guides, or rod rings, are whipped to the rod, the size of these rings being determined by the type of

LEFT The reel is attached to the rod at the reel seat using various types of fittings.

reel, the line to be used and the weight to be cast. There are some rods without rings, the line being instead threaded through the rod's hollow centre, but these have yet to become universally popular. Rods are tapered from the butt to the tip in varying degrees, depending on the rod's purpose. The rod has what is termed a 'test curve', which is the weight needed to compress the rod to an angle of 90°. The rod's action will also vary, from through action to tip action, terms that refer to the rod's flexibility from the butt to the tip.

BELOW Rod tips vary greatly according to their purpose.
(TOP) A heavy duty boat rod.
(MIDDLE) A spinning rod.
(BOTTOM) A lightweight trout fly rod.

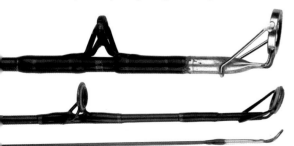

These technical aspects are a little difficult to explain, but have great relevance to how a rod is intended to perform. In an effort to describe it in simple terms, imagine flicking an object like a rubber with a ruler and visualise the rubber flying across a classroom. Now imagine doing the same with a floppier piece of plastic. Returning to angling, a line is attached to the flying object, which has to be retrieved and may be extremely heavy if a fish has taken the bait. The rod now has to cushion the strain on the line.

A rod is therefore designed to meet the following criteria:
- To cast or place the bait.
- To absorb any stresses placed upon the line during casting.
- To absorb the stresses of hooking and landing fish.
- In some cases, to indicate a fish's bite at the tip of the rod.
- To transmit the sensation of a fish pulling at the end of the line to the angler.
- To give anglers pleasure in its use.

Types of rod

There are many types of rod, including poles; match or float rods; leger or quiver-tip rods; carp or pike rods; spinning or lure rods; beachcasting rods; boat rods; and fly-fishing rods.

Poles

A pole is a rod that is used without a reel to place, or swing, bait into position. Basic poles were prevalent before the introduction of the reel, and poles made of cane were traditionally used for roach fishing on such rivers as the Thames. Although they went out of fashion some time ago, they have made

ABOVE Poles can present bait with great accuracy.

a big comeback since the introduction of modern rod-making materials, which enable them to be extremely long (in excess of 42ft 6in, or 13m) and light in weight, while remaining relatively rigid. A length of elastic is attached to the interior of the pole and connected to the line to act as a buffer and help to prevent line breakage. Poles are often used in freshwater match fishing to present bait precisely, as well as to catch large numbers of fish quickly.

Short poles, or whips, are often only a few feet or metres long. I bought a 10ft (3m) whip for my five-year-old son;

with no reel to become entangled with the line, it was the ideal first rod, and by dangling a float with the bait suspended beneath it, he was able to catch large numbers of small fish. These simple beginnings are enough to excite and stimulate a beginner, and whips can be purchased for relatively small amounts of money. Specialist poles can be extremely expensive, however, and are not usually bought by newcomers to the sport.

To summarise:
- Poles are generally used in freshwater fishing to catch coarse fish from still water or slow-moving rivers and canals.
- Poles are widely used in competition fishing.
- Poles are good for presenting bait accurately at short ranges.
- Short poles, or whips, make ideal first rods for youngsters.

Match or float rods

Match or float rods typically measure between 12 and 15ft (3.7 and 4.6m) in length. Very light in weight, they are designed for float-fishing with light tackle, and are likely to have a test curve of between 12oz and 1lb 4oz (340 and 560g). The lines used with these rods have a small diameter and a low breaking strain (1 to 6lb, or 453g to 2.7kg). The rod rings are arranged so that the line is kept clear of the rod (a line can otherwise cling to a wet rod and impede the trajectory of the float when an angler is casting a light weight).

Match or float rods are used to catch many different species of fish in a variety of waters. On rivers, they are primarily used to catch roach, dace and grayling. The long rod gives excellent control of the tackle as the float is allowed to drift (or is trotted) downstream, also enabling the line to be lifted from the current, thus allowing a straight run downstream. In still waters, the rod is used to target most coarse species, and this is the rod that a newcomer to coarse fishing should purchase. General float-fishing (see pages 236 to 239) for coarse fish will give the novice practice in all of the basic angling skills, including casting, playing fish and general watercraft.

Leger or quiver-tip rods

Leger or quiver-tip rods are designed for fishing bait on the bottom. They are generally 9 to 12ft (2.7 to 3.7m) in length and are usually used with slightly heavier lines than those used with match or float rods. This is because they are used to cast weights ranging from 12 to 4oz (14 to 113g). A tip section, known as a quiver tip, with a very small diameter that flexes easily, thereby registering when a fish has bitten, is built into some rods. The tip's test curve is likely to be around 2 to 4oz (57 to 113g), while the main rod will have a test curve of between 1lb and 1lb 8oz (453 and 680g).

Leger or quiver-tip rods are used for catching a wide range of medium-weight coarse fish, such as bream, tench, small carp and roach, from still water. When

BELOW Gazing intently at a pair of quiver tips.

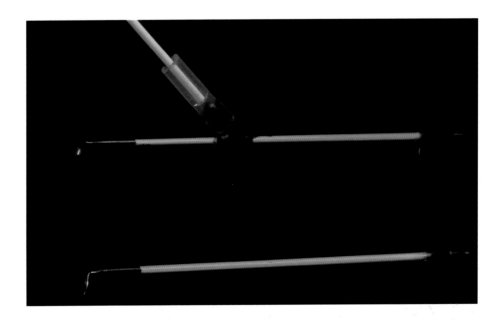

fishing in rivers, barbel, chub and bream are likely to be targeted.

Carp or pike rods

If I had to choose one rod for fishing, it would be a 2lb (907g) test-curve carp or pike rod. Such a rod, which can be used for many differing purposes, can be pushed into service to fish for a vast range of species throughout the world. I have landed bass, salmon, flounder, grey mullet, pollock and many other species of fish, including, of course, carp and pike, with a rod like this.

ABOVE The top quiver tip has an attachment for a beta light, so that the tip can be seen in the dark.

Carp or pike rods are designed to cast weights ranging from 12 to 4oz (14 to 113g) over medium to long distances. They have a test curve of between 1lb 8oz and 4lb (680g and 1.8kg) and a length that ranges between 10 and 13ft (3 and 4m). They vary in action, from tip action with a powerful mid-section designed for distance-casting, to soft, all-through action to tire out big fish at close ranges as the rod absorbs their powerful lunges.

Spinning or lure rods

Artificial lures are mainly used to catch predatory fish, and spinning or lure rods are the tools that cast these lures. These rods range from 5 to 11ft (1.5 to 3.4m) in length, and tend to have a fairly stiff action because they need to transmit movement to the lure rather like a puppeteer transmits movement to a puppet. When a fish grabs the lure, the hook must take hold immediately because a fish will not hang onto a lure as it does to a natural bait.

There tends to be a big difference between the lure rods designed for the American and the European markets (although these differences are starting to diminish as American and European anglers explore each other's techniques). In the United States, anglers generally prefer short rods, termed 'bait-casting rods', which are used single-handedly to cast lures for freshwater bass, northern pike and

BELOW Spinning rod launches a lure into a lake.

muskellunge. These rods and casting methods are now becoming widely used throughout Europe and the United Kingdom. English anglers have, however, traditionally preferred to use longer rods with which to cast their lures to salmon, pike and bass. I use both types of rod, depending on the prevalent conditions and my personal preference at the time. Different lures work better with some rods than with others, which is why it is useful to own a range of spinning or lure rods (and I have more than half a dozen, all designed for a specific purpose).

In lure-fishing, the rod is held throughout, from casting out to retrieving, and one can become very fond of a particular rod. I have an old, hollow-glass spinning rod, produced by a company called Milbro (which I believe no longer trades), with which I caught my first salmon over twenty years ago. I still carry it to the river whenever I'm targeting salmon on spinner or bait, and as I am wandering beside the river, asking questions of each likely lie, the rod really feels like an extension of my arm. I have total confidence in this rod, despite its age.

Beachcasting rods

Beachcasting rods are designed for shore fishing, primarily in salt water. The environment in which sea anglers fish is, on the whole, relatively harsh, and exposure to tidal currents, weather extremes, rocks and seaweed make the business of keeping the bait where it has been cast very demanding, which is why sea anglers use heavier gear than freshwater anglers. The most commonly used

TOP RIGHT The beachcaster is used for putting bait out into a harsh environment.

BELOW In the hands of an expert, the beachcaster can propel a bait to fish far out in the surf.

49

beachcasting rods cast around 5oz (142g) of lead, are around 12ft (3.7m) long, and have a test curve of over 4lb (1.8kg). The optimum casting weight varies between rods, depending on the purpose for which the rod has been designed.

Some beachcasting rods are designed

ABOVE A pair of beachcasting rods sit expectantly on a tripod.

RIGHT A sea angler's view out into the surf as the sun slowly sets.

primarily for casting over long distances using specific casting styles. In expert hands, such rods may launch a weight as far as 656 or 984ft (200 or 300m). Although a rod like this may be extremely powerful, it may give the angler little enjoyment when playing fish, and bite detection may also be poor. This is why compromises have been made in the design of most beachcasting rods in order to make them good, general-purpose tools.

There are two distinct types of beachcasting rod. Firstly, light, bass-type rods that cast 2 to 4oz (57 to 113g) and can be held by the angler for long periods. (These are, in effect, no more than heavy carp rods.) And, secondly, rods that are generally used for casting 4 to 8oz (113g to 227g) of lead, are fished in a rod-rest, and whose terminal tackle ensures that a fish hooks itself.

Boat rods

An enormous range of boat rods is available to the angler. A boat rod, which typically measures 5 to 7ft (1.5 to 2.1m) in length, is not used for casting, so that its main functions are to absorb the pulls of a fish, to act as a lever and to impart a pleasurable sensation to the angler. Twenty years or so ago, boat rods were divided into categories exclusively determined by the breaking strain of the line with which they are used, ranging from the 6lb to the 130lb (2.7 to the 59kg) class, this rating system being based on the guidelines of the International Game Fishing Association (IGFA), an organisation that keeps world-wide records of fish landed on different line classes (and many anglers set out to land large fish on light lines and set new records). These rods are generally used to lower a bait down tide from the side of a boat or to troll a lure behind a boat in motion.

The other type of rod that is today used for boat-fishing is the up-tide rod. These rods, which are normally around 9½ ft (2.9m) in length, are used to cast bait some distance up tide from a boat. An anchor-like weight is used to hold the bait in position on the seabed, away

RIGHT This Nile perch was landed using an up-tide rod.

from the disturbance created by the boat. This method has proved highly effective in shallower water, where fish can be scared by the vibrations emitted by a boat as the tide rushes by. It also allows the use of lighter tackle, which gives the angler better sport. Up-tide rods are versatile rods because young anglers can use them as shore rods. They are also ideal when targeting many fish, such as Nile perch or mahseer in the wild waters of India or Africa.

BELOW The rod takes the strain as the skipper waits with the net.

Fly-fishing rods

Fly-fishing (see pages 183 to 201) is a way of fishing that is fundamentally different to the types of angling for which all of the aforementioned rods are used. In fly-fishing, the line provides the casting weight, while the lure is a hook to which materials are adjoined that are intended to simulate a living creature. The rod acts as a pivotal lever when throwing the line that carries the hook and lure to their destination.

In common with all of the other rods used for casting, fly-fishing rods are rated according to the weight that they cast, which, in this case, is the weight of the line. Fly-fishing rods are rated on a scale that is referred to as AFTM (after the American Federation of Tackle Manufacturers that instituted it). The scale starts at 3 (very light) and goes up to 12 (very heavy). Fly-fishing rods range from 6 to 15ft (1.8 to 4.6m) in length.

The rod that you will need depends upon the fishing you intend to do. If you intend to fish a tiny brook for trout, for example, a weight 3 line would suffice, while if you intend to fish for tarpon on the Florida Keys, a weight 12 line would be more appropriate. Remember that the rod must always match the line. Perhaps the most distinctive feature of a fly-fishing rod is the position of its reel, which is situated near the bottom of the butt.

BELOW The reel sits near the bottom of the butt of most fly rods.

The reel

The purpose of the reel is to store the line, as well as to release the line on the cast and to retrieve it when required.

There are three categories of reel: the centre-pin reel, the fixed-spool reel and the multiplier reel. All three generally incorporate a form of braking system, which is generally referred to as a 'drag'. This utilises friction to control the release of the line if a powerful fish is pulling hard enough to break it or pull the hook free. Additional braking can be applied to the spool by the angler's thumb or finger. The drag setting is paramount when big fish are likely to be hooked.

Centre-pin reels

The centre-pin reel has a spool that revolves on a central pin. Having been used for thousands of years, this type of reel is the oldest extant design, the other two types having been widely used for a mere century or so. Most centre-pin reels are made from machined aluminium, plastic or carbon fibre.

The centre-pin reel is a delight to use when trotting rivers for roach, dace and grayling at close range. When combined with a lengthy, well-designed float rod, a top-quality, well-engineered reel enables anglers to control their tackle with ease. Centre-pin reels are also used for close-range fishing for barbel and carp, when they provide direct contact with the fish. In addition, they allow anglers to prevent fish from reaching the sanctuary of snags (trees or branches embedded in a riverbed), making them ideal in snaggy situations. Large centre-pin reels are sometimes used by boat anglers, too, when they again provide direct contact with the fish, while fly-fishing reels are also centre-pin reels.

These reels are not, however, used for fishing at long distances. The only way that anglers of old could cast any distance with these reels was to coil the line around newspaper or a similar material to enable it to travel away unhindered. Can you imagine the hassle of having to do this on a wet, windy day?

LEFT A classic centre-pin reel.

Fixed-spool reels

As its name suggests, a fixed-spool reel
comprises a fixed spool, the line being
put onto the spool by a bale arm,
which is driven by a series of gears
operated by a reel handle, the spool
being moved bobbin-style to
ensure the smooth lay of the line.

ABOVE AND LEFT Fixed spool
reels.

When the cast is made, the bale arm is disengaged and the line is pulled from the spool's lip by the momentum of the weight being cast.

Being relatively easy to use and not prone to tangling, fixed-spool reels are ideal for newcomers to angling. The secret of trouble-free casting is to load the spool to its optimum level, which is generally around 14in (65mm) from the lip of the spool. The less line there is on the spool, the greater the resistance, and the further the weight flies, the greater the resistance, too, leading to loss of distance.

This type of reel is the number-one choice for 90 per cent of all bait fishers for coarse-fish species. Fixed-spool reels are also used by a large number of sea anglers because they can cast bait a long way.

ABOVE The bale arm lays line upon the spool, which moves bobbin-style.

Multiplier reels

The multiplier reel has a revolving spool that turns around a central pin, but unlike the centre-pin reel, it has a gear system that enables the line's speedy recovery. Perhaps the major difference between the multiplier and other types of reel is that it is attached to the top of the rod. Certain rods are therefore designed slightly differently for multiplier compatibility, with the rod rings generally being smaller and the reel seat often being designed to give the most comfortable grip possible.

The spool is mounted on ball bearings, ensuring its smooth operation and the potential to make long casts. The multiplier is the reel of choice for most boat fishers out at sea, and is particularly suited to fishing for large species of fish like shark, skate and marlin. Smaller multipliers are widely used for bait-casting and bait-spinning. The multiplier is my own preferred choice for most beachcasting situations, mainly because it is so pleasing to use (there is not a great difference in the distance that can be achieved using a fixed-spool or multiplier reel).

Beginners would be ill-advised to make their debut with a multiplier reel, however, because they are prone to what

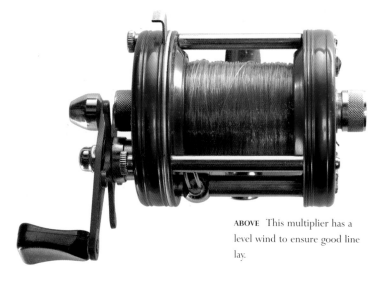

ABOVE This multiplier has a level wind to ensure good line lay.

ABOVE Well-engineered
multipliers are a joy to use.

are called 'bird's nests'. Bird's nests occur when the weight that has been cast slows down after its initial launch towards its destination, but the spool is still spinning extremely fast following the acceleration powered by the cast. If the spool is not slowed, it will continue to feed out line that the weight does not require, resulting in a nasty tangle, or bird's nest. Although most modern multipliers have sophisticated braking systems (either centrifugal or magnetic) that help to control the rotating spool during the cast and thus reduce the occurrence of bird's nests, smooth casting is probably the greatest factor in the reduction of tangles.

Mastering a multiplier reel will be well worth your effort, not least because large fixed-spool reels are ungainly tools.

RIGHT The thumb controls the revolving spool as the bait is lowered to the seabed.

BELOW A multiplier used for distance beachcasting: the angler uses a rubber strip to improve grip during powerful casts.

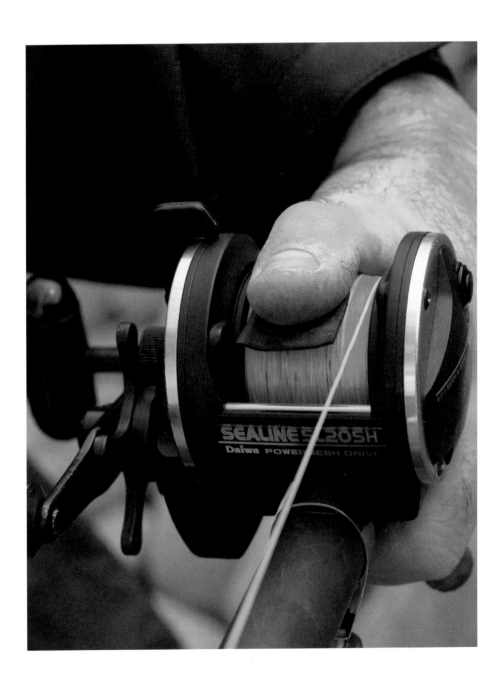

The line

The line is the vital connection between the angler's world and the mysterious world of the fish.

Until the 1950s, fishing line was made from natural materials, such as silk, cotton and horsehair, which were prone to rotting and needed drying after use, while hook lengths had to be soaked before use to make them sufficiently supple to be attached to a hook. By contrast, if they are stored out of direct sunlight, modern lines (which are developing rapidly, becoming ever stronger and thinner in the process) retain their strength for years.

The most commonly used line is currently nylon monofilament, which

ABOVE Braided line has made a big impact with its incredible strength-to-diameter ratio.

has revolutionised the angling world by making casting and bait presentation far easier. The big disadvantage of this line is its potential to inflict harm on wildlife if it is carelessly left on a bank or shoreline, or even if it is disposed of via a waste bin, when it may end up on a landfill site, where birds may become entangled in it (this is why it is best either to burn a line or to cut it up into short lengths before disposing of it). Nylon monofilament lines should be regularly replaced; exactly how frequently depends on how often they have been used, but certainly at least once a year.

Braided lines manufactured from Kevlar and other synthetic materials have made a big impact on angling. Such lines have even thinner diameters than nylon monofilament, as well as little stretch. This lack of stretch both provides a far superior bite indication and can lead to longer casts. In lure-fishing, it furthermore gives the angler an excellent feeling of how the lure is working and enables hooks to be driven home into fishes' mouths with minimum effort. When using a braided

ABOVE Line should be cut into short lengths before disposal as it can harm wildlife.

line, it's important to increase the breaking strain used, firstly to allow for the line's lack of stretch, which can result in its sudden failure, and, secondly, to minimise the potential loss of expensive terminal tackle and lures. Care must also be exercised when the end tackle becomes entangled (snagged) in some unseen rock or debris. It will be necessary to pull until the lure breaks. To do this with bare hands can result in nasty cuts, and for this reason wear gloves or wrap the lure around a suitable piece of smooth wood. Remember that braided lines present the same sort of environmental hazard as nylon monofilament. They are

BELOW Monofilament line revolutionised the angling world.

generally a lot more expensive than nylon monofilament, but last far longer (sometimes for more than a season).

Another type of line, wire line, is used in boat-fishing to combat strong tides. Such lines require special, roller-type rod rings. Because the modern braided lines mentioned above offer all of wire's benefits, but without its tendency to kink and break, I can see no future in wire lines, however. For fly lines, see pages 191 to 192 of the section on fly-fishing.

When purchasing a line, you will need to think carefully about the properties that are of the most importance to you. Lines are rated in breaking strain (bs) and diameter. Some will be stretchy, while others will have little stretch; some will be soft, and

Remember that the line that you choose must be:
- Strong enough to land the type of fish that is likely to be hooked.
- Suitable for casting the required distance.
- Unlikely to scare the fish away from the bait.

others less so, and with greater memory (in other words, they will retain twists from being stored on the reel).

Hook links, lengths or traces

The hook link, length or trace may sometimes be part of the main line, but is usually a separate section of line attaching the hook to the main line. There is a hook link for every situation, and anglers must choose carefully if they are to maximise the effectiveness of their set-ups.

The optimum length of the hook link will be determined by several factors, including the water conditions, the species of fish anticipated, the terrain and the angling pressure.

In clear water conditions, fish are likely to be aware of a visible line, which is why it may be wise to use as light a breaking strain as possible for the hook link. Indeed, it is good practice to use a hook link with a lighter breaking strain than the main line whenever it is practical to do so. This will ensure that if a fish breaks free, it will not leave metres of line trailing behind it and will also reduce the amount of line lost if the terminal tackle becomes snagged. In freshwater bait fishing, a hook link of clear, monofilament line is ideal. Modern fluorocarbon lines are also excellent because their light-reflective properties greatly reduce their visibility under water.

If the species of fish targeted has sharp teeth or abrasive mouths (like a large proportion of predatory fish), you will need a wire trace. Remember that it is the angler's responsibility always to choose tackle that is strong enough to land any fish that he or she is likely to hook. In waters that contain several different predatory species, it may therefore be necessary to use a wire trace in case you hook a species that you have not directly targeted. If you were fishing for perch with small live bait or spinners in water containing pike, for example, a wire trace would be essential, even if it reduces the chances of catching perch. The type of wire trace that you choose will depend on the species and size of fish targeted. Care must be taken with wire, which will become weakened if it becomes kinked or corroded.

The terrain will also determine the strength and characteristics of the hook link. Rocks or gravel are likely to fray the line, for example, so that a relatively heavy and thick line will be required in terrain like this. If there are fallen trees or other such fish havens present, a strong line will be needed to prevent the fish from reaching them.

Angling pressure – where fish are targeted by a large number of anglers – will also influence the choice of hook link. In many coarse-fishing venues, the fish will have been caught and returned to the water many times, and such fish as carp and barbel are capable of developing a cunning that enables them to detect lines and hook links. A very wide range of special hook links has been developed to counteract this problem and enhance the presentation of the bait.

NEXT PAGE The angler expectantly cradles his rod as the sun sinks.

The hook

The hook is the final link in the chain between the angler and the fish, its purpose being to hold the bait and secure the fish.

Early fishhooks were made of wood or bone. Some were gorge hooks that wedged into the fish's throat, totally unacceptable devices in today's world, when conservation is a major consideration. Most of today's hooks are made from tempered-steel wire and have seven major features: the eye, shank, bend, gape, throat, barb and point.

Careful consideration needs to be given to the type of hook required for each situation. Generally recognised hook sizes are based upon the Redditch scale. The smallest hooks in use are probably size 22. Such a hook would be used to mount a single maggot or tiny bloodworm. At the other end of the scale, a size 16/0 would be used to mount a whole fish for shark fishing. It is essential always to match the hook size to that of the bait being used, while

BELOW A typical hook.

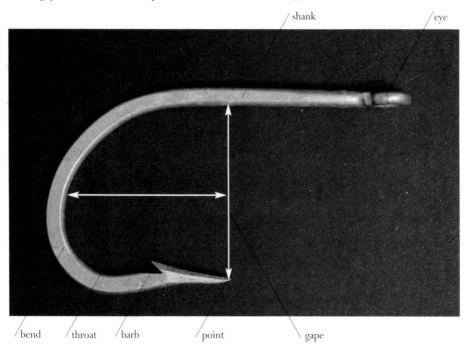

shank   eye

bend   throat   barb   point   gape

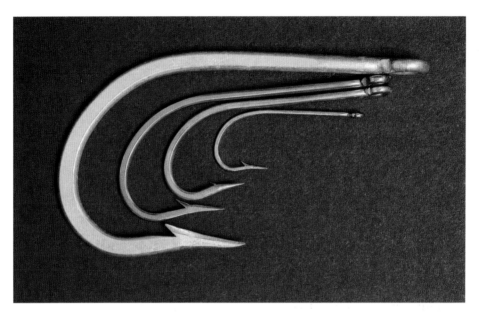

ABOVE Hooks vary greatly in design.

the hook point must be free to penetrate the mouth of the fish easily. When using soft bait, it may be practical to bury the hook within the bait. If the bait is hard, it is essential to leave the hook exposed. (I will look at this issue in greater detail when discussing various baits and how to present them, see pages 122 to 171.)

Manufacturers produce a vast range of hook designs, each of which has a specific function. The temper of the wire will determine the use to which a

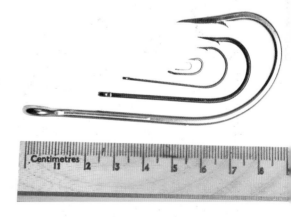

ABOVE Hooks sizes 22 up to 12/0

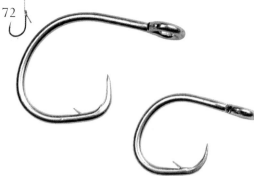

hook may be put.

Fine wire hooks penetrate more easily, for example, but are also more prone to straightening during a battle with a large specimen. On the other hand, a fine wire hook will also be lighter and present bait more naturally. A compromise will probably therefore have to be made.

The ideal hook is light, strong and capable of maintaining a secure hold within the mouth of the fish. The heating of the carbon steel that is used to make the hook determines its brittleness. A hook that is so brittle that it suddenly breaks is waste of money, while a certain amount of flexibility has to be incorporated into the hook's shank and bend.

Hooks should always be carefully inspected before use for signs of weakness or corrosion, as well as to ensure that their points are extremely sharp. Many modern hooks have been chemically sharpened, a process that produces an exceptionally sharp point. Once such a point has become dulled or blunted by rubbing against stones, for example, it is almost impossible for it to regain its sharpness, however. A sharpening stone is essential for the maintenance of hooks that have not been chemically sharpened.

In some instances, bronzed hooks that corrode easily are desirable. When fishing for shark, conger and other large

BELOW A hook file is essential for keeping non-chemically sharpened hooks sharp.

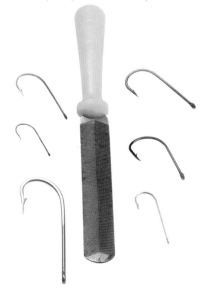

ABOVE Carefully sharpening a hook point.

sea fish, for example, it may be difficult to remove the hook from the fish, so that in order to avoid causing the fish unnecessary distress, it is often better to cut the trace as near as possible to the fish, after which its extremely effective digestive juices will dissolve the hook. It is better to remove hooks from fish whenever possible, however, especially double and treble hooks, which are effectively a combination two or three single hooks to create greater hooking power. Treble hooks are widely used on lures to achieve a more effective hook-up ratio, double hooks being used in some flies for the same reason. Trebles are also used to present fish baits to pike and other predatory species.

The hook's barb is often a bone of contention among anglers. The purpose of the barb is to prevent the fish from shaking itself free of the hook. It will only work if the hook has penetrated beyond the barb, however, which is why a big barb is not desirable. Many freshwater anglers furthermore use barbless hooks to reduce the amount of damage that hooks can cause to fish that are to be returned to the water (indeed, this is mandatory on many waters).

Remember that the hook must always be chosen to match the quarry, the quarry's environment and the size of the bait or lure being used.

ABOVE Treble hooks widely used on lures.

The weight

Once the line has been cast, the weight carries the bait and hook to their destination and then keeps the bait there. The weight may also be used to assist in the hooking of a fish by creating an anchor point that pulls the hook into place within the fish's jaws. In addition, the weight is used when float-fishing to cock the float and sink the bait to the desired depth.

Until recently, most weights were made of lead on account of its heaviness. Environmental concerns have now forced manufacturers to offer alternative

ABOVE A selection of weights used by the freshwater angler.

materials for their smaller sizes, however, with the result that most weights weighing less than 1oz (28g) are now lead-free. Each weight has been designed for a specific purpose, so that the choice of weight will be determined by the particular situation that the angler is facing. In many instances, the location of the fish will determine the weight needed, and consequently also the rod with which to cast it. Of the huge range of weights available, many are designed for carp fishing. Some are designed primarily to achieve distance, while others are designed to cling to the riverbed in running water or a steep-sided lake. The shape may be aimed at hooking fish effectively.

The smallest weights that anglers generally use are split shot, which are usually employed when float-fishing for smaller species or when giving weight to bait if free-lining or using a light leger.

ABOVE Split shot is attached to the line by pinching it carefully in place.

ABOVE Split shot – SSG (Left) and Number 6 (right).

Split shot range in size from the tiny dust shot (the size of a pinhead) to swan shot (the size of a pea).

Olivettes are similar to split shot, but have a slightly more streamlined shape.

They are often used for pole-fishing.

For general legering, a small, bomb-type weight is used, namely the Arlesey-type weight. The original was designed by the late Richard Walker for perch fishing on a lake of the same name during the 1950s, and forms the basis of most of the weights used for casting at any distance in both fresh and salt water.

Some weights have been designed to carry loose feed or groundbait to the area that is being fished. Swimfeeders, for example, which are weighted cylinders, full of holes, that are filled with bait or groundbait. There are two basic types of swimfeeder: the open-end and block-end swimfeeder. Open-end swimfeeders are plugged with groundbait that disperses in the water, while block-end swimfeeders have

ABOVE A selection of weights used by the sea angler.

RIGHT A block-end feeder allows maggots to escape into the swim.

sealed ends so that the loose feed, typically maggots, escapes through the holes. A third type of feeder, called a method feeder, is also widely used. This weight is designed to allow a paste-like groundbait to be moulded around it, producing a ball of bait that slowly dissolves to form an appetising mound beside the hook.

The weights that are used in sea angling are generally heavier, due to the need to cast them over long distances and keep the bait in position. The breakaway lead, a weight designed during the 1970s, has wire arms that dig into the seabed, thus anchoring the tackle into place, despite the tidal pressure. On retrieving the terminal tackle, the wires fold back so that they give no resistance. These weights are also used in a form of boat-fishing termed up-tiding (see page 379).

In boat-fishing, casting is not always required, and the weight can simply be lowered over the side until it reaches the required depth or the bottom. In strong tidal currents, it may be necessary to use weights in excess of 2lb (907g). Remember that smaller-diameter lines can enable the use of lighter weights.

The float

Floats generally serve two purposes: firstly, to indicate a bite, and, secondly, to suspend the bait at the desired depth beneath the surface. The prevalent conditions, along with the type of bait and tackle being used, will determine the size of the float.

If you have decided to use a float, you will need to select it with care. There are floats designed for still water, windy weather, rivers, poles, pike

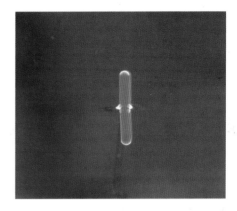

ABOVE Buoyant optimism.

BELOW Sea-angling floats.

fishing and so on. In salt water, it is sometimes necessary to use a large float. In shark fishing, for example, a toilet cistern or partly inflated balloon may be used to suspend the bait.

It is important to weight the float correctly in the water. Ideally, only a small portion of the float should be left showing above the water. Cocking the float correctly (so that just the tip shows) will ensure that the fish feels little resistance when taking the bait, and if a fish's suspicions are not aroused, you will have longer to respond to its presence and set the hook.

Not only does a float give the angler a point on which to focus, but its appearance of apparently continual, buoyant optimism is delightful. (I believe that it was the angling writer H T Sheringham who described a float as giving much delight in its appearance, and even greater pleasure in its disappearance.)

The swivel

A swivel's primary function is to connect two sections of line. It also

BELOW Swivels connect lines and reduce twist.

ABOVE A three-way swivel gives three points of attachment.

helps to reduce any twisting of the line and therefore improves the presentation of the bait. In many instances, the swivel furthermore acts as a stop to prevent a weight or float from sliding downwards and becoming entangled with the bait. The only branch of fishing in which the use of swivels is uncommon is fly-fishing.

Swivels are rated in size in much the same way as hooks (see pages 70 to 74). Note that it is important to select a swivel that is much stronger than the line being used. Never buy cheap, poor-quality swivels because their failure can lead to the loss of a big fish or people in the vicinity being injured during a powerful cast.

Some terminal-tackle set-ups incorporate the use of three-way swivels that enable three points of attachment: to the main line, to the hook and to the weight.

Sundry items

In addition to all of the tackle items outlined above, there is an enormous range of accessories and tools that are used in the making of rigs and end tackles (these items will be covered as and when their uses arise). Some widely used items are beads that can be used as buffers between weights and swivels, for instance. Brightly coloured beads are sometimes also used as attractors, especially when fishing for flatfish in salt water. Carp anglers are particularly well catered for, with many specialist components being available for rig-making. Sea anglers have also developed a great variety of rig-making components that I shall discuss later (see pages 118 to 121).

There follows an introduction to some other useful items of tackle.

FAR LEFT The angler uses various sundry items.

LEFT This plaice was attracted to the bait using beads.

Bite indicators

I have already mentioned that quiver-tip
rods (see page 44) and floats (see page
77) are bite indicators, but there are
many more, too. They fall into two
groups: audible and visual, and sometimes
a combination of the two is used.

Although sea anglers tend to watch
their rod tips intently for an indication
of a bite, they sometimes use audible
indicators as a back-up. Most multiplier
reels have a check or ratchet that can be
set so that it emits a clicking sound if a
fish takes the line from the reel, a
warning that can prevent expensive rods
and reels being dragged into the sea.
Some anglers clip a bell to the tip of the
rod, which rings when a fish rattles the
rod's tip. (Many view these bells as
being a little amateurish, but I think
that there is something rather endearing
about hearing the tinkle of a bell on a
cold, calm, frosty night as another
whiting takes the bait.) Luminous or
reflective paint or tape is often added to

RIGHT The beach angler carefully monitors the
rod tips for indications of interest in his baits.

the tips of rods to enable them to be
seen in the beam of a headlight or
lamp, and beta and star lights (luminous
sections of tube) can also be attached to
rod tips to make them visible in the
dark.

    Freshwater anglers have a far wider
range of bite indicators available to
them. In addition to the

aforementioned quiver-tip rods, there
are swing-tips, which consist of a length
of rod-tip-like material that is attached
to the top of a rod by means of a screw
attachment and a length of flexible

BELOW Homemade drop-off indicators suitable
for pike fishing.

tube. This is then allowed to hang at an angle below the rod's tip, and when a fish pulls, the swing-tip rises, indicating a bite. (These indicators were once widely used for bream fishing, but have fallen out of favour in recent years.)

Butt-style indicators, which are most commonly used for specimen angling, are fitted between the reel and rings near the butt of a rod. When a fish takes the bait and pulls on the line, the indicator will either rise or fall, depending on the direction in which the fish moves away or the set-up of the terminal tackle being used. The indicator usually consists of a bobbin of some type. A piece of bread paste or dough was traditionally moulded around the main line and allowed to hang some distance beneath the rod, and silver paper, the tops of bottles of washing-up liquid and corks have all been utilised by anglers over the years. These days, however, state-of-the-art indicators, with easy-release line clips, luminous inserts and adjustable weightings or sensitivity, have become the norm. In many cases, these butt indicators are used in conjunction with audible alarms. The indicators rely on the movement of the line to trigger an alarm caused by the connecting or breaking of an electrical circuit, which will typically emit a bleep and flash a light.

Pike anglers and anglers who target some other predatory fish use drop-off alarms, some of which are audible. These consist of a line clip attached to the rear rod-rest (see below). When a fish pulls the line from the clip, the indicator drops free, alerting the angler and enabling the fish to swim away without feeling any resistance.

Before the advent of audible alarms, anglers sometimes utilised a metal wheel hubcap, or a similar object, and a coin placed on the reel spool. When a fish pulled the line from the spool, the coin dropped with a clatter into the metal receptacle, thus alerting the angler.

Rod-rests

In static forms of fishing, where the rod is not held, a rod-rest is required. The type of rest will depend upon the required position of the rod and the type of angling method being used. For simple float-fishing, for instance, the rod is rested upon a rest and positioned close at hand so that the angler can strike instantly on receiving an indication of a bite.

Anglers using quiver-tip rods will need to position the rod at an angle to the water, supported by a front and rear rest, again in a position that allows them to react immediately.

If the angler is legering (see page 330) using a butt indicator, the rod should be pointed in the direction of the main line as it enters the water. Front and rear rests are essential, and the front rest (which may incorporate an audible alarm) must allow enough space for the main line to pass through unimpeded. The front and rear rests need to be capable of supporting the rod in strong winds, and should ideally prevent the rod from being pulled into the water when a big fish takes the bait.

If a bank consists of stone or concrete, so that a bank stick on the rod rest cannot be driven into the ground, a rod pod will be required. This is a platform that allows the rod, or rods, to rest in the correct position. Rod pods, which are used widely by carp anglers, have the advantage of being easily carried, complete with rods, from swim to swim (pools in rivers that provide good fishing).

When fishing from a beach, a sand spike can be used to hold a rod firmly in an upright position, but note that sand spikes are only practical on sandy beaches. The sea angler needs a tripod that secures rods firmly in position, with the tips held high to enable the angler to see bite indications. The line must also be held clear of waves and weed when fishing from a beach. Most sea-angling tripods are designed to hold a pair of rods, and incorporate clips on which spare traces, for example, can be hung. During strong winds, the stability of the tripod can be improved by hanging a weight from a central point, thus anchoring the tripod's feet firmly to the ground.

When fishing from a boat, rod-holders may sometimes be incorporated into the sides to support the rods safely. Alternatively, special rests can be purchased that are clamped to the sides, allowing the rods to rest with most of their length outside the boat. Not only does this arrangement gives the angler more space on board, it also ensures that the line is kept away from the boat, with which it could become entangled.

BELOW A rod pod supports a pair of rods.

Disgorgers

When you have successfully landed a fish, you will need to extract the hook, which you can do with the help of a disgorger. The type of disgorger that you will need depends on the type of fish, its dentition and where it has been hooked.

ABOVE This hook is easy to remove with a simple disgorger.

LEFT A pair of pliers are useful for removing hooks from large fish.

A plastic, tube-like disgorger is often suitable for small fish. After sliding the line into the slit provided, this device is inserted into the fish's mouth and slid down onto the hook's shank; a gentle push, twist and pull should be all that you need to do to release the hook.

For larger fish, a pair of forceps is ideal for gripping and extracting the hook. For smaller fish, a pair of 6in (15.2cm) forceps will suffice, whereas a pair of 12in (30.5cm) forceps would not be too long for pike or larger fish. For large, toothy fish like pike, a pair of long-nosed pliers or a Baker hook-out-style disgorger are preferable.

A T-bar is the answer for large sea fish, such as conger or small shark, and I have also used a piece of rope to good effect. The idea is to slide the T-bar or rope into the bend of the hook and then use gravity to detach the fish from the hook.

If the hook is deep, it may be better to cut the trace as near to the hook as possible, a decision that will be made according to the angler's experience and the fish's species. Note that extracting a hook from a large fish like a shark is downright dangerous, which is why extreme care needs to be exercised.

Landing nets, gaffs and tailers

Having got a fish to the side of the water, you will only be able to lift it directly if it is small. Any larger, and lifting it from the water will put pressure on the hook's hold or possibly break the line. When the water is not supporting the weight of the fish, you are therefore likely to lose it unless you use some kind of landing tool, although it may sometimes be possible to land or beach the fish by hand on a gently sloping shelf of sand or gravel.

A landing net is generally the best piece of equipment for landing a fish. A net is certainly the kindest option for the fish because it will do the fish no harm. All nets used in fresh water should be constructed without knots to avoid damaging the fish's scales (it is, in fact, illegal to use knotted nets in the United Kingdom). The size of net will be determined by the target species, and a useful general maxim is always to err on the large size when selecting a net. No fish is likely to be lost because the perimeter of the net is too large, but many have been lost due to it being too small.

A pan-style net is suitable for most small- to medium-sized freshwater species. For larger species, such as carp or pike, a specimen-sized net is required, with arms whose span measures around 40in (102cm). (This may seem large, but believe me, when a pike measuring more than 20lb (9kg) is wallowing on the surface, it won't appear too large at all.) Large, circular nets have advantages over the more commonly used, triangular specimen nets, one being that they are easy to carry and can be used with a sling when being carried on the back. I use a large, round net for lure-fishing for pike, for salmon fishing, for specimen-trout fishing and also for some sea fishing. In some locations, an extending handle will be necessary if the net is to reach the water. When sea fishing from high walls or piers, it is sometimes necessary to use a drop net with which to land a fish. This consists of a net fixed to a frame that is lowered to the water by means of a rope; the net is drawn over

RIGHT Success, the fish is safely in the net.

the fish, which is then lifted towards the angler.

A gaff hook is used to land some sea fish, but note that this tool should only be used if the fish is to be retained because it may seriously injure the fish. It may sometimes be possible to gaff a fish carefully through the jaw, thus causing no harm, but this requires quite a lot of skill. Gaffs are not generally used in freshwater fishing anymore because a net is generally far more effective. The

ABOVE A salmon rests in the folds of the landing net.

exception is when landing large species like Nile perch, which, when played out, can be safely landed by slipping the gaff hook under the chin.

The only other tool used for landing fish is the tailer, which was once widely used in salmon fishing, but seldom these days. The tailer is a loop of wire that is placed around the wrist, or bony ridge, of the fish's tail before being pulled tight (this technique will work with salmon, but not with trout or sea trout, which do not have a wrist to grip). The only other species that a tailer may be of use for are tope and small shark.

Unhooking mats

Gravel and hard banks can do severe damage to a fish that is flapping about on the ground by removing its essential scales and slime, and an unhooking mat will protect the fish from such harm while the hook is being removed.

Large, freshwater species, such as carp, pike, catfish, bream and barbel, should be unhooked on an unhooking mat. This may be a sheet of padded foam covered in plastic, a large piece of bubble wrap or a commercially manufactured mat sold by tackle retailers. A patch of soft grass is the next best thing to a hooking mat, but note that carrying a hooking mat is compulsory in many fisheries.

BELOW This large perch has been photographed on an unhooking mat.

Clothing

In the past, anglers tended to make do with any old clothes for their fishing excursions, and as a result often suffered in inclement weather. It is imperative that you are comfortable and are not being made miserable by being too hot, cold or wet, so take the weather and terrain into account when deciding what to wear.

Your clothing must be designed to protect you from the weather and elements that are most likely to prevail while you are fishing. If rain or spray is indicated, a waterproof outer layer is vital. I personally avoid one-piece waterproof outfits because they tend to make one feel too hot when undertaking any type of exertion. A bib-and-brace-style over-trouser and good-quality waterproof jacket are ideal because the jacket can be removed, leaving the bib-and-brace over-trouser to keep the back warm, legs dry and inner garments clean.

RIGHT Flotation suits (left and right) offer protection against the elements and give a greater chance of rescue if the angler is unfortunate to be swept into the sea. The camouflage jacket (centre) is more in keeping on the banks of lakes or rivers.

Several layers of loose-fitting garments will keep the cold at bay far better than one or two thick, woolly jumpers. If you are anticipating extreme conditions, put on thermal underwear, followed by trousers, a shirt or T shirt, a fleece and perhaps a smock to keep you clean and resist the wind.

The extremities of an angler's body are the most vulnerable to the cold, and because a large percentage of the body's heat is lost through the head, a good hat is essential. A neck-warmer will cover the gap below the chin and soak up any water that finds its way down the back of the neck. Fingerless mittens protect the hands while leaving the fingers free to tie hooks and so on. I find neoprene mitts superb because they keep the hands warm, even when it is wet. Avoid cold feet by wearing either boots that have been specially designed for cold weather or a pair of thermal socks and waterproof boots that are a couple of sizes too large for your feet. (Always ensure that your boots have plenty of room for your feet because tight-fitting boots reduce the circulation, leading to painfully cold feet.) Chest-waders (long, waterproof boots that extend to the chest) are an alternative to bib-and-brace over-trousers, but note that great care must be taken when wearing waders because they can make it extremely difficult to escape from the water should you fall in. And whatever footwear you choose, make sure that its sole has a suitable grip.

LEFT Brightly coloured flotation suits are suitable for sea angling.

BELOW Wellington boots are widely used.

If the water is clear and the fish are likely to be close to you, it would be wise to wear some camouflage because if a fish spots you and becomes alarmed, it is unlikely to take the bait. If you are going to be wandering down a wooded riverbank, it would therefore be sensible to wear green or brown. If you are going to be lowering your line from a boat into the depths of the ocean, camouflage is of little consequence, however. In fact, when sea fishing, it is better to wear bright clothing to increase your visibility should you fall overboard or be swept from rocks by a large wave.

If you are fishing in a hot climate, your prime consideration should be protecting yourself from the sun. The most effective colour for reflecting hot solar rays from the body is white, while a less conspicuous compromise is khaki. To prevent sunstroke, it is important to wear a hat with a brim and to keep your neck shielded from the sun. (And it is not just in tropical climates that sunstroke can strike: after spending many a long day beside a lake or river in the United Kingdom, I have suffered

This hat gives protection to the neck when fishing in tropical sun.

blinding headaches caused by a mixture of the sun, concentration and fatigue.) Another crucial item is a good-quality pair of polarising sunglasses, which not only protect the eyes from the sun's harmful, ultraviolet rays, but can also give the angler a valuable window into the underwater world. Indeed, these glasses' ability to reduce surface glare can enable you to locate fish and features beneath the water's surface, and they have helped me to hook a number of salmon from clear, fast-flowing rivers.

Mobile anglers will find the waistcoats traditionally aimed at fly-fishermen ideal for carrying all of the little bits and bobs required for a roving approach to angling. Tackle belts can also be worn for carrying lures, tools and so on.

To summarise, the angler's clothing needs to be comfortable and to give full protection from the prevailing elements, thereby ensuring that the angler is free to concentrate on enjoying the job at hand, namely catching fish!

BELOW Polarising glasses give valuable protection from the sun's ultraviolet rays.

Tackle carriers and holders

Once you have acquired all of the tackle you need, you will have to carry it to the water's edge. The amount of tackle that you take with you will, no doubt, be determined by your approach to the session ahead. If you are going to be mobile, for example, you will need to carry the minimum of gear, while if you are anticipating a long fishing session, you will need a mountain of equipment. Between these extremes lie a wide variety of requirements.

For roving trips, it may not be necessary to carry a bag if all that you require fits into the pockets of your waistcoat or tackle belt, when you will just need a few small tackle containers in which to carry hooks and other spares. Most angling sessions will require you to carry your tackle in a bag or box, however.

Your choice of tackle carrier or holder will depend on the factors outlined above, and to some extent also on the terrain. Not only will your tackle box, bag or holdall need to be both large enough to hold your tackle and easily transported, it must be capable of protecting the tackle from being damaged and from rain, spray and mud.

A backpack or rucksack is ideal for many angling situations. Different sizes are sold by tackle shops and walking or outdoor-activity retailers. I often find it difficult to determine the size that I need, however, for the bigger the bag, the more I seem to cram into it. I therefore find myself perspiring as I struggle to the water's edge overloaded with everything that I might need and a little bit more, just in case.

A seat box is also suitable for many angling scenarios, especially match angling. Most are designed to house all of the angler's gear in a tidy, organised manner, and to keep everything dry and clean. You can, of course, also sit on a seat box. Plastic seat boxes have now replaced the wickerwork creel of the past.

Bite indicators, reels, scales, cameras and items of a similar size can be housed in separate bags within the main tackle carrier. Small items of tackle, such as hooks, weights and swivels, should be stored in plastic

NEXT PAGE Loaded up with tackle.

boxes, however, which can be bought from tackle and tool shops and Do-It-Yourself stores. These boxes are typically divided into compartments that store items separately. There is nothing more annoying than arriving at a venue to find a box's contents strewn over the bottom of your bag, however, so make sure that you buy boxes with strong fastenings and close-fitting lids to keep everything within confined to the correct compartment.

Because carp and long-session anglers sometimes camp out by swims for days or weeks at a time, they often have to carry a vast amount of kit. In such instances, using a trolley or wheelbarrow to transport equipment may spare their back and legs.

Rods should be transported in a bag or holdall, some of which are designed to carry rods that have already been made up and are ready to fish, thus saving valuable time at the start of a session. A Velcro strap is sometimes used to hold the rods together for transportation. Because rods generally need to be transported by car, make sure that a rod will fit into your car before purchasing it. (Although rods can be transported on a roof rack, this makes them vulnerable to theft.) Indeed, my foremost consideration when buying a car is whether my rods will fit into it! An estate car or hatchback is an ideal rod-transporter, and some anglers have four-wheel-drive cars that give them easy access to beaches and perhaps even the luxury of fishing from the vehicle.

To sum up, your tackle carrier must usually be transportable. If you are going to be climbing a cliff to reach your angling spot, you will need to keep your hands free, making a big, cumbersome box and massive rod holdall inappropriate choices, for instance. If you can park next to your swim, however, transportation isn't an issue because you will be able to pack everything that you may need into your car. Finally, when choosing a tackle bag, ensure that it is robust and of good quality because there is nothing worse than the strap of your rucksack breaking when you still have a mile or more to walk.

Seats

Although a seat is not required for many mobile forms of angling, static anglers need to be seated comfortably. Freshwater match anglers usually sit on their seat boxes or tackle stations, while sea anglers generally make do with their seat boxes (see above) or a handy rock, or simply lie back on the shingle gazing up at their rod tips.

BELOW A seat box combines as tackle carrier and seat.

Freshwater specimen anglers are generally those who require a seat, and carp anglers who have adopted a static approach will need a comfortable seat or bed. Indeed, many carp anglers have a bed-chair, along with a day chair or guest chair.

The river angler will need a lightweight chair that can be easily carried from swim to swim. A piece of plastic-covered foam or a car mat will sometimes be sufficient.

Shelters

The most common form of shelter is the angler's umbrella, which can be securely anchored to a bank with guy ropes to protect the angler and his or her gear from the wind, rain or sun. (And there is something rather cosy about sitting under an umbrella on a wet day, listening to the rain pitter-patter on the canvas.) Remember that it's important to secure the umbrella firmly to prevent it from floating away downstream after having been uprooted by a gust of wind.

Sea anglers sometimes use purpose-designed beach shelters to protect them

and their tackle and bait from the
elements. Such shelters are really only
practical on steep beaches with little
tidal rise and fall, however.

Long-stay specimen anglers require
a bivvy (bivouac) or tent to house them
and their gear. Many modern anglers'
shelters are extremely well made, easy
to erect, incorporate windows (and
sometimes porches) and are generally

ABOVE The bivvy – essential for long-stay anglers.

comfortable places in which to await
the action. Some anglers who camp
beside lakes take their home comforts
to the extreme, furnishing themselves
with portable televisions, radios and
even anglers' showers (some sleep in
the bivvy overnight and go off to work
in the morning).

Lights

Depending on where they are fishing, and what they are fishing for, nocturnal anglers need a light of some sort, and sea anglers who are constantly watching their rod tips require a powerful light or lamp that will last for the duration of the session.

Sea anglers generally keep a light on constantly to enable them to watch their rod tips and to light up the surrounding area. A point that many sea anglers overlook, however, is that there are times when a light should not be allowed to shine on the water, notably when the water is clear and the fish are at close range, because the light will

BELOW A selection of headlights suitable for the night angler.

alarm the fish. (This is also why freshwater anglers generally only use a light for baiting up and retackling.) Paraffin pressure lanterns were once the most popular lamps in use, but have now been surpassed, to some extent, by excellent pressure lamps that run on lead-free petrol. The hiss of a lamp as it illuminates the beach sounds comforting, and a pebble that has been heated on its top has brought comfort to many a cold hand.

In recent years, the headlight has dominated the anglers'-light market. Anglers utilised old miners' lamps powered by bulky, acid-cell batteries for a long time, but such lamps have now been superseded by light-weight units that are sold with chargers and battery packs, giving anglers ample light for sessions lasting several hours. And light-emitting diode (LED) lights today extend the life of many headlights and torches, some of which give up to eighty hours' continual illumination. In fact, all that is needed for most night angling is a rechargeable headlight and a small back-up light in case of battery or bulb failure.

Food and drink

If you are out angling for more than a couple of hours, you will need to take some food and drink to sustain you. For fishing sessions lasting only a few hours, a Thermos flask filled with a warm drink and a box of sandwiches should suffice. For longer sessions, you will require a portable stove (available from camping shops) on which to prepare a little hot food and perhaps to boil a kettle. Don't forget to take along a box of matches, too.

On the subject of forgetting things, I have forgotten to take just about everything at some time or other over the years. And there is nothing more frustrating than arriving at the water's edge, only to find that you have no reel or bait or that you have condemned yourself to an uncomfortably close encounter with thick, cold mud because you left your Wellington boots at home. I have now learned my lesson and keep a few checklists on the wall of my shed to remind me of what I need to take with me at the start of a day's fishing.

RIGHT Contemplating the river with some coffee.

Knots and rigs

It's no use buying the best tackle that money can buy if you have not learned the basic skills of tying knots and creating rigs.

Knots

Knots are needed to connect the line to terminal tackles, such as hooks and swivels, as well as to the reel spool, and to join two lines together. It is vital that knots are tied correctly. Poor knots have caused many a big fish to be lost, and there is little that frustrates an angler more. Having put so much effort into hooking a fish, only to lose it because of an inadequate knot, is unforgivable. To reel in after losing a fish and see a telltale kink in the line near the hook is sickening, not least because the fish that you lose is always a big one.

Although a vast number of knots are used in angling, you will only need to master a few to start off with. These are the tucked half-blood knot; the grinner; the loop; the water knot; the blood knot (for joining lines of equal diameter); the leader knot; the knotless hook attachment; and the stop knot.

The tucked half-blood knot

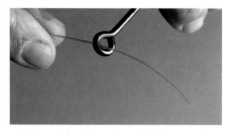

1. Thread the line through the eye of the hook.

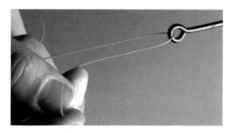

2. Pull a short length of line through the eye.

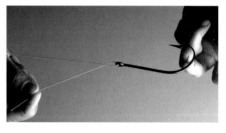

3. Twist the line by turning the hook.

4. Repeat at least five times.

5. Hold the loose end of the line.

6. Pass the loose end through the loop formed at the hook eye.

7. You now have a second loop through which to pass the end of the line.

8. Wet the line with saliva.

9. Carefully start to pull the knot tight.

10. Then tighten the knot fully.

11. Trim the tag end using line clippers.

The grinner

1. Thread the line through the hook eye twice.

2. Form a large loop through which to pass the end of the line.

3. Pass the end of the line through the loop five times.

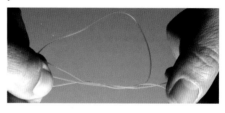

4. Begin to pull the knot tight carefully.

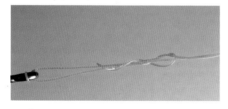

5. Wet the line with saliva and continue to tighten the knot.

6. Trim off the tag end. (A tag end can be left to help hold bait in position.)

7. The completed knot.

The loop

1. Take the end of the line and fold it over.

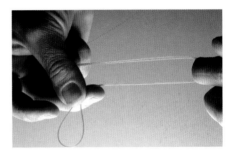

2. Form a loop in the end.

3. Cross over the two double lengths of line.

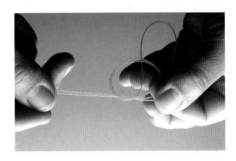

4. Tie a simple overhand knot.

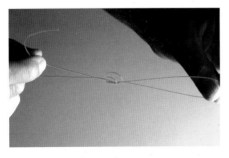

5. Wet with saliva and pull tight.

6. The finished loop.

The water knot

1. Take two lengths of line.

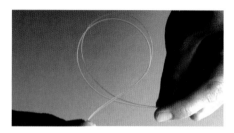

2. Form a loop with the two lengths.

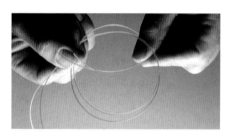

3. Pass the two ends through each other to form a loop.

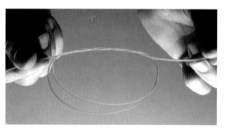

4. Repeat this four or five times.

5. Moisten and gradually pull tight.

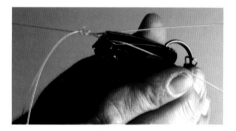

6. Trim the ends. If a dropper is required leave one end long to attach hook.

The blood knot

1. Take the two ends of line to be joined.

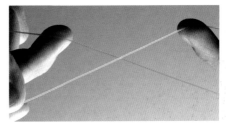

2. Start to twist together.

3. Continue to twist.

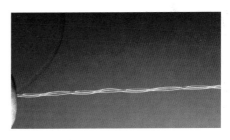

4. Make at least ten turns.

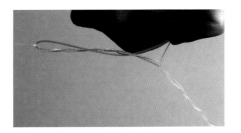

5. Form a gap in the centre of the twisted section.

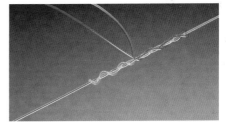

6. Insert both ends of line moisten and pull tight.

7. Trim the line ends.

The leader knot

1. Take the shock leader.

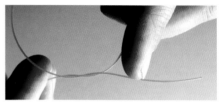

2. Tie an overhand loop.

3. Repeat.

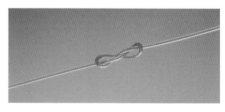

4. Pull partially tight to form two loops.

5. Insert thinner-diameter main line.

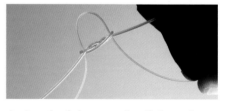

6. Into both loops and pull through about 25cm (10in).

7. Wrap the thin line around leader.

8. Make at least six turns.

9. Pass the end of the line back in through the loop formed.

10. Pass the line back in through the new loop.

11. Start to slowly tighten.

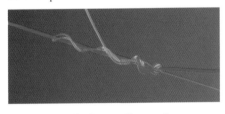

12. Moisten before pulling tight.

13. Trim off line ends.

14. The completed knot.

The knotless hook attachment

1. Take a hook length and form a small loop in its end.

2. Wrap line around hook shank and line.

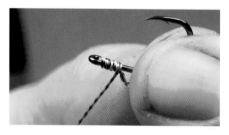

3. Pass the line through the hook eye.

4. Pull through until desired length remains.

5. Insert line end, back through hook eye.

6. Pull tight.

7. A baiting needle can now be used to attach a boilie or other suitable bait.

The stop knot

1. Lay a loop of line beside mainline.

2. Start to twist around the main line.

3. Make around six turns.

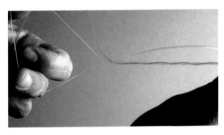

4. Pass one end of line into loop.

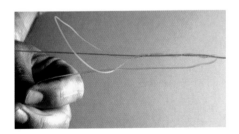

5. Start to pull tight gradually.

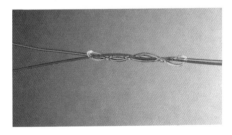

6. Moisten before tightening fully.

7. Trim ends to leave protruding tags.

Rigs

Rigs are the terminal tackle component set-ups at the business end of the main line. They need to be as simple and functional as possible, as well as strong and reliable. They must not be prone to tangling and must help to present the bait to the fish in a manner that does not deter the fish, but promotes its effective hooking.

There are a large number of rigs covering many situations, with apparently endless variations. I shall now introduce a selection of rigs and describe their construction and purpose.

The free line

The free line is the simplest rig of all. The hook is attached either directly to the main line or to a short hook length, either by means of a swivel or by joining the two lines. This rig is suitable for close-range work, preferably when the fish can be observed.

The running leger

The running leger is used in various forms throughout most branches of angling. A leger weight is threaded on to the main line and then stopped, often with a bead and swivel, with the hook length being attached to the swivel. In theory, the fish can take the bait with the line running freely through the eye of the weight. The sensation of the bite will then be transmitted directly to the rod tip, or to whichever bite-indication set-up is being used.

• The basic running-leger set-up for carp and freshwater species.
• The running leger for pike and predators.
• The boat angler's running leger, used for up-tide or down-tide angling.

The paternoster

In the paternoster, the main line is fixed to the top of a three-way link of some type, with the second link being connected to the weight and the third to the hook. Not being prone to tangling (if constructed carefully, at least), this rig is particularly good for fishing at long range.

There are several variations of the basic paternoster:

- The running paternoster.
- The sea angler's paternoster.
- The sea angler's two-hook paternoster.
- The sea angler's pulley rig; and the carp angler's helicopter rig.
- The basic paternoster, for use in fresh water.
- The running paternoster.
- The sea angler's paternoster.
- The sea angler's two-hook paternoster.
- The sea angler's pulley rig.
- The carp angler's helicopter rig.

Although paternosters are effective rigs, they have a distinct downside, namely the possibility of a fish becoming tethered to a snag by the rig if the main line breaks, a possibility that must always be taken into account and, if possible, prevented. Using a weak link to the weight is a wise precaution because it ensures that if the weight becomes snagged on the bottom, only the weight will be lost. It is sometimes possible to use a hook length that is lighter than the main line, which will ensure that a fish that breaks free will only leave a small length of line trailing from the hook. The golden rule, however, is to use as strong a line as is reasonably practicable. And if you are fishing for fish with sharp teeth, such as pike, make sure that you use a wire trace.

Float rigs

Floats (see page 77) are used to suspend the bait at the proper depth, and, in most situations, to alert the angler to a fish taking the bait. It is essential to weight floats so that they sit on the water correctly.

The main float-fishing set-ups are as follows, but many other variations can also be used.

The light, still-water float

The light, still-water float is the set-up used to target a wide range of fish in lakes and ponds. The hook bait can be fished at a range of depths, from the surface to the bottom. Various floats can be used to cater for the prevailing conditions and size of species being targeted. A pole rig incorporates the same basic features.

The running-water float

Although a larger, more buoyant, float is used for the running-water float, the basic set-up is the same as for the light, still-water float. Split shot are positioned according to the conditions, and in relation to the presentation of the bait. In fast-flowing water, it may be desirable to sink the bait quickly by bunching the split shot near to the hook.

The sliding float

The sliding float is used for fishing the bait at a depth greater than the length of the rod. In this set-up, a stop knot is incorporated in the line at the desired depth and a float is allowed to slide freely on the line. When the rig is cast out, the weights sink, pulling the line through a ring at the base of the float. When the stop knot is reached, the float cocks, suspending the bait at the desired depth.

The lift method

The lift method is a simple, but effective, rig used mainly for tench and carp fishing. The weight, which is concentrated close to the hook, is allowed to rest on the bottom, with the line being tightened until the float cocks. When a fish takes the bait, the float lifts as the weight is dislodged, at which point the angler strikes (or else if the float sinks beneath the surface).

The floating bait-controller

In the floating bait-controller set-up, the float is primarily used as the casting weight. The line is threaded through an eye in the float, and a hook link is attached in a similar way to the running leger (see page 118). A stop can be incorporated to fix the float into position. The floating bait is fished on a hook length that is partially greased so that it floats.

The float paternoster for pike and predators

In the float paternoster for pike and predators, the paternoster rig (see page

118) is combined with a float to provide bite indication by means of the float. It is advisable to incorporate an upper wire trace to avoid a bite off should the line come into contact with the predator's teeth.

The free-roving predator float

In the free-roving predator float, the bait is suspended beneath the float and allowed to drift. If live bait is used, it can similarly be allowed to rove freely around the swim.

The sea float rig

Floats used in salt water are generally larger than those used in fresh water. Sliding floats are commonly used for sea float rigs.

The shark angler's float

In shark fishing, the float seldom acts as a bite indicator, its main purpose instead being to suspend the bait at the correct depth. When a shark takes the bait, the stop detaches, allowing the fish to swim off with the bait without feeling any resistance. The angler sets the hook (though multiple hook rigs are sometimes used) when he or she is confident that the bait has been properly taken.

Bait

Bait can be divided into the following categories: natural, manufactured and artificial.

Successful anglers always make sure that they have the best bait, but what is the best bait? The answer to that question depends on many factors, and angling successes or failures often rest upon the choice of bait. Because each species of fish responds better to particular bait, the species targeted obviously determines that choice.

The angler must be prepared to think carefully about bait and presentation, however. Water clarity, location and a host of other factors will also influence your options. If you are fishing in heavily coloured water, for example, a big, smelly bait will be required to attract fish, while a small, visible bait maybe more productive when fishing in clear water.

Many successful manufactured and artificial types of bait are never found naturally, yet still tempt large numbers of fish. In some instances, this is because anglers have deliberately weaned the fish on to the bait. In many other cases, however, it is simply because the fish's natural instinct tells it that the bait is edible. In general, freshwater anglers use more manufactured and artificial bait than sea anglers.

Anglers use hundreds of types of bait to catch fish throughout the world, but I shall now outline my own personal favourites, for both fresh water and salt water.

Freshwater bait

For freshwater bait, I use worms, maggots, bread, boilies and pastes, particle baits, meat baits, floaters, fish

ABOVE Lobworms or night crawlers are my number-one bait for freshwater fishing.

baits, imitation baits and groundbait.
These are among the most commonly
used categories of freshwater bait, and
give the angler plenty of room for
experimentation. The proper
application of bait and groundbait is
fundamental to successful angling, so
remember to give it careful
consideration.

Worms

I should imagine that every species of
freshwater fish has been caught after
being tempted by a variety of the
humble worm, the traditional natural
bait and my number-one bait when
fishing in fresh water. All worms make
particularly effective bait in rivers
following heavy rain, perhaps because
fish would naturally expect to find them
in the water as a result of being swept
from the riverbank by the rising water.

There are several varieties of worm
available to the angler, and the
lobworm, or night crawler, is the most
commonly used for large fish. These
worms can be dug up from the garden
or bought from tackle shops. My
favourite method of collecting them is

ABOVE What fish could resist this tasty offering?

to stalk them on a damp night. After
dark, the worms emerge from their
underground world to search for food
on the lawn or flowerbeds. If you creep
along slowly with a torch, you will be
able to see them and seize them before
they disappear down their holes. If you
manage to grab one, hold it firmly until
you feel its grip falter, then pull it
steadily from the hole. If the worm
breaks, store the parts separately from
the healthy, intact worms and use them
as groundbait. Catching lobworms in
this way is almost a sport in itself, and

it takes a little practice before you become proficient in the art. (Until you try it, you would never believe the speeds that a worm can attain!)

After obtaining your worms, you will need to store them carefully. They will stay healthy for weeks in a bait box full of damp moss or newspaper if kept constantly damp and at a low temperature (and you should ideally have a fridge dedicated to storing bait). If you want to bring any unused worms home after a day's fishing, invest in a small cool box and place an ice pack

ABOVE This barbel was tempted with maggots.

OPPOSITE PAGE Maggots are highly attractive baits.

BELOW This carp fell to lobworm bait.

inside it, but apart from the worms, which will die if they become warm, and if you don't discover their corpses quickly, they will really stink!

A trick that you can use that will sometimes tempt extra fish to the bait is to inject air into a lobworm with a syringe. (Caution: great care must be taken when doing this to avoid accidentally injecting air into your fingers, a mistake that could prove fatal.) That done, add a split shot to the hook link and suspend the worm several inches from the bottom of the water. The split shot will dictate the distance, and should generally be sufficiently heavy to sink the worm (this can be determined by lowering the baited tackle into the margins of the water for close observation).

The red worm and brandling are commonly used as bait, too. Both can be purchased from tackle shops, and brandling can also be collected from manure heaps. These worms are generally fished on finer tackle to tempt a wide variety of fish species. They can be fished in bunches, and may prove as effective as lobworms in certain conditions.

The efficiency of worm hook baits can be greatly increased by turning them into groundbait and loose feed, and chopped worms are highly effective at stimulating fish within a swim. Worms can be chopped up with a pair of scissors, a knife or ideally a pizza-cutter on a chopping board. The chopped worm can then be scattered into the swim, either by hand or with a catapult. It can also be added to groundbait or put into a feeder. In addition, concentrated worm extract can be purchased from tackle dealers to add to groundbait.

Maggots

Maggots are probably the most widely used bait in coarse fishing. Although they are classed as natural bait, I don't

suppose that fish come across many maggots under natural circumstances, yet maggots are nevertheless highly attractive to many species of fish. Their greatest benefit is therefore as attractors, and loose feed can be applied to the water to encourage fish to feed confidently, thus making them easier to tempt.

Maggots can be purchased in a variety of colours, the most common being red, white and bronze. The colour that you should use will depend upon the preference of the local fish to a large extent. Many anglers believe the coloured maggots to be more effective on certain days, and although I tend to buy a mixture of colours, I have a preference for reds on the hook.

The success of maggots as bait will be determined by their application as loose feed. In float-fishing, maggots are generally sprayed into the swim using a catapult. If you are fishing a river, they must be deposited into the river upstream to ensure that they drift into the swim at the appropriate depth. If you put the maggots into the wrong area, you may draw the fish downstream and out of the swim. The speed of the current and depth of the swim will dictate the point at which the maggots should be introduced.

The swimfeeder (see page 75) is the ideal tool for introducing maggots to the water when legering (see page 330), and there are a large number available to suit different swims. For running water, select a feeder that remains on the riverbed (the size of the holes will determine the rate at which the maggots escape). On large, fast rivers, you will need to use large feeders and cast them constantly, thereby supplying a steady trickle of bait to stimulate and attract the fish.

In still water, large quantities of maggots can be used to bring big species, such as carp, tench and bream, into a swim. If there are soft silt deposits on the bottom, live maggots may bury themselves in them and thus become hidden from the fish, however, which is why it is sometimes better to use dead maggots as feed (keep a supply by freezing any maggots left over from angling outings).

One way of pepping up the

effectiveness of maggots as bait is to flavour them. A wide variety of spray-on flavours is available, ranging from sweet to savoury; alternatively, powdered spices (my favourites are curry or paprika) can be sprinkled over the maggots the night before going fishing.

To discourage maggots from turning into casters (chrysalises), you will have to keep them cool, and ideally in a fridge (which may not go down well with other members of your household, so either be discreet or invest in a dedicated bait fridge). Adding a sprinkling of dry groundbait to the maggots will help to prevent them from sweating.

A word of warning regarding maggots: many anglers have horror stories to tell about escaping maggots, including me. My friend and I once returned to his house after a long, wet day's fishing on the riverbank. As we unloaded my car, I looked at several pints of maggots wriggling away in an open-topped bait bucket in the boot. 'What about these?' I asked. 'They'll be okay. They won't climb out – they're dry', he responded confidently, so I slammed the door shut and headed inside for a hot meal and a bath. When I opened the boot the next morning, there were maggots crawling everywhere! And despite having attacked it with a vacuum cleaner as soon as I got home, for weeks every warm day caused flies to hatch in the car.

Bread

Bread is a cheap and very effective bait that is used to tempt a wide range of fish species. It is also extremely versatile and can be presented in many ways, including as flake, crust and paste.

ABOVE Bread flake proved effective for these roach.

Flake

Flake is simply a piece of bread whose centre is squeezed onto a hook. I prefer to use cheap, doughy, sliced bread for flake. It is essential that the bread is fresh, otherwise it will not stay on the hook and can cause frustrating fishing.

The size of hook used for flake will depend entirely on the size of the bait. The ideal for small species, such as roach, is a thumbnail-sized bit of flake on a size 10 hook. For larger species like carp, a walnut-sized lump of flake on a size 4 hook may be required.

Whatever size of bait is used, it is important to ensure that the hook's point is showing. For legering, the bread is squeezed onto the shank and eye of the hook, leaving a fluffy tail around the hook's point.

When float-fishing, the bait is often best presented by pinching a corner of the flake and pushing the hook gently through it. You may initially find this presentation frustrating, however, because you will need to put fresh bait on the hook every time that you cast it. A friend of mine demonstrated this to me while we were trotting for roach on England's famed Hampshire Avon. He insisted that if the bait came back, it had not been put on correctly, the idea being that the bait should in no way impede the hook from striking home on a fish that is intercepting the bait.

Another way of presenting flake is to use a bread punch to form tiny pellets of flake, which are then lightly hooked. This is a very effective bait for roach when fished in conjunction with liquidised bread.

LEFT It is important to ensure that the hook point is not masked by the bait.

Crust

To prepare crust, simply tear pieces from a loaf of bread, ideally unsliced crusty bread. Crust is an extremely buoyant bait, and is ideal when fishing for carp in warm weather on a dark, still, summer's night. Having scattered a few pieces over the surface of the water (crust is more effective when it is not used generously), the angler then waits in suspense, watching for signs that the carp are feeding. The carp will be heard as they slurp down the floating crusts, at which point the angler lowers, or casts, the bait near the feeding fish. If anglers keep themselves concealed from the carp, the crust (which should be offered on a size 6 to 4 hook) can be lowered into the margins of the water, which is an exciting method to use, especially after dark. Tension mounts as they approach the bait, and if all goes well, the bait will be devoured in a swirl of carp, whereupon the angler may suddenly find him- or herself standing, rod arched, as a powerful carp surges away in an attempt to free itself of the hook. (Such encounters were frequent before the onset of modern methods. For an insight into the sport's early days, I recommend BB's enchanting book *Confessions of a Carp Fisher*, and Richard Walker's famous book, *Stillwater Angling*.)

ABOVE Carp slurp down floating crusts.

RIGHT Bread crust is a traditional bait referred to in several classic angling books.

Smaller species, such as chub and rudd, also take floating crust. When fishing for these species, use size 10 or 12 hooks with crust baits the size of a thumbnail.

Another way of presenting crust is to suspend it on the bed of a lake or river, either by adding split shot to the trace or by allowing the crust to rise directly from the weight.

Paste

Paste is made by removing the crust, wetting the bread and then compressing it within a cloth to remove the moisture. The paste is then moulded onto an appropriately sized hook (the paste should be soft enough to allow the hook to pull free on the strike without affecting penetration). Paste can be flavoured easily with commercially prepared products or simple household ingredients, such as Marmite or custard powder.

Paste can also be used in conjunction with crust to form a balanced bait that sinks slowly to the bottom of the water. This is ideal when soft silt covers the bottom because the bait will be clearly visible to the fish.

Bread as an attractor

Like most bait, bread is far more effective when it is fished among loose feed, or an attractor, which can either be hook-sized samples or smaller particles. Bread is used as an attractor in the following three ways.

1. Breadcrumbs (finely ground bread) are often used as the bulk ingredient for groundbait. This forms a cloud in the water that stimulates the fish without overfeeding them.
2. Stale bread can be soaked, placed in a bucket and mashed, either by hand or with a potato-masher. The mashed bread can then be thrown into the swim by hand or in a cage-feeder.
3. Fresh bread can be made into perfect groundbait by placing it in a food processor and liquidising it into tiny particles. These particles can then be squeezed into balls and either thrown into the swim or squeezed around a method-style feeder prior to casting.

Boilies and paste

A boilie is a paste bait that is immersed in boiling water to create a hard crust, making it resistant to the attentions of small fish. It also means that the bait can be left in the swim for long periods of time before breaking down. Since the late 1970s, boilies have become the most widely used bait for carp throughout the United Kingdom, and, I suspect, also throughout Europe.

The ingredients used in the making of boilies are extremely varied, although typical ingredients are ground-up trout pellets or semolina to which egg is generally added as a binder before the bait is rolled and boiled. Boilies can furthermore be coloured and flavoured to give the bait a distinctive, fish-attracting character.

BELOW Boilies are the most widely used modern carp bait.

The subject of specialist carp bait is very technical, so I shall only outline it briefly. If you want to learn more, you will need to read such specialist books as *Carp Fever*, by Kevin Maddocks, and *Carp, Now and Then*, by Rod Hutchinson, which are today only sold by second-hand book-dealers. During the late 1970s, Fred Wilton was generally credited as introducing the high nutritional value (HNV) bait theory. Wilton argued that carp could detect the food value of bait, so that if HNV bait were to be introduced into the carps' environment, the fish would eventually be weaned onto it and would then eat this food in preference to more natural sources of nutrition. Although this has proved a controversial theory, it cannot be denied that such baits, which include boilies, have proved both highly effective and beneficial to the growth rates of fish.

Due to their widespread use, boilies have become an effective bait for many species other than carp, including tench, bream, barbel and even roach. The size of the boilie used will depend, to some extent, on the species targeted.

Fortunately for the modern angler, boilies are now widely sold over the counter by angling shops, removing the need to undertake the laborious task of mixing and rolling them. The variety of bait that can be bought is astonishingly large, which can sometimes make choosing difficult, in which case try to seek local advice or simply ask tackle dealers which baits are their best-sellers (that way you will at least end up with a bait that attracts fish in local waters).

The boilie has encouraged the evolution of a range of bait presentations, the most important being the discovery of the hair rig during the late 1970s. This rig involves attaching the bait with a short length of line or similar material (see opposite), while the hook is left bare and is pulled into the fish's mouth with the bait. Being completely uncluttered, the hook easily finds purchase within the fish's mouth. This presentation is often used in conjunction with a heavy weight, a set-up termed a 'bolt rig'. As the fish moves away with the bait, the weight causes sufficient resistance for the hook to prick the fish, and as the fish then

1. Hook and hair rig loop.

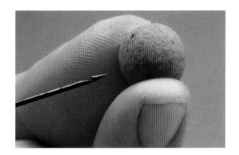

2. Insert baiting needle into bait.

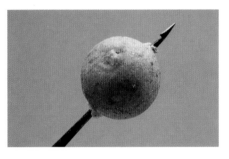

3. Push carefully through leaving point and barb showing.

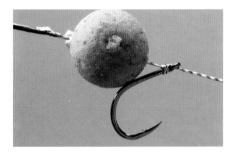

4. Attach loop to barb and pull through bait.

5. The baiting needle is removed.

6. Insert a bait stop into loop.

7. Pull tight and trim off bait stop.

8. Boilie and hair rig ready to cast.

swims off in panic, the hook is driven home against the anchorage of the weight. The fish has thus hooked itself, as the bite indicator indicates to the angler. It is an effective mode of fishing and has led to a minority of anglers becoming lazy, and, some would say, unsporting. Remember that although fads and fashions will always affect the angling world, intelligent anglers should not follow the herd, but should instead adapt and evolve their angling skills in order to stay ahead of both other anglers and their target fish.

Boilies should be used in conjunction with attractors (which are also called free offerings or loose bait), and several methods have been developed to enable the angler to introduce these free offerings into the water. Catapults, throwing sticks and bait-droppers are the most commonly used, while some anglers use remote-controlled boats to deposit the free offerings near the hook bait. Another very effective way of introducing a small amount of bait near to the hook is by using polyvinyl acetate (PVA), a plastic-like substance that dissolves when it

comes into contact with water, which is sold in various forms by most good tackle shops. Boilies can be threaded onto a PVA string, tied to the terminal tackle, and introduced to the water, whereupon the PVA melts, leaving several free offerings next to the bait. Alternatively, bags made of PVA can be filled with broken boilie particles, or other dry ingredients, to attract fish to the hook bait.

Boilies are made by boiling paste baits, which are themselves made from a wide range of ingredients. When used as bait, they are generally fished on the

ABOVE Baits are put into a PVA bag, which dissolves in the water, helping to ensure fish are attracted to the hook bait.

hook rather than on a hair rig. Although they will not stay on the hook for long, they sometimes have more instant appeal to fish than other types of bait. To enhance a boilie's attractiveness to fish, paste can also be moulded around the harder boilie. Small paste baits are highly effective in commercial fisheries, and help anglers to win many matches when fished beneath a float on a pole.

Particle baits

The term 'particle baits' covers an enormous range of baits used by anglers, particle baits being small baits that are generally introduced into the swim in sufficient quantities to encourage the fish to become partially preoccupied with them. I suppose that the maggot could be termed the ultimate particle bait because the basic principles applied to fishing with maggots (see page 125) are relevant here, too. Although many anglers link the use of particle baits with carp fishing, such baits were in widespread use long before the rapid growth in carp fishing stimulated by Richard Walker during the 1950s.

Hemp seeds are one of the most effective particle baits in use. Tiny seeds that are boiled until they split open, revealing white kernels, they are more effective if soaked in water for several days so that they ferment in their juices. Single seeds can be fished on a tiny hook when the target is a small species, such as roach, or can be carefully presented in greater numbers on larger hooks when targeting such species as carp. Hemp is generally used as an attractor, however. Its pungent odour draws fish into the swim, and its tiny particles sink into the debris on the lake- or riverbed, stimulating the fish to root about in a feeding frenzy. A larger, more easily presented, bait is then fished in this area.

ABOVE Hemp seed is a brilliant attractor.

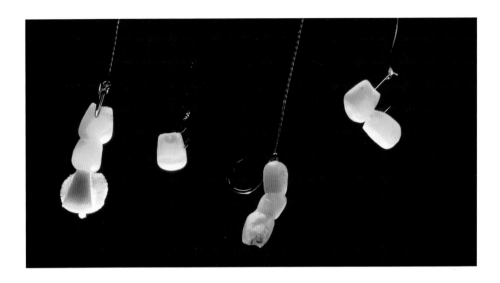

ABOVE Sweet corn can be presented on a hook in various ways.

LEFT Effective bait straight from the tin.

Sweet corn was widely used by anglers during the late 1970s and early 1980s, and has remained an extremely effective bait, particularly for carp, with several record-winning fish having succumbed to its sweet taste and bright colour. Bream, barbel, tench, roach, rudd, trout and a host of other species find this bait attractive, too. Because it is sold by most supermarkets and can be used directly from the tin, it is furthermore a very convenient bait. Single kernels can be attached to an appropriately sized hook, while multiple kernels can be fished on a hair rig. Sweet corn can also be placed in blender and pulped before being added to groundbait.

ABOVE A tiger nut is fished on a hair rig.

LEFT Tiger nuts are an effective carp bait.

BELOW A bait drill is used to enable the nut to be attached to the hair rig.

Supermarkets, seed merchants and tackle dealers sell a host of other types of particle baits as well. A few such particle baits are: peanuts, tiger nuts, tares, beans, maples, cockles, sultanas,

ABOVE AND RIGHT Trout pellets are effective particle baits and are often fished on a hair rig.

peeled prawns, sunflower seeds, wheat, maize, pigeon food, trout pellets and chick peas. Although many of these baits are used primarily for carp, some are also effective for other species. Remember that many seed- or nut-type baits will need careful preparation in order to enhance their effectiveness and make them safe for fish to eat, which will usually involve soaking and boiling the baits to soften them and release their fish-attracting oils and aromas.

Meat baits

Mention the term 'meat baits', and most coarse anglers would at one time have thought of luncheon meat, a highly successful bait that has been catching several species, including carp, barbel, chub, tench and bream (and carp, barbel and chub in particular have an appetite for luncheon-meat bait), for many years. It is also a convenient bait because it can be used straight from the tin, being cut into cubes or broken off into small chunks before being either impaled on the hook or hair-rigged.

There are several brands of luncheon meat, and each has its own properties – some are more buoyant, harder or softer than others, for instance – and aroma. I suggest that you try out several brands to see which works best for you (my favourite is Bacon Grill). To pep up the bait a little, you could add some flavour or colour, and I have two ways of doing this. One is to cut the luncheon meat into bait-sized pieces, place them in a plastic bag containing either a liquid flavouring or a

RIGHT Luncheon meat.

powder, such as curry powder, give the bag a good shake and then leave the bait in the bag until it's time to go fishing. The other is to follow the same procedure, but to store the bag of bait in the freezer, which seems to help the bait to absorb the flavour. Luncheon meat can also be lightly fried to give the bait a light crust, which helps it to stay on the hook. You could flavour the fat in which you fry the meat with spices or herbs, too, my favourites being garlic, paprika and curry powder.

In addition to luncheon meat, many other meat-based baits will catch fish, too. Sections of pepperoni sausage, garlic sausage and Campbell's meatballs, for example, make excellent baits, particularly in heavily coloured water, where a strong scent trail is vital.

Finally, pet shops are packed with treats for cats and dogs that are equally appealing to our scaly quarry. Many of these are packaged in small, resealable sachets that be tucked away in your tackle bag for a change of bait on a difficult day.

Floating baits

Floating baits, which are also known as surface baits or floaters, are widely used for carp fishing (and I have already mentioned that floating bread is used as carp bait, see page 129). Several other baits make good floating baits, too, although floating boilies, which can be bought or made, are not generally used as surface baits.

The most popular surface bait is probably the Pedigree Chum Mixer that is sold in pet shops and supermarkets, a small dog biscuit that is extremely buoyant, the ideal size to present to carp in particular, and that can also be coloured or flavoured to give extra appeal. Several other brands of dog and cat biscuit can be used in the same way, which is as follows.

Because dry dog biscuit is very hard, you will need to soften it up before using it. Do this by putting some biscuits into a plastic bag, adding hot water (with a little flavouring if you like) and then draining off the water. The baits will have absorbed the moisture within an hour, when they will be soft enough to put on the hook and

ABOVE Dog biscuits make superb floating carp baits.

introduce to the water as floating feed (they can also be presented on a hair rig). My favourite way of attaching these pet-food baits to the hook is to superglue a few dry baits to the shank.

Having introduced some free baits into the water, it is wise to observe the fish feeding confidently before casting out a hook bait, and then to cast the bait beyond the fish before drawing it back into their midst. These baits are generally fished in conjunction with a controller (a float that gives weight when casting).

Fish baits

Because they prey on other fish, predatory fish (such as pike, zander, catfish, perch and eels in the United Kingdom) need to be targeted with either dead baits, live baits or lures (see pages 172 to 182). There are thousands of species of predatory fish in the world, and the principles described here, which apply in UK, can be adapted for use when fishing for them.

Dead baits are the most widely used baits for pike fishing in the United Kingdom. Perhaps strangely, sea-fish dead baits like mackerel, sardines and herring prove just as effective, and sometimes even more so, than naturally occurring freshwater dead baits. These baits can be purchased from tackle shops or fishmongers and stored in the freezer until required.

Dead baits can be fished whole or in sections, when the head or tail is commonly preferred. Using a section of bait will allow its blood and juices to escape into the water quicker, and will

BELOW Mackerel is a fine bait for pike

LEFT Dead baits can be injected with flavours to enhance their appeal.

BELOW This brown trout attacked the live bait that was intended for perch.

therefore attract fish faster. The bait will also need changing more frequently as a result, however. The effectiveness of the baits can be improved by injecting them with a flavour and fish oil, such as pilchard. Dead baits can be presented in a variety of ways. Treble hooks are often used to mount a bait, for instance, with two size 6 trebles (which should be attached to a wire trace to resist the pike's sharp teeth) being applied to the flank of the bait.

It seems that sea-fish dead baits seldom appeal to zander, perch or eels, species that prefer small, freshwater dead or live baits. The use of live baits is controversial. Some people regard it as being a cruel and unjustified

practice, but I don't. Indeed, I find it an exciting, and, at times, highly effective method. If you share my opinion, note that live baits should always be caught in the venue that you are fishing because it is illegal to transfer fish from water to water; it is important to obey this law to prevent the spread of disease, which can decimate a fishery.

ABOVE A perch live bait.

When presenting live baits, you will need to give careful thought to your hooking arrangements. As always, the hook must match the size of the bait. And although treble hooks are used for pike fishing, single hooks are better for most other species, a large, single hook being both adequate for the task and easier to remove from the fish's jaws.

Imitation baits

There has been an influx of realistic imitation baits made from soft foams and plastics into the angling market in recent years. These are often used in conjunction with the real thing to enhance bait presentation. A floating piece of foam can be shaped to imitate the bait and can then be fished alongside the real bait to provide higher or neutral buoyancy, for instance. At other times, however, they are used on their own. I suspect that the fish will need to be stimulated into feeding heavily on the real baits before they will take these facsimiles, although because some of them can be flavoured, a fish may sometimes take a solitary offering.

Groundbait

The purpose of groundbait is to attract fish into the swim and stimulate feeding. This mixture should ideally not overfeed the fish because hungry fish will feed further and thus be catchable, whereas fish with full stomachs will feed no more. Always remember this when introducing groundbait or loose feed to the water (the maxim 'feed little and often' is a good one to bear in mind).

You will need to take the species that you are targeting into careful consideration, as well as the numbers inhabiting the water in which you are fishing. Carp, for example, are large fish that devour large amounts of food, so it stands to reason that if large numbers of carp are present, large quantities of groundbait should be applied. If you are targeting a small shoal of roach, however, only a small amount of feed will be required. Groundbait can also be applied as a secondary attractor in certain situations: for example, introducing groundbait to the swim to attract small fish may in turn attract the predatory fish that the angler is targeting.

Many groundbait mixtures designed for specific situations are available from tackle shops, so read their labels carefully and think about what you need. Combining different mixtures or adding the groundbait to a bulk ingredient like breadcrumbs (see page 130) may sometimes be very effective. It is also often helpful to add particles of the hook bait to the mixture, good examples being liquidised sweet corn, ground hemp seed and chopped worm.

The groundbait can be introduced to the water by hand, in balls, by catapult, or by means of a block-end or method feeder, which requires a stiff mixture. Indeed, the consistency of any type of groundbait is extremely important. If there is a strong current, the groundbait will need to be a heavy mixture that will sink to the bottom before slowly breaking up. In still water, it may be desirable for the groundbait to form a cloud in the water, to break up on contact with the water and then slowly to sink down through the swim.

NEXT PAGE The method feeder is encased in groundbait. The hungry carp or bream are encouraged to feed on this ball of food and in so doing find the hook bait which is fished on a short hook length.

Saltwater bait

Although some of the baits used in freshwater fishing can also be used in salt water, there is generally a greater emphasis on the use of natural baits in sea angling. The way in which these baits are offered to the fish seldom reflects what the fish naturally encounters, however.

I once read an apt analogy: a cow grazing in a field will eat many blades of grass, but it is difficult to determine exactly which blade of grass it will eat today; if you translate this scenario into a fish grazing upon the seabed, your bait is the equivalent of that blade of grass.

Remember that the bait will need to be able to attract the attention of the fish in a vast expanse of water, drawing them to it by both its appearance and smell. It must also be placed where the fish are the most abundant (see pages 33 to 37).

I shall now outline the most generally used saltwater baits.

RIGHT This pollock has taken a whole mackerel bait intended for shark.

NEXT PAGE Fresh mackerel are a superb bait.

Fish baits

Fish baits are among the most widely used baits for sea angling, and can be adapted for use in lots of situations. The big advantage of many of these baits is that they can be purchased ready frozen and stored in a freezer until required. Indeed, many species, such as mackerel, can be caught in large numbers during their season and then

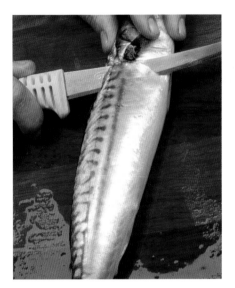

1. A sharp knife is essential.

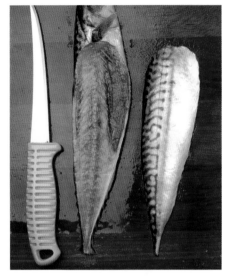

2. One fillet makes a bait for large fish.

3. Cut into strips for smaller bait.

4. Perfect bait for many sea fish.

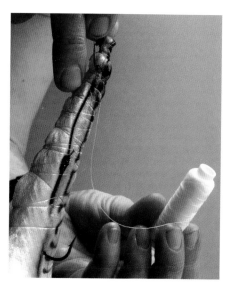

1. A fillet can be attached securely to the hook with shirring elastic (bait elastic.)

2. A strip of mackerel can be hooked lightly when boat fishing to give a more tempting presentation.

be immediately frozen.

Oily-fleshed fish like mackerel, herring and sardine make superb baits, with a fine, fish-attracting aroma. These baits can be cut into sections or strips or fished whole, depending upon the species being targeted. Remember that the size of hook must match the bait, and that the bait must be placed on the hook in such a way that the quarry is easily hooked.

Many small species of fish can be fished whole as live baits. The visual attraction of the fish is of the most importance in this instance, combined with the vibrations that it emits as it flutters in the water. (Predatory fish have sensors in their lateral lines that detect this movement, enabling them to

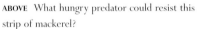

ABOVE What hungry predator could resist this strip of mackerel?

TOP RIGHT A whole mackerel is used to tempt large predatory fish like shark.

RIGHT Mackerel with shark hook (12/0) and a length of pipe cleaner that can be used to secure tail, thus improving presentation.

home in on their prey from a considerable distance.)

Sand eel is a popular bait that can be purchased blast-frozen from tackle shops. These small fish are the staple diet of many sea fish and birds, although their numbers have been sadly

ABOVE A small blue shark is brought to the side of the boat. The mackerel bait is clearly visible in its jaws.

RIGHT The head of a mackerel is good big fish bait.

depleted by commercial harvesters, who use them in fertiliser or animal feed. Their streamlined shape makes them ideal for distance-casting, and they are threaded on to appropriately sized hooks as bait (they are the number-one bait for shore-caught ray in the United Kingdom). Live sand eel can be obtained from sandy beaches after dark or purchased directly from netsmen. When lightly hooked, they make superb

bait for bass, pollock and a wealth of other fish species.

The greater sand eel, or launce, is similar to the sand eel, but, as its name suggests, is much larger. These fish can be bought blast-frozen or caught from a boat using special strings of feathered hooks. Live sand eels are used to make good catches of pollock, bass and cod from offshore reefs.

Squid is another popular fish bait that attracts a wide range of species.

ABOVE A squid fresh from the ocean.

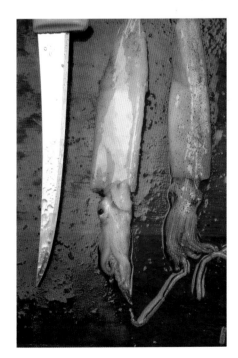

RIGHT Calamari squid are a popular bait.

LEFT This fine pollock took a live launce.

The most readily available squid is calamari, which can be bought frozen in small boxes and stored until required. When fishing for cod, conger, ray and bass, it is best fished whole on a large hook, or on a pair of hooks termed a 'pennel rig'. Alternatively, the squid can be cut into strips to be fished on a small hook to attract lesser species. Long, thin strips can also be cut to wave tantalisingly in the tide. Squid is ideal as an attractor when fished in conjunction with another bait, and the addition of squid strips to worm bait is considered essential when targeting plaice over the famous Skerries and Shambles banks off southern England.

All fish baits are best used fresh: being firmer, the flesh stays on the hook, as well as being generally more attractive to the target fish. Your own sense of smell is a good guide to the freshness of the bait, as is its appearance: squid, for example, is white when fresh, but turns pinkish as it decays.

1. Open the squid out.

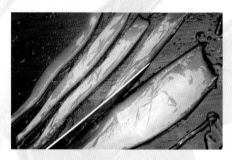

2. Cut into strips.

3. A fine bait on its own or combined with a different bait to form a cocktail.

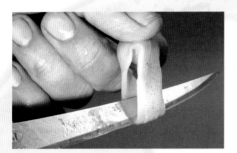

4. 4. Alternatively cut the squid into segments and then cut each section to form a strip.

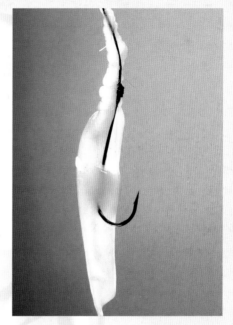

5. A squid strip.

LEFT A whole squid on what is termed a pennel rig.

Marine worms

There are many different species of
marine worm, most of which end up as
food for fish. Anglers should
concentrate on marine worms that are
easy to obtain and suitable for impaling
on a hook. Note that the hooks used for
marine-worm baits should be of a
thinner gauge of wire (fine wire) than
that used for many other baits to
prevent the worm from breaking up as
it is being threaded onto the hook.

Marine worms can be dug from the

ABOVE Lugworm

BELOW Tell-tale lugworm casts make location
simple.

ABOVE Digging for lugworm.

RIGHT A fresh blow lug.

shoreline or purchased from angling
shops. They need to be stored and
transported in a cool container and
protected from rainwater and sun, both
of which quickly kill them. Newspaper is
the best medium in which to wrap them

because it absorbs excess moisture.

The most popular bait used in the United Kingdom is the lugworm, of which there are several varieties. The ones most often used by anglers are the black, or yellow-tail, lug and the blow lug. The black lug can be found well down the beach, near the low-water mark, while the blow lug can be located nearer the top of the beach. All lugworms leave telltale casts in the sand or mud, helping the angler to pinpoint the areas in which they proliferate. Be warned, however, that digging up worms is hard work and requires a good deal of effort. (I do not envy bait-diggers who do it for a living. Bear this in mind when you go to buy your worms: would you venture out into the wind and rain to dig up worms for the amount of money that you are being asked to pay in the shop?) When digging marine worms of any type, it is good practice to backfill the holes, which helps to preserve the marine environment, ensures that the area is repopulated by worms and avoids causing a hazard to boat-owners and anyone else who is wading out from the

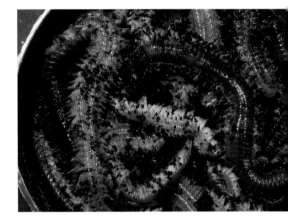

ABOVE King ragworm.

RIGHT Always backfill your holes after digging bait.

shoreline. When collecting marine-worm bait, remember never to dig close to boat moorings and to abide by local byelaws because certain anglers' inappropriate practices can lead to the loss of other anglers' freedoms.

The lugworm can be fished either singly or in bunches, depending on the species of fish sought. If you are targeting flatfish and small whiting, you will require a size 2 to 1/0 fine-wire hook, while larger species, such as cod and bass, need a 2/0 to 6/0 hook. Remember, too, that worm baits can be

ABOVE Lugworm has tempted many fine cod.

enhanced by the addition of other baits to form 'cocktails' that will attract fish.

Ragworms are another family of marine worms of interest to the angler. The two species most commonly used are the harbour rag and king rag. The harbour rag is abundant in most estuaries, and can be dug up quite easily (remembering always to follow good practice). It makes an excellent bait for many small species of fish, especially flatfish. Harbour rags are fished in bunches on small, fine-wire hooks; it is best to thread several worms on to a hook headfirst, leaving their tails to trail attractively (to fish, anyway) in the tide. The king rag is a much larger ragworm that can grow up to 3ft (91cm) in length. It attracts a wide variety of species and is generally fished singly, depending on both the size of the worm and the fish species being targeted.

Shellfish

Shellfish are probably only eaten in large numbers by fish following a storm, when they are dislodged from their anchorages. Mussels and razor fish make excellent baits for a wide variety of species, either on their own or, more frequently, as part of a 'cocktail' bait.

Mussels can be collected from rocks or groynes at low water, or else bought

LEFT Razor-fish shells are often to be found on a beach following a storm.

BELOW Mussels are effective baits, particularly when used with other baits in a cocktail.

from a fishmonger. They should be carefully removed from their shells with a blunt knife and whipped to the hook with fine elastic. These baits can be frozen, either ready prepared on a hook and trace or wrapped in aluminium foil or clingfilm.

Razor fish can be collected using a special spear-like tool at low water on certain sandy beaches. It a craft that requires considerable effort to learn, which is why you may prefer to buy your razor fish frozen, from a tackle shop.

Most other types of shellfish will also prove effective as bait, depending upon the locality that you are fishing and the species of fish present.

Crabs

The common crab forms a major part of the diet of many sea fish, and is often found in the stomachs of fish after they have been cleaned. The strange thing is that such crabs are often hardback crabs, which are seldom effective on the hook.

The prime time to use crabs as bait is when they are moulting (as crabs grow, they shed their shells and grow

ABOVE The peeler crab is often protected by a larger hardback crab.

ABOVE Peeler crabs tend to be less aggressive than hardback crabs.

new ones). Before it has shed its shell, a crab is termed a 'peeler crab', or 'peeler', and this is the time when the entire outer shell can be removed, leaving a soft interior that can either be mounted whole or cut into sections for

LEFT The outer shell is peeled from the crab.

LEFT The legs can be peeled to provide small baits.

ABOVE Peeled crab ready for use.

RIGHT The crab is secured to the hook with the help of baiting elastic.

mounting on the hook. (Don't overlook the legs, which make excellent bait for small fish or can be mixed with other baits to form a 'cocktail'.) Crab baits are generally best held to the hook with fine elastic. This type of bait gives off an enticing scent trail that is highly attractive to many species of fish, particularly bass, cod, wrasse and eel.

After shedding its shell, the crab is at its most vulnerable to attack by many

RIGHT Peeler crab can be found beneath seaweed.

BELOW A hook-shaped tool can be used to reduce back strain when searching for crabs.

or ridge tile partially buried in the mud. The crabs seek refuge in these sanctuaries as they prepare to moult, and the angler checks their moulting status regularly before storing them in a cool shed or fridge prior to use. (When the crab's shell starts to lift from its back, it is perfect for freezing.) In warmer climates, crabs moult all year round, while in cooler climates, their main moult will often take place during the summer.

LEFT Crabs can be harvested by using traps consisting of guttering or ridge tiles.

BELOW Bait collecting can be hard work.

species of fish. At this stage, the crab is termed a 'softback' and has a jelly-like feel and makes a perfect bait.

The hardback crab is of limited use to anglers. Small hardback crabs make reasonable baits for wrasse, but few other fish seem to take them when they are presented on a hook.

Common shore crabs can be found on the beach under rocks or weeds that are well below the high-water mark. In many regions, anglers harvest crabs by laying traps that consist of sections of guttering

Apart from the common shore crab or greenback crab, there are several other varieties of crab that the angler can use as peelers or softback bait, including the edible crab, the velvet swimmer, the spider crab and the hermit crab. (The hermit crab makes its home inside the shells of shellfish, typically whelks, from which it can be carefully extracted and used in the same way as other crabs.)

Prawns

Prawn is an extremely effective bait in some areas, particularly in clear water due to its lack of strong scent. It is best fished live on relatively light tackle.

Prawns can be collected by either using a dip net at low tide or by lowering a baited drop net beside a harbour wall.

Groundbait

Although groundbait is not used as much in sea angling as it is in freshwater fishing, it can nevertheless be extremely effective in some situations, and will draw fish from a wide area if introduced carefully.

The most commonly used saltwater groundbait is rubby-dubby, or chervey, which consists of ground-up fish, fish oils and bran and is an essential element of shark fishing (see also pages 392 to 399). This evil-smelling mixture should be placed in a large onion sack and tied to the side of the boat, after which the action of the rolling boat will cause tiny fragments to break off and drift in the tide, providing a tempting scent trail that stretches out behind the boat. Using its keen sense of smell, the shark will then home in on the source to find a juicy bait suspended in mid-water.

A similar mixture can be used to attract fish when fishing from the shore. An onion sack containing bread, or a rubby-dubby mix, suspended from a harbour wall will prove an effective bait for grey mullet and other species, which can be caught using light tackle, as used for freshwater angling. I have found that canned cat food, especially the fish-flavoured varieties, is an excellent additive for saltwater groundbait.

LEFT With a bucketful of bait its time to do a bit of fishing.

Lure-fishing

Lure-fishing can be a highly enjoyable and effective method of angling. It offers many advantages over other forms of angling, too: because it needs little preparation (it does not require the collection of bait, for instance), it is ideal for anglers with limited time, enabling them to go fishing at a moment's notice. Just casting out and reeling in the lure is not guaranteed to bring results, however. Indeed, careful thought is required, and because many anglers fall into the trap of turning to

BELOW Lure anglers can roam freely casting here and there.

lure-fishing as a last resort when other methods have failed, they may quickly lose interest in this form of angling.

The fish that are most likely to be caught with a lure are predatory species like pike, perch, bass, trout, salmon and game fish, such as tuna. This is why most lures are imitations of fish or anything that will trigger an aggressive response in the targeted species. Lures come in all shapes, sizes and colours. They are designed to be used in a variety of ways, and are generally brought to life by anglers, who act almost as though they were puppeteers.

One of the joys of lure-fishing is being able to wander freely along the bank or shoreline, casting into each likely spot. Successful lure anglers should be confident and expect a fish on every cast. They should search the water methodically, and, informed with the knowledge of what each lure is designed to do, select appropriate lures for every situation that they encounter. This section will give you an overview of the various groups of lure available to the angler, as well as an understanding of how they are applied.

ABOVE A spinner consists of a blade that revolves around a central shaft.

Spinners

Spinners are lures that consist of a blade that revolves around a central shaft. The bright, flashing blade visually attracts predatory fish, which are also stimulated by the vibrations that it gives off. Spinners are generally fished using a steady retrieve. To reduce line-twist, the use of a swivel is recommended. In some instances, it is necessary to add a weight to the line to improve the casting distance and position the spinner at the required depth in the water.

ABOVE Spinner baits are a variation on the traditional spinner.

LEFT A small pike that attacked a spinner bait.

The spinnerbait is a variation on the traditional spinner. This lure is shaped like a coat hanger, with a revolving blade on one arm and a single, large, weighted hook on the other. The spinnerbait is cast out and retrieved like a spinner. Its design causes it to emit lots of flashes and vibrations, while the upturned hook ensures that it is almost snag-free and can therefore be cast close to weed beds and reeds with little risk of losing it.

Spoons

As its name suggests, the spoon lure is spoon-shaped. Spoons, which are sold in a variety of shapes and colours, flutter in the water as they are retrieved, flashing their sides like injured fish. The density and weight of the spoon determine the depth at which it is fished, as, to some extent, does the speed of the retrieve.

ABOVE AND LEFT A selection of spoons.

Plugs

Plug lures, which are usually crafted from wood or plastic, are carefully designed for use in specific situations. They typically have two or three treble hooks attached to their underside and a lip that helps them to dive, also imparting movement as they are retrieved. Each type of plug works at a specific depth, which may be indicated on its packaging.

Floating plugs dive down to a certain depth and swim at that depth during the retrieve, but if the angler stops winding the reel, the plug will float to the surface. This is useful when fishing near to snags (submerged obstacles) because it enables the plug to be floated over them. And having a range of floating and sinking plugs will enable the angler to search the water from top to bottom.

BELOW A selection of plugs.

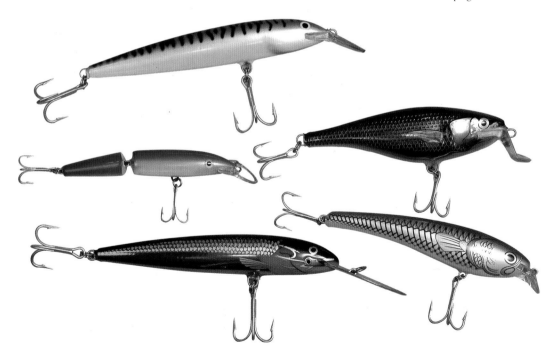

ABOVE It is wise to carry a good selection of different coloured plugs.

from aggressive fish like pike or bass. This method, which is the most productive during hot summer weather, enables the angler to fish next to fish-holding weed beds.

Plugs are manufactured in a huge range of colours, of which the angler should carry a variety because there are days when certain colours will work better than others. There has been much discussion over the years about how to decide which colour is best in relation to light values and so on, but my advice is, after careful consideration, to choose the lure that inspires the most confidence in you. A fish that is looking up at a plug will probably only see it as a silhouette anyway, in which case the colour may not matter.

The jerk bait is a plug lure that has recently become popular in the United Kingdom. This large plug has little action of its own, the angler instead imparting movement by retrieving it in jerks and pulls. Being large and heavy, it must be used with a special rod and heavy, braided line, and is therefore not a suitable lure for the beginner.

An erratic retrieve will often lead to an aggressive attack by a hungry predator. Some plugs are specially designed for fishing on the surface of the water, the disturbance that they create often resulting in explosive takes

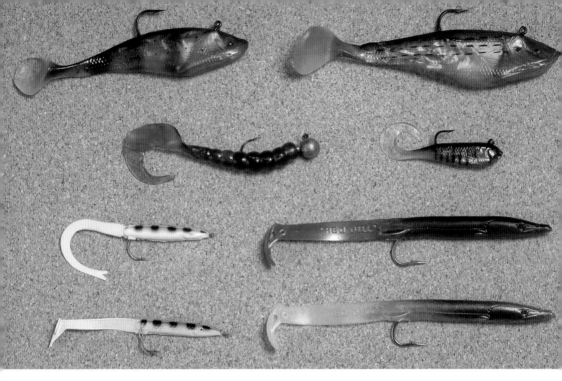

ABOVE The top row of lures are soft plastic ones that will tempt a wide range of predatory fish including bass and pike; those in the second row are more suitable for perch or chub; the bottom two rows are rubber eels suitable for bass, pollock and cod over reefs or wrecks.

Soft plastic lures

Soft plastic lures are often fished on large, single hooks and frequently have tails that wiggle enticingly in the water on the retrieve. Many anglers believe that the softness of the lure encourages the fish to hang on to it for a moment or so longer than it would to other lures, enabling the hook to be set more easily. They are a valuable addition to a lure collection and can often be fished far slower than other lures, too, especially if they have neutral buoyancy.

Rubber eels and worms

Rubber eels and jelly worms are typically used for tempting fish in salt water. When angling in deep water over wrecks and reefs, these lures are lowered to the bottom on a long trace and then slowly retrieved, causing the aggressive fish that inhabit these environments, such as pollock and cod, to attack them with heart-stopping takes.

Smaller jelly worms are also used on little, jig-like hooks to tempt small freshwater predators like perch and freshwater bass.

ABOVE Traces of Hokia lures suitable for mackerel and pollock.

BELOW Mackerel feathers are used for catching large numbers of predatory shoal fish for bait.

Feathers

Feathers consist of single hooks to which feathers or plastic have been whipped, in imitation of small fish like sand eel or whitebait. In sea fishing, feathers are fished in strings above a weight. They are either cast from the shore or lowered from the side of a boat, and are retrieved with a pumping motion to impart movement.

Feathers can effectively catch large numbers of shoal fish, such as mackerel, for bait. They can also be tipped with fish strips to catch fish like whiting or pollock.

Pirks

Pirks are heavy lures that are used to fish either directly beneath a boat or through a hole in the ice in arctic climates. They are made from chrome or painted lead, and have a hook fixed to the bottom.

Boat-anglers use pirks with heavy rods to impart action, pumping the rod up and down as the boat drifts over a wreck or reef. In some cases, a string of large feathers is fished in conjunction with the pirk to make large catches of prime table fish like cod and ling.

Anglers fishing in holes in the ice of Canada and other such northerly countries use pirks in conjunction with short, specially designed rods. Holes are drilled into the thick ice of many large lakes, with shelters being erected above to keep the anglers warm as they work their baits or lures in the dark, icy water below.

ABOVE These heavy Pirks are suitable for cod and ling, which inhabit deep water wrecks or reefs.

Summary

In summary, it is important to remember the following when lure-fishing:

- There is an enormous range of lures to suit different situations.
- The angler should take the species of fish being targeted into careful consideration.
- The prey of the targeted species may influence the size and colour of the lure required.
- The lure must be given life by the angler and should trigger a response in the fish.
- The lure must be put into the predator's taking zone.
- The tackle that the angler uses will affect how the lure behaves.
- A wire trace is needed when angling for fish with sharp teeth.
- Sharp hooks are essential.
- Because the lure appeals primarily to a fish's visual sense, water clarity is of great importance, although vibrations are more important in coloured water.
- Think 'size, colour, action' when deciding which lure to use.

Fly-fishing

I would guess that the term 'fly-fishing' originated many years ago, when anglers fished for trout using hooks that were dressed to imitate the flies that fell into the water. Fly patterns have evolved since those far-off days, with many of the creations now being used bearing no resemblance to any fly seen in nature. Some of these imitate a food source; others are designed to trigger a response in the fish. And the fly rod is today used to target a far wider range of fish species than ever before.

Many anglers fly-fish solely for the satisfaction that the method gives. Because it is considered a more sporting approach than using bait or spinning, it is the only technique permitted by many trout fisheries. There are also times when fly-fishing is the most effective way of tempting fish. All in all, it is a useful weapon in the angler's armoury.

The stocking of large reservoirs with trout – rainbow trout in particular – has led to a substantial increase in the number of practising fly-anglers, who were previously limited to fishing streams or rivers for salmon or trout. Because many of these waters were strictly limited to the wealthy upper classes, a degree of snobbery was once

LEFT A fly-fisherman and tranquil waters.

BELOW Still water trout fishing is very popular.

NEXT PAGE Casting a fly is very rewarding.

associated with the sport of fly-fishing, which is generally no longer the case.

The huge increase in the popularity of trout fishing has resulted in the opening of many small, commercial, still-water trout fisheries, which have met a demand for large, specimen trout. Because this type of fishing is sometimes too easy, and because they relish the opportunity to travel further afield, many anglers seek greater challenges. Fly-fisherman now target such large game fish as tarpon and barracuda, along with powerful fish like bonefish. There has also been a growth in fly-fishing for sea bass, and even for such coarse fish as carp.

BELOW This carp was taken on a floating dog biscuit imitation.

RIGHT Chasing rainbows in a large reservoir.

What is fly-fishing?

In fly-fishing, the lure or fly is cast out using the fly line as the weight. The basic principle is that the line is lifted from the water and thrown back behind the angler. When the line straightens and starts to bend the rod back, the angler begins the forward cast and punches the line and fly forward, using the rod as a loaded spring. This action can be repeated to extend the length of line while it is airborne. The line is worked out or shot through the rod rings until the desired distance is reached. This is known as 'false casting'.

The most important aspect of fly-casting is timing: if the timing is perfect, fly-casting is a joy to watch and to perform. (And taking tuition from a qualified instructor is a valuable step towards becoming a proficient fly-caster.)

Casting sequence.

1 The angler starts with the line straight out in front of him.

ABOVE The airborne fly line is the casting weight.

2 He starts to lift the line.

3 He accelerates into the back cast, so flicking the line back over his shoulder.

7 At the same moment he begins the forward cast, using the loaded rod to push the line forwards.

4 He pauses with the rod at "1, o'clock."

8 The line will travel forwards.

5 The loop of line will now unroll.

9 The line lands in a straight line in front of the angler.

6 When the line has straightened behind him, the angler starts to pull down with the line with his left hand.

10 The angler can now start to fish out the cast by retrieving the fly or allowing it to drift across the flow of the river.

The fly-fisher's outfit

The fly-fisher's outfit is determined by the water that he or she is fishing and the species present. The rod (see page 55 for fly-fishing rods) should be matched to the required line, and the reel (see page 57 for centre-pin reels) must be of a sufficient size to hold both the line and the backing, the backing being a thinner line that is used to extend the main line if a powerful fish causes it to run out.

Another factor that will greatly influence the choice of outfit is the pleasure factor: because lighter rods and lines demand less physical effort, they are generally more pleasing to use.

Fly lines

Fly lines are rated on a scale known as the AFTM (set up by the American Federation of Tackle Manufacturers). The lightest line is a weight 3, and the heaviest a weight 12. The size of the fly will, to some extent, determine the weight of the line needed to propel it to its destination. The large flies used for pike will need heavy lines, while the large hooks will require a

LEFT In action on a small commercial trout fishery.

powerful rod to drive them home, for instance. A tiny fly used for trout will need only a light line to propel it, however, and therefore a correspondingly light rod.

Fly lines are manufactured in an enormous range of colours and designs, some of which are outlined below. Each is designed to give the optimum performance in its role. Remember that each type of fly line has a different density, which means that it will either float or sink, so that the line that you choose will depend on where, and how, you intend to present your fly.

The double-taper (DT) line

The thickest part of the double-taper (DT) fly line is the mid-section, from which point it tapers so that each end section is thinner. Although it is ideal for presenting the fly delicately, it is not the best line for distance-casting.

The weight-forward (WF) line

The weight-forward (WF) line is the ideal fly line for most situations. The weight of the line is concentrated in its forward section, behind which is a thinner section that facilitates the easy shooting of the line to a relatively great distance.

The shooting-head (SH) line

The shooting-head (SH) line consists of a heavy section of fly line attached to a light backing line that shoots out easily through the rings. This fly line is designed for casting over extreme distances.

The floating line

The floating line is used to present either a dry fly on the surface of the water or a wet fly, nymph or lure near to the surface. A long leader (line tip) will enable a nymph to be fished at a specific depth beneath the surface, however.

The intermediate line

The intermediate line is used to fish wet flies or nymphs near to the surface of the water without causing a wake or disturbance that may alarm the fish.

The sinking line

Sinking lines are sold in various densities that sink at different rates. A slow sinking line will sink at a rate of around 2in (5cm) per second, while a fast sinking line will sink at a rate of around 8in (20cm) per second. These lines enable the angler to sink the fly to the depth at which the fish are feeding.

The sink-tip line

The sink-tip line has a floating main section and a sinking tip, giving the angler the option of fishing a nymph-type fly deep in the water, along with the bite-indication advantages of a floating line.

Fly types

The type of fly or lure that should be chosen depends upon the species of fish being targeted and the prevailing conditions. Because all flies or lures are designed either to imitate a food source or to trigger a response in the targeted species, anglers must try to imagine what type of lure or fly is required for the particular situation that they are facing. Anglers should observe the sort of natural food that the target species takes and then set out to imitate this food source with a fly or lure. A marrow spoon can be used to examine the contents of a trout's stomach, giving a clue as to the type of fly or lure that may be successful. Experienced anglers

ABOVE Choosing the fly.

will be able to make an educated guess regarding the type of fly that is likely to stimulate a response in the fish.

Remember that as well as being of the appropriate size and colour, the fly must be fished at the correct depth. Note that a fish will rarely only take a fly that perfectly matches a real water creature, and that a fly may exaggerate one of the creature's features to increase the likelihood of a fish taking the offering.

FAR LEFT Fly-fishing for saltwater estuary bass.

LEFT There are many lures and types of fly to choose from.

The dry fly

The dry fly is fished on the surface of the water to imitate a naturally hatching fly, or else one that has been blown onto the water. This is a particularly exciting type of fly to use because the fish can be seen rising to meet it. And the moment that a trout gulps a fly from the water's surface is one of the most exciting moments in angling.

The fly that you choose should depend, to a certain extent, on the type of fly that you can see on the water, and you should ideally choose a matching one. This is particularly important when fishing in chalk streams that contain large, wild fish, but is not so significant when fishing in most of the waters that have been stocked with 'uneducated' fish – those not fished for before.

When fishing a dry fly on a river, it is normal practice to cast the fly upstream. If you are fishing in clear water, it may be possible to cast the dry fly to a fish that you have spotted, but if you are fishing in a fast-flowing stream

BELOW The dry fly is fished on the water's surface to imitate the natural insect.

and cannot see any fish, you will have to cast at likely lies (areas where fish may be situated).

When fishing still waters, the dry fly is often either fished static or allowed to drift with the breeze. On Ireland's large lakes, anglers use a technique known as 'dapping' during the early summer, when the mayfly emerges from the water in all of its glory. Dapping is when a suitable artificial fly (or even a real mayfly) is mounted on a lightweight hook and allowed to brush the surface of the water, carried by a light silk line blowing in the wind. The angler uses a special, long rod to control this line as it floats in the breeze in front of a drifting boat.

The wet fly

As its name implies, the traditional wet fly is fished beneath the water's surface. These flies may either imitate a real water creature or be formed according to a general pattern designed to stimulate a trout to take them.

When fishing on a river, the wet fly is most often fished by casting down and across the flow. The fly will then drift across the current until it is suspended directly beneath the angler, ready for recasting. A large area of river can be covered if the angler takes a step downstream after each cast.

When fishing still waters, the angler will need to impart life to the fly by retrieving it in a careful and thoughtful way.

The nymph

Nymphs are imitations of aquatic flies in their larval stage, before they hatch. It was G E Skues who developed the art of nymph-fishing in the crystal-clear

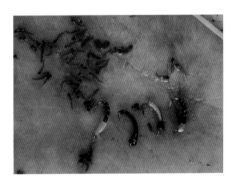

ABOVE Nymph patterns imitate the larval stage of aquatic flies.

chalk streams of southern England. Having witnessed trout darting from side to side as they took the nymphs swimming in the water, he realised that the trout could be tempted by artificial nymphs if a dry fly had failed to work.

In running water, the nymph should be fished upstream in the same way as a dry fly. The nymph must be of sufficient weight to sink quickly to the depth at which the trout are feeding, which you may be able to ascertain with the help of polarising glasses. You should then carefully judge the path of the nymph as it drifts past the trout. As it takes the nymph, you will see the white of the trout's mouth, whereupon a flick of the wrist and a tug of the line (known as a 'strike') should set the hook before the trout discovers the deception. If the trout is not visible, watch the tip of the line, or leader, as it enters the water; it should twitch or dip as a trout takes the nymph, and this is the point at which to make your strike.

In still water, you will need to retrieve the nymph in order to give it the appearance of life. Imagine how your nymph appears in the water and compare it to the real thing. Because the real insect will not move at great speed, remember that your retrieve should generally be very slow, with just an occasional twitch to induce a take from a trout that may otherwise have ignored the offering. Watch the tip of the line carefully to receive advance warning of a take because by the time you feel a tug, it may be too late.

The nymph is most often fished on a floating line with a long leader. Some nymphs have weighted bodies to help them to sink quickly, but others are very light, with greased leaders to make them float after being suspended within inches of the surface. Some have polystyrene heads tied into them to ensure that they sit on the surface, almost like a dry fly.

An effective method of fishing a nymph is to use it in conjunction with a site bobbin (see page 85) attached to the end of the fly line. When a trout takes the nymph, the bobbin will sink beneath the surface like a float. A large, bushy dry fly can also be used in conjunction with a nymph. The dry fly will suspend the nymph at a taking depth, and will also indicate when a trout has connected with it.

The lure

Lures may be tied to hooks to imitate a tiny fish (fry) or some other life form, such as a tadpole or large nymph, although they often bear no resemblance to any real creature. Lure-fishing was developed on the large reservoirs where anglers fished for rainbow trout, which would attack the lures with gusto, especially shortly after the water had been stocked.

Lures are fished at various speeds to prompt a trout attack, and you will need to experiment in order to discover the speed required. Some lures have been developed for use in a specific way. Boobies, for example, are extremely buoyant lures that are generally used in conjunction with a fast sink line and short leader: the line having been allowed to sink to the bottom, the booby then rises from the bottom, often provoking a savage response from the trout. Some anglers even fish this fly completely static

LEFT Casting a lure in an estuary can give good sport.

RIGHT Lures often bare no resemblance to a real creature.

(which may, however, be in breach of some fisheries' rules).

A huge array of lures is available, all designed to tempt both fish and angler. I suggest that beginners purchase a small selection of different colours, types and sizes. To list every lure and its application would require a book in itself, however, and I therefore advise either reading up-to-date trout-fishing magazines to learn about the latest developments or chatting to other anglers on the bank.

ABOVE A selection of salmon and sea trout flies some of which are tied on tubes and fitted with treble hooks.

To summarise, you should fish a lure until you have discovered the correct combination of lure, speed and depth. Note that this may change as the day progresses, however, and that other anglers will make catches using a completely different approach.

Salmon and sea-trout flies

Anglers fish for salmon and sea trout primarily in rivers, although they can also be caught from certain lochs and lakes. The salmon does not feed in fresh water, which is why its readiness to take a fly or lure is the subject of great debate among anglers. It is not known whether the salmon takes a lure as a reflex instinct from its feeding days at sea or as an aggressive reaction to something having intruded into its territory. It is fascinating to observe a salmon in a river as it is shown a lure or bait: it will often totally ignore the offering, while on another occasion it may attack the lure with no hesitation, and on yet another day, it may lazily open its mouth and gently engulf the fly or bait.

Most flies used for fishing salmon are fished downstream and across, in the same way that wet flies are fished for trout. Note that salmon take up lies that are well known to experienced anglers or ghillies (angling guides who

ABOVE Sea trout take a fly best after the sun has set.

are normally employed by the owners of fishing waters).

Although the sea trout is the same species as the brown trout, it has developed the urge to migrate to sea, where it feeds on richer sources of food than those found in the river of its birth. The sea trout will return to its home river to reproduce, however, and will grow to a far larger size than its non-migratory brother or sister.

Sea trout can be caught on either specially created flies or some trout flies.

It is best fished for after dark, when it seems to lose much of its daytime caution, and special lures have been created for this exciting branch of angling. I strongly recommend reading Hugh Falkus' excellent book, *Sea Trout Fishing*, which is the definitive book on fishing for sea trout and contains a large section devoted to fishing the fly at night.

The rainbow trout of North America also develops a migratory strain, termed the steelhead. It is fished for with flies and tactics similar to those used for salmon.

RIGHT Sea flies imitate
sand eel, fry and prawns.

BELOW Pike flies.

Pike flies

Pike are fierce, predatory fish that can
provide the angler with good sport. The
lures that are used to tempt them are
imitations of the real fish or water
creatures that the pike are likely to
devour. Large flies are created using
bright materials that will attract the
pike's attention, while other lures are
bulky in order to create a wake, disturb
the water and thus similarly draw the
pike to them. If the lure is to resist the
pike's rows of razor-sharp teeth, a wire
trace is essential.

Sea flies

Fly-fishing in the sea is growing in popularity all over the world. Bass, pollock and mackerel can provide excellent summer sport in the United Kingdom, while strong fighting fish, such as bonefish, tarpon and even sailfish, are targeted in tropical climates.

Sea flies often have bright, silvery lures in imitation of sand eel, prawn and fry. The tackle used needs to be resistant to salt water's corrosive properties, and it is best to rinse all tackle in fresh water after use. For the same reason, the flies used for saltwater fishing should be tied on stainless-steel hooks.

RIGHT Fly fishing in saltwater takes the trout angler into a new environment.
BELOW School bass give great sport on trout weight tackle.

Flies for coarse fish

Several species of coarse fish can be caught on the fly. Chub, roach and dace are among some of the species that will readily take small trout flies or nymphs, while carp can be tempted with artificial floating dog biscuits crafted from cork or deer hair.

Casting

Casting is one of the most important skills that an angler needs to learn: delivering the bait and terminal tackle to wherever it is that the fish are situated is obviously a fundamental requirement for regular success.

When casting, your two basic aims should be achieving distance and accuracy. Anglers fishing a stream with a spinner will not need to cast very far, but will have to cast with great accuracy if they are to cover the water adequately without the line becoming entangled in the far bank or an obstruction. By contrast, sea anglers who are fishing from a shallow beach may need to propel their juicy bunch of lugworm for more than 100yd (90m) if they are to stand any chance of tempting the bass or cod patrolling the surf.

Some anglers become obsessed with casting enormous distances, and at times cast beyond the fish that they are

FROM TOP TO BOTTOM The skill of casting lies in timing and loading the rod to give maximum performance.

seeking, but skilful anglers are able to place their bait wherever the fish are, be that 10 or 150yd (9 or 140m) away. And long, accurate casts take plenty of practice to achieve, especially when you consider that a carp angler who is fishing a large gravel pit may need to land his or her bait on a patch of weed-free gravel the size of a table top, 100yd (90m) from the shoreline.

ABOVE Long casts may reach the fish on this vast Irish surf beach.

The tackle chosen for a day's fishing will be largely dictated by the casting needs of the day ahead, as well as the style of fishing or species of fish and the terrain over which you will be fishing. There are many factors that will affect both your casting and the tools that you require. The rod needs to be matched to the weight that is being launched, for example, and the line will need to be strong enough to land the fish that you are seeking.

LEFT Watching bait sail out into the distance is very rewarding.

ABOVE Multiplier reel loaded with line and shock leader.

Note that the main line's diameter will have a dramatic effect on the casting distance. The thinner the line, the less air resistance there will be to hold back the end tackles. The cast can put enormous pressure on the line during the initial power stroke, however, which is why it is essential that anglers who are striving to cast long distances use what is termed a 'shock leader', a length of heavy-duty line that takes the strain and ensures that the lead weight does not fly off, endangering anyone in the vicinity. (A lead weight leaves the rod tip at a frightening speed during a powerful

RIGHT The fixed-spool reel needs to be loaded to within a short distance of the spool's lip.

cast, and has been responsible for more than one death over the years.) As a rough guide, the shock leader should have a ratio of 10lb (4.5kg) for each 1oz (28g) being cast, as follows:

1oz (28g) =	10lb (4.5kg)
2oz (57g) =	20lb (9kg)
3oz (85g) =	30lb (13.6kg)
4oz (113g) =	40lb (18.1kg)
5oz (142g) =	50lb (22.7kg)
6oz (170g) =	60lb (2.7kg)

This length of heavy line can also play a part in protecting the part of the line close to the fish from abrasive rock and shingle. Moderate-sized sea fish can be lifted from the sea using the shock leader, too. Remember that all tackle components need to be very strong; good-quality

ABOVE A strong lead link is essential to ensure safe casting.

swivels and lead links are essential.

A leader is only required when powerful casts are to be made. (Although many forms of fishing do not require a leader, it is a must whenever heavy weights are being thrown for long distances.) There are also times when it may be necessary to employ a heavy main line and dispense with the leader: when beach fishing after a storm, for example, when large clumps of weed may build up on the line and collect on the leader knot, making the line almost impossible to retrieve.

The line is, of course, stored and released on a reel, either a fixed spool or a multiplier (see pages 58 to 61), and the correct loading of the line onto the reel spool is extremely important to ensure trouble-free casting. Fixed-spool reels should be loaded to within a short distance of the lip, thus avoiding friction, for instance.

Now let's look at the angler's different casting needs and the mechanics of casting. Note that when describing all of the casting sequences, I shall use times on an imaginary clock face (12, 3, 6 and 9 o'clock, for example) to indicate the required direction.

Short-range casting with a fixed-spool reel: underarm cast

This short-range casting technique is described on the assumption that a fixed-spool reel is being used. The same basic casting technique can be used with a centre-pin reel, a loop of line being pulled from the reel to allow the bait to reach its destination.

Note that if you are using an artificial lure, you should begin the retrieve and work the lure back to your feet. If you are using bait on a leger tackle, the bait must be allowed to settle on the bottom before the line is tightened.

1 Holding the rod in the 12 o'clock position with your casting arm, stand facing the water.
2 Ensure that the weight is hanging approximately one-third of the rod's length from the rod tip.
3 Trap the line with your finger and release the bale arm.
4 Move the rod to the 8 o'clock position.
5 Keeping your eyes fixed on the destination of the bait, flip out the bait, releasing the trapped line in accordance with the forward momentum.
6 End the cast with the rod pointing to the 12 o'clock position.
7 Engage the bale arm and tighten the line.

LEFT The start of the underarm cast.

The standard overhead cast

The standard overhead cast is the cast that is most commonly used in angling. It can deliver bait or lures over short to moderate distances.

ABOVE Determine where you need to cast.

LEFT The rod needs to be fully compressed to make a long-distance cast.

1 Determine where you need to cast your line. Now line it up with a point on the horizon.

2 With the point on the horizon at 12 o'clock, stand comfortably, with your legs slightly apart.

3 (I am assuming that you are right-handed, but if you are left-handed, adjust my instructions accordingly.) Grip the rod butt with your left hand and the rod at the reel seat with your right hand. If you are using a fixed-spool reel, use a finger to trap the line and disengage the bale arm.

4 Hold the rod with the rod butt (at 12 o'clock) pointing at the target and the rod tip (at 6 o'clock) behind you, with the weight hanging beneath it.

5 Imagine that the rod is a lever. Your left hand should be at approximately eye level and your right hand gripping the reel seat over your right shoulder at nearly ear level.

6 Ensure that the line is not tangled around the rod tip and that the weight or hook is not entangled in an obstruction.

7 Looking ahead at your target, cast out by pulling down your left hand briskly and pushing your right hand forwards. (Note that the butt will start at 12 o'clock and that the tip will finish at 12 o'clock.)

ABOVE The weight sails to its destination.

8 When the forward motion dictates the right time, release the line and allow the weight to sail to its destination.

9 When the weight hits the water, stop the line from spilling from the reel. If the water is deep, allow the weight to sink to the bottom by releasing the line from the reel before tightening it again.

Long-distance casting

Remember that the distance that you need to achieve will determine the amount of power that you should apply to the cast. Also note that there are some instances when you may need to propel your bait and terminal tackle to a range that cannot be achieved using the overhead thump. This is one of the reasons why novice anglers should seek the aid of a qualified instructor to help them to progress and develop the techniques necessary to reach a distant spot on the horizon.

The sport of tournament-casting has evolved from the angler's desire to cast great distances, and special tackle has been designed to enable casters to propel weights over unbelievably long distances. The world record now stands at a distance exceeding 300yd (274m), the equivalent of three football pitches! The human desire to compete against one another is the driving force in this sport, not the need to catch fish.

Although long-distance casting is not always necessary, it is a useful weapon in the angler's armoury. I have enlisted the help of casting instructor Hugh Parkyn

ABOVE A carp rod is used to reach a distant feature.

to demonstrate the basic steps in making a long-distance cast (see page 211). The ground cast is the basic starting point, enabling the angler to begin to compress the rod at the start of the forward cast. Remember that the rod is a tool that needs to be fully compressed if its maximum potential is to be exploited. The reel needs to be finely tuned and well maintained. The multiplier reels favoured by many

ABOVE A rubber thumb guard helps to grip the reel spool during powerful casts.

BELOW Casting instructor Hugh Parkyn uses a length of plastic guttering as a launch pad.

casters have braking systems to reduce the risk of bird's nests or overruns, but a smooth, well-timed cast is nevertheless the key to avoiding tangles. Making long casts is not all about strength and brute force: timing is undoubtedly the key. Watch a skilled caster, at work and it will all look effortless.

Before you cast, ensure that you have an adequate shock leader and a reliable link to the weight because the force generated during a distance cast is phenomenal. If you were to cast across a field, this would become fully apparent because the lead weight would bury itself to a depth of up to 6in (15.2cm) in the soil.

The basic ground cast

1. The weight and terminal tackle is placed on the ground at 8 o'clock. The angler's feet are pointing towards the target at 12 0`clock.

2. The rod is held with the butt pointing skywards, the left hand gripping the butt.

3. The angler is poised like a spring, the left hand pulls, the right pushes and the body unfurls.

4. The rod is fully compressed.

5. At the moment that forward momentum is achieved the reel spool is released to allow the bait and weight to speed to their destination.

Pendulum casting

The full pendulum cast is the ultimate cast used by most tournament-casters and anglers to achieve long distances, and a well-executed pendulum cast is a joy to behold.

3. Hugh watches as the sinker flies many metres out to sea.

1. During the pendulum cast the weight is fully airborne throughout.

2. The rod is brought to the starting position with the rod already loaded.

LEFT This ingenious bait clip holds the bait in position behind the weight throughout the cast then releases upon impact with the water.

Terminal tackle has evolved, allowing anglers to cast baited rigs to long ranges without damaging the bait. Reducing wind resistance is the primary aim of any rig designed for distance, and carp anglers sometimes use PVA string with which to tie their baits neatly to the weight and reduce air resistance. Various clips can also be incorporated into rigs to hold the bait closely behind the lead as it travels through the air, clips that ingeniously release the bait and hook upon impact with the water.

Delivering bait successfully with a good cast is rewarding, and a major boost to the angler's all-important confidence. Remember that casting is the key to placing the bait in the right spot, and that having bait in the right spot is essential if fish are to take the bait, so practise often and seek qualified help if possible.

BELOW A lure is sent on its way in a freshwater lake.

Chapter 2

Catching fish

Having outlined the various environments in which we fish, and described the basic tools that are necessary to perform the craft of angling, it's now time for me to introduce you to the practicalities of angling.

Although anglers do not target all species of fish (of which there are at least 30,000), they do aim to catch a large number. Fish species generally fit into the following categories: sea; freshwater; small; small to medium; medium to large; large; predatory; non-predatory; and opportunist, a mixture of predatory and non-predatory fish. (Putting fish into categories is difficult, however, not least because each species may have its own peculiarities that do not fit a typical definition.) If you are starting out as an angler, you would be wise to start off fishing waters that contain large numbers of small- to medium-sized fish because catching them will give you confidence and enable you to practise the basic

LEFT The angler asks a question with each cast into the river.

rudiments of angling. From this basis, you can then progress to the field of angling to which you feel you belong. Many people enter the sport at too high a level (often because they have been introduced to angling by well-intentioned friends who are entrenched in their own path), and can then become disillusioned by their perceived lack of success. Trying to catch large, specimen fish from the outset, for instance, will either result in failure or rapid success with a lack of accomplishment, both of which can prompt an early exit from the sport.

Let's look at some of the options available to us in pursuit of our quarry, the fish. In the tackle section (see pages 38 to 93), I tried to make it clear that each item of tackle is a tool with a specific job. Now we will consider how to put these tools to good use.

Before casting a line and hook bait into the water, you will need to think about the following questions.

- What would you like to catch?
- What lives within the water that you are about to fish?
- What species are you likely to catch?
- Where are the fish likely to be?
- What is the best way of getting a bait or lure to where the fish are? If this is not possible, how are you going draw the fish within your reach?
- How will you get the bait near the fish without scaring it away?
- What sort of bait is likely to attract the fish that you are seeking?
- How will you land the fish once you have hooked it?

Although these questions may seem a little simplistic, I believe that they form the basis upon which we should move forward.

At this point, I should point out that before embarking on a fishing trip, you will probably need a licence and a permit. The requirements for these vary greatly from country to country. In the United Kingdom, you will need a licence if you are intending to fish in fresh water and are over twelve years of age. (Although a licence is not required for fishing in salt water in the UK, it is in some other areas of the world.) The licence fee should be paid to the government body responsible for fishery management and regulation, which, in the UK, is currently the Environment Agency. A permit is, in effect, the granting of permission from the landowner or owner of the fishing rights for you to fish their waters, for which a fee will normally have to be paid. These systems are not universal, however, which is why you should make enquiries before venturing out, rod in hand.

I will now set out a series of ventures to different waters in search of different species, and will try to give you some ideas about how to proceed. Remember that you will catch fish as a result of asking the right questions and arriving at the correct solutions. Before setting out to fish any venue, you must decide what you are trying to achieve, and should also enquire whether the fish that you are seeking inhabit that water. (You should be able to find the relevant information in angling publications and from local tackle shops and angling clubs.) You should then check the rules that apply to that venue. Many game fisheries offer only fly-fishing, for example, while coarse fisheries often impose restrictions on baits, hooks and lines, for instance (and I remember turning up at a fishery with a bucketful of bait, only to find that it was banned).

A trout stream

I started my angling career at a small, clear-running trout stream containing wild brown trout. Although small, these fish fight hard, and can provide anglers with an interesting challenge.

ABOVE The clear waters of a small trout stream.

RIGHT A wild brown trout has been deceived.

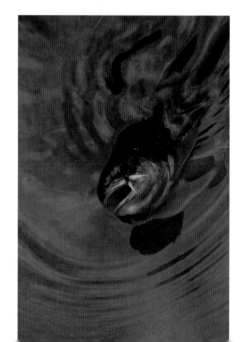

One of three methods is likely to be successful when trying to catch wild brown trout: fly-fishing, bait-fishing using a free line or lightly weighted set-up, or using a spinner. The weather conditions and state of the stream will greatly influence the method employed.

LEFT Casting a dry fly upstream.

BELOW On the way to the water.

Tackle required
Fly-fishing

- A 7ft (2.1m) long fly rod, 4 to 5 AFTM.
- A matching double-taper floating line.
- A leader of 2 to 3lb (907g to 1.4kg) bs.
- A selection of dry flies, nymphs and small wet flies.
- Fly floatant to help dry flies stay afloat.
- Line snips for cutting line.
- A small pair of forceps.
- Maybe a net, depending on the size of the trout, although you can probably manage without one.
- A priest (small club), if you intend to keep the fish.

Bait- or spinner-fishing

- A 7ft (2.1m) long lightweight trout-spinning rod.
- A 3 to 6lb (1.4 to 2.7kg) bs line.
- Size 8 to 12 barbless hooks.
- A few split shot.
- Line clips.
- A disgorger.
- Natural baits.
- A small selection of spinners.

Assessing the situation

Approach the stream with caution, trying not to show yourself to the fish, which you will not be able to catch if they become alarmed. Because fish always lie with their heads pointing into the current, approach them from downstream to avoid disturbing them. Stay low on the horizon as you study the water, looking at how it flows and estimating its depth. Also take note of any features, such as shade, trees, bridges, weirs, weed beds, rocks and bends. Look for deeper areas of water, and, most importantly, look for fish (wearing polarising glasses will be of great help in this). Try to imagine where you would position yourself in the stream if you were a fish. Look for a spot where a fish may receive any food that is floating downstream (the biggest fish are likely to be lurking in the best of such spots).

OPPOSITE PAGE, TOP A beautiful wild brown trout.

OPPOSITE PAGE, BOTTOM Approach fish carefully, keeping low to avoid shadows on the water.

LEFT Searching in the shaded stream.

A prime position for trout is a deep channel overhung by trees, providing both food and shelter, and I remember learning as a child how bridges and tunnels formed by overgrown brambles held the biggest fish in the stream. Getting a fly to these trout is not always easy, however, and an innovative casting style may therefore be needed. A fly can sometimes be catapulted into the lie or dapped (bobbed by the wind) onto the surface. If you have time before your fishing trip, visit the water without a rod and have a good look at the entire length of water because if you bring a rod with you, you may be tempted to linger too long in a swim while a perfect pool awaits you at the far end of the fishery.

ABOVE Catapulting the fly into a difficult lie.

BELOW The reward of the innovative cast above.

Having carried out a full reconnaissance of the stream, the next decision that you will have to make is which bait and method to use.

Fly-fishing

Insects and small forms of aquatic life make up the bulk of the trout's food, and the artificial fly is probably the most effective and enjoyable method to employ when angling for this fish. Ideally, you will be able to see flies emerging from the water, enabling you to select a suitable imitation (and the purist fly-angler may even tie an imitation there and then on the bank).

ABOVE The artificial fly is probably the most enjoyable and effective method to use on small trout streams.

RIGHT Working upstream, casting with a dry fly.

Don't be concerned if you can't see any insect life, however: if you select the pattern of fly recommended to you by someone in the local tackle shop, for example, and present it to the fish correctly, you still have a good chance of connecting with it.

Your options are a dry fly, a wet fly or a nymph (see pages 194 to 196). If the weather is warm and the fish appear active, my first approach would probably be to cast a dry fly upstream. I would advise selecting an appropriate fly (such as a Greenwell's glory), and tying it carefully to the end of your light leader, which you should have treated with a floatant to within 6in (15.2cm) of the fly; also treat the fly with a floatant to help it to repel the water and sit correctly upon the water's surface.

Now creep to the water's edge, downstream from the pool that you intend to fish, and, crouching low, start to extend the line by false casting. Drop the fly delicately on to the surface and allow it to drift downstream with the current. Then retrieve the line and mend any bows formed by the current by flicking the line upstream. (It is important to avoid what is termed

'drag', when a fast current pulls on the line, dragging the fly unnaturally quickly across the surface, because any wise trout would refuse such an offering.) Next, systematically cover the water until a fish has been tempted, and on witnessing a trout rising to the fly, flick your wrist to set the hook. Timing is all-important here, and you will need to practise perfecting it. On a fast stream, it is unlikely that you will be too fast, but on a slow stream, it is possible to pull the fly from the fish's mouth before it has closed it and returned to its downward-pointing position.

OPPOSITE PAGE Selecting a fly.

ABOVE Dropping the fly delicately onto the water's surface.

BELOW Crimson-spotted beauty of brown trout from a small stream.

Once you have hooked a trout, keep the rod held high to absorb any lunges that the fish makes. Always keep the line taut and play the fish carefully towards your hand or the waiting net. Wet your hands before handling the fish, and, if possible, grab the hook's shank, thereby shaking the fish free. If the hook is embedded firmly in the fish's mouth, however, remove it with a small pair of forceps. Note that although it is preferable to return wild trout to small streams, it is acceptable

ABOVE Dry fly has tempted this small trout.

BELOW Wet your hands before handling the fish.

to keep the occasional sizeable fish for the table, in which case you will need to dispatch it quickly using a priest (a small club).

As you work your way upstream, casting either at rising fish or into likely spots, you may be advised to try using different fly patterns. If the fish refuse to rise, try a nymph, for instance, or perhaps cast a wet fly downstream or upstream. If you are sharing the water with others, remember to observe angling etiquette. Never push in front of other anglers or disturb the water that they are about to cover. If they are following you, do not linger for an unreasonable amount of time. It is often best to have a friendly chat about the areas that you intend to fish and to reach an amicable decision on how best to share the water fairly.

When you have covered all of the

BELOW The crystal clear waters of the river Test in Southern England. Dry fly fishing developed on its hallowed banks.

likely lies, it's time either to retire for the day or to take a break and rest the lies for a while before covering the stream again. At the end of your day's fishing, try to remember the best spots on the river to revisit. With luck, you will have enjoyed your trip, caught a few fish and not suffered from too many tangles (and if your fly does become entangled in a tree, try to retrieve it rather than leaving the line dangling and in danger of ensnaring birds).

Bait-fishing

If it has rained and the stream's level has risen and the water has become coloured, a fly may not be the most effective approach, and a bait or spinner may instead bring better results (that is, if the rules that apply to the water permit their use). If the stream is running very high, you will need to search out slacker areas of water or eddies out of the main current, but if the level has risen only a little and the water is only slightly coloured, you may be able to catch fish in the same areas that you would target with a fly (see above).

Following a rise in the stream's level, the ideal bait is a worm. This can be fished with sufficient weight (a couple of split shot will probably be enough) to suspend it so that it is just trailing along the bottom. The important thing is that the bait trails along with the current in a natural manner.

Approach the stream stealthily and flick the bait slightly upstream. Allow it to sink to the bottom and then encourage it to drift through the swim. The bale arm should be open as you hold the line lightly between your fingers, paying it out slowly as it is drawn out by the current. Carefully watch the line between the rod tip and water. If it suddenly twitches or becomes taut, briskly tighten it to set the hook. Also remain alert for a sudden tug. Work your way upstream in this way, flicking the bait into any likely spot where trout may be found.

On hot, sunny, summer days, it is also possible to catch trout from small streams by dapping a live insect, such as a grasshopper, onto the surface. This can be an exciting angling method, which will sometimes turn up bigger-than-average fish from overgrown areas. To tempt trout in this way, push the tip of your rod carefully between the bushes and lower the insect on to the water below.

Using a spinner

As the water fines down, or subsides, following a spate, trout will often snatch at a small spinner fished down and across the stream like a wet fly (see above). Having checked that spinners are permitted, use the same tackle as for bait-fishing (see above), with the addition of a small swivel to help to reduce line twist. It is a good idea to flatten the barbs on the hooks to enable their easy removal.

LEFT A shimmering spinner.

A small still water

A small, enclosed still water is the ideal location for a beginner to embark on an angling adventure because fish stocks are often high in such waters, ensuring plenty of bites and action. The fish will not generally be large in size, although it is surprising what can lurk in the depths of small waters.

The water is likely to contain a variety of species, such as carp, rudd, tench, bream and perch. And although we could use several angling methods, we will concentrate on float-fishing and free-lining.

OPPOSITE PAGE A still water in summer.

ABOVE Anglers wait patiently.

RIGHT Sunny summer reflections upon calm waters.

Tackle required

Float-fishing

- A 12ft (3.7m) long float rod.
- A fixed-spool reel.
- A 3 to 8lb (1.4 to 3.6kg) bs line.
- Size 6 to 18 hooks.
- A selection of floats.
- Split shot.
- A plummet
  (a weight with a cork base).
- Baits: maggots, worms,
  bread and sweet corn.
- A rod-rest.
- A disgorger.
- A seat.
- A pair of scissors.
- A landing net.

Free-lining

- A 10ft (3m) long whip or pole.
- Pole floats

Free-lining is the simplest form of angling where a hook is attached to the main line with the addition of no other terminal tackle. In some cases a couple of light weights such as split shot may be added to the trace. In essence free-lining is used for close range fishing with bites detected by sight when the bait is visible, or by touch as the act of the fish taking the bait is transmitted through the line.

Assessing the situation

The intimacy of a small still water makes locating fish simple because they can often be seen, and even if they are not visible, you know that they cannot be too far away. On arriving at the still water, it is advisable to walk around it surveying it. Try to avoid alarming the fish as you do so because fearful fish will be less inclined to feed on your bait. Look for signs that the fish are feeding, such as coloured water, as well as for the fish themselves.

If you can't see the fish, try to imagine where they are likely to be. The weather and water temperature will

LEFT The smile says it all.

have a considerable influence on their location: if the weather is cold, the fish will probably be in the deeper water, for instance, while if the sun is shining on one side of the pool, it may be warming the water slightly, thereby encouraging greater activity. On larger waters, fish are greatly influenced by wind direction, and although this factor is far less relevant on small waters, it may still have some bearing on the situation, even if it only helps you to decide on the most comfortable angling spot.

Look for features that could provide shelter for the fish, too, such as weed beds, overhanging trees, sudden changes in depth or any form of structure within the water. Fish tend to rest in these areas, which offer safety from danger, and if bait is located close to these spots, it is more likely to be found by the fish.

It is a good idea to introduce a few baits into different swims to visit later in the day should your first choice of swim not prove productive or need resting.

Float-fishing

Having chosen a swim that you think looks promising and introduced some free offerings, set up a simple float tackle, such as a size 12 hook attached to a hook length of 4lb (1.8kg) bs line. Using split shot, weight a float so that its brightly coloured tip is showing just above the water's surface (the correct loading is often marked on a float's side). Lock the float in position using two small split shot.

LEFT Free offerings such as this sweet corn can be introduced with a catapult.

BELOW The angler's arm rests upon the rod in readiness for the disappearance of the float.

You will now need to determine the depth of the water that you are fishing using a plummet, which is a weight with a cork base. Pass the hook through the eye of the weight and insert it into the cork. The plummet will now sink the float when it is lowered into the water, and the float's position on the line can be altered by sliding the locking shot gently up or down. To find the depth, keep adjusting the float until the plummet does not pull it under the water. Having indicated the exact depth of the water in front of you, the plummet can now be removed from the

ABOVE Accurate introduction of free offerings will pay dividends.

line and the bait can be attached instead.

The free offerings that you introduced into the swim earlier should now have sunk to the bottom, and it is here that you should now present your bait by fishing with a short length of line laid upon the bottom. Cast the baited tackle past the baited area and then draw it back into position. Allow the float to cock and tighten the line to the rod tip.

You can now lay your rod on a rod-rest, with your hand resting on the butt ready to set the hook when the float indicates a bite.

To keep the fish interested, trickle in a few baits every few minutes and soon, it is hoped, a few fish should come your way.

It is often advisable to open up further possibilities by introducing other baits into different areas of the water: a few chunks of floating bread may entice some carp to feed on the surface, for example. And if you see carp taking these baits, you could remove your float and try to catch one on a piece of floating crust. Attach the crust to a size 8 hook and then lower or flick it into the vicinity of the feeding carp. When a carp engulfs the bait, pause for a second as the carp turns downwards before setting the hook. The fun should now really begin as the carp tests your light tackle to its limit.

At the end of the day, pack away your gear and ensure that you have left no litter behind.

RIGHT A fish is drawn to the waiting net.

A large still water

LEFT Daybreak is a magical time.

A wide variety of fish species are present in large bodies of fresh water. We will assume that the water that you are going to fish contains carp, tench and bream. Today we intend to target primarily carp.

ABOVE A fine specimen carp.

BELOW A bream caught at distance from a large still water.

Tackle required

Note that the distance that you will have to cast the bait and the weight of the terminal tackle will, to some extent, determine the tackle used. The size of fish that you are seeking will obviously also be of some relevance. If large carp are present, for example, you will need to ensure that they can be landed if hooked. If bream or tench are your quarry, a reduced tackle strength will provide increased sport. If the fish are in the margins, you can either leger or use a float. A set-up similar to that used in the small still water section (see page 232) will suffice, too, as long as allowances are made for the larger-sized fish.

ABOVE LEFT Location is the key.

ABOVE Arriving at the water loaded up with all the tackle required.

OPPOSITE PAGE All set up for a long wait.

Carp fishing

- A 12 to 13ft (3.7 to 4m) long rod with a 2 to 3lb (907g to 1.4g) test curve.
- A fixed-spool reel holding more than 200yd (183m) of 10 to 15lb (4.5 to 6.8kg) bs line.
- A leader line of 30lb (13.6kg) bs.
- 2 to 4oz (57 to 113g) weights.
- Hook-length material.
- Size 2 to 12 hooks.
- Bait, such as loose feed, boilies, groundbait, particle baits.
- A hair rig, semi-fixed leger rig or free-running rig.
- A rod-rest.
- A pair of audible bite indicators and a butt bite-indicator bobbin.
- Line clips.
- An unhooking mat.
- A pair of forceps.
- PVA string or a PVA bag (optional).
- A catapult, method feeder, throwing stick or bait-rocket or bait-dropper (optional).
- A seat.
- Food, antiseptic wipes, shelter and cooking facilities (optional).
- A weighing sling, carp sack, bank stick and retaining cord (optional).
- A camera and tripod (optional).

Assessing the situation

ABOVE Binoculars are useful for fish and feature location.

A large expanse of water is a more daunting proposition to the angler than a small pond or lake. The first problem is the location of the fish because it is likely that such water contains large areas that are not heavily populated by the fish that you are seeking. You will therefore need to study the water carefully, with the help of a pair of binoculars, looking for clues as to where the fish may be found.

If there are any other anglers fishing the water, where are they fishing? It is a good idea to approach them to ask them about the water and what it contains, but do not bombard them with questions. If they are amicable, they may give you useful information, but don't be offended if they are reluctant to impart too many details. Just wave them a cheery goodbye and continue with your reconnaissance of the water.

The surrounding land will give clues about the likely contours of the ground beneath the water. If a bank slopes steeply into the water, it is likely that the slope continues beneath the surface. Conversely, if the bank is a gentle incline, the water is likely to be shallow near the shoreline. Look for any rivers or streams that enter a lake because they may have created deep channels beneath the water's surface. Weed beds or areas containing any form of structure are worth investigating, too. A gravel pit is likely to contain gravel bars that form either patrol routes for fish or areas where their food accumulates.

The wind will have a considerable influence on the location of the fish in large masses of water. The windward bank often proves the most productive source of fish, partly because higher oxygen levels may make the fish more active; partly because warmer water from the water's surface is driven into the bank, promoting insect life to hatch; and partly because food may be carried there by the wind. All of these factors make the windward bank a promising area to explore.

The banks of the water may indicate which areas are the most heavily fished. And if well-worn swims reveal that many anglers have fished there, ask yourself why. If they are near to the car park, it is likely that the anglers were lazy and did not want to carry their kit too far. If this is not the case, however, it is likely that the swims are productive areas to fish

and merit further investigation.

It is useful to have a map of the water, which you may be able to obtain from the owner of the fishery; if you are lucky, the water depths around the lake will be marked on it. Failing that, it is helpful to discover the depth of the lake or area that you are intending to fish. One option is to gain access to a boat with an echo-sounder, but if this facility is unavailable, you will need to resort to other means. A marker float and heavy weight are useful tools for this job. First select a carp rod that is capable of casting a weight of 2 to 3oz

BELOW A marker float is used for exploring the contours of the swim.

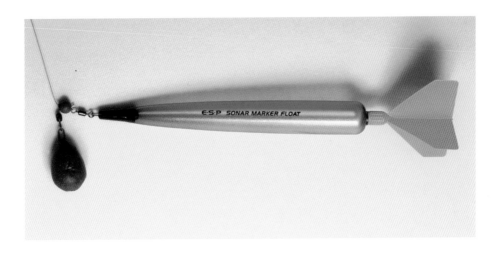

(57 to 85g). Thread on a weight and then a bead. Tie the float to the end of the line, cast it out into the lake and allow it to sink to the bottom on a tight line. Now gradually release the line 1ft (30cm) at a time, measuring it against the rod as you proceed, until the float appears on the water's surface. This will give you the depth of the water at that point. Now wind the float back down to the weight and drag it towards you. As you feel the weight progress, it will give you clues about the consistency of the bottom. You can then release the float again to measure the depth at various points in the swim. The ideal depth at which to fish depends, to some extent, on the water. Look for changes in depth, the start of a slope or a depression in the bottom. When you have found an area that you consider to be worth fishing, you can leave the marker in place to give you a target at which to introduce loose feed and eventually your hook bait.

RIGHT A PVA bag full of tempting baits will help the carp locate the hook bait.

Carp fishing

Having found an area that you think is worth fishing, you will need either to

attract fish to it or keep them there with bait. There are several ways of introducing bait and groundbait into the area, most of which require casting over some distance.

In some cases, you will not need

much loose feed and can either fish a solitary bait or a few offerings in the immediate vicinity. One method of doing this is by tying baits to the hook using PVA string, which dissolves shortly after contact with the water, leaving a few loose offerings near to the hook bait. You could alternatively use a PVA bag to hold a few small baits or a mixture of dry baits.

In other instances, it may be desirable to introduce substantial quantities of bait with which to attract and hold shoals of fish. If one is available, you could use a boat to deposit the bait, with a marker lowered over the side to mark the location. (Many anglers now use specially designed remote-control boats for this purpose.)

ABOVE Bream will often take baits intended for carp.

BELOW A PVA stringer ensures loose offerings in the vicinity of the hook bait.

ABOVE A PVA stocking can be filled with bait and then trimmed off to be cast out into the lake.

BELOW A remote-controlled boat is a wonderful tool for delivering bait to distant swims with great accuracy.

Generally, however, the bait will need to be introduced by being launched some way from the bank. Catapults can be used to fire individual offerings or large balls of compacted groundbait a considerable distance, or to scatter boilies around a fairly tight area (although this takes practice). A method feeder can also be employed to deposit compacted groundbait around the hook bait, while boilies can

ABOVE LEFT A throwing stick can launch boilies over 100m (300ft).

ABOVE RIGHT The method feeder is highly effective for carp, bream and tench.

BELOW A catapult can fire a ball of groundbait far out into the lake.

ABOVE A method feeder is cast out into the lake.

alternatively be deposited using a throwing stick, a device that, in experienced hands, can launch baits over 328ft (100m).

Small particle baits, such as hemp seed and maize, can be delivered to the area using a bait-rocket or -dropper, a cylinder whose bottom is made of a buoyant material. The cylinder is loaded with bait before being cast out with a powerful rod dedicated to the purpose, and when it lands on the water, it turns over, depositing the bait beneath it.

LEFT AND BELOW A bait rocket is filled with particle baits.

A large bed of bait may be needed to hold the attention of a shoal of fish and encourage them to feed with confidence. A bait bombardment will obviously cause a considerable disturbance in the water, which, on waters that are heavily fished, may draw fish that have become accustomed to equating the sound of splashing with a meal in the vicinity. On lightly fished waters, the disturbance will, however, probably drive the fish away for a few hours before, it is hoped, they return to feed on the carpet of bait. You will therefore need to take these factors into consideration in conjunction with the amount of time that you will be spending at the water.

Deciding on the amount of feed to introduce is difficult, with many issues to consider. Some anglers invest large amounts of time and money in pre-baiting the lake that they regularly fish in a campaign that often lasts for a season or a long session. The baits that they use are often of high nutritional value, and are flavoured to impart a taste that the fish can recognise. Over a

BELOW Boilies are an effective and easy-to-use bait.

ABOVE A fine reward for correct use of bait.

period of time, the carp are gradually weaned onto the bait as they increasingly come to accept it as a safe and valuable food source, causing anglers to enjoy great sport for a while. The carp eventually become wise to the deception, however, and begin to associate the bait with danger, forcing anglers to search out new bait and start the weaning process all over again. (When carp become suspicious of bait, it is said to have been 'blown'. I remember having considerable success with sweet corn when fishing for carp in clear water many years ago, and could observe the carp as they fed eagerly on the bright-yellow grains on the lakebed. The following season I tried the same tactic, but was astonished to see the carp bolt away in panic at the sight of the bed of sweet corn. It was time to change the bait.) As a beginner, you should not be fishing a water that demands a serious baiting strategy, however. The water should instead hold a good head of fish that are likely to respond to a wide variety of baits.

Having considered where, and how, to introduce the bait, you must now decide how to present your hook bait. The most widely used carp hook bait is the boilie (see pages 131 to 135), which is easy to apply to the hook and can easily be flavoured and tailored to the carp's taste. It is often helpful to fish a boilie over a bed of particle baits, such as pellets or hemp seed, because feeding on the particles will encourage the carp to root around in the sediment on the lakebed and suck in the boilie while actively feeding.

It's important to ensure that the rig with which you present the bait does not alarm the carp through association with a previous experience. The carp must take the bait into its mouth with the hook, which must then take hold and penetrate the carp's flesh, something that the combination of a heavy weight with a sharp, exposed hook point should ensure. If you are a

BELOW The trap has been set and the rods sit expectantly.

beginner, you will probably feel more confident using a ready-constructed hair rig, which you can buy from a tackle shop. Note that because the weight must be heavy enough to be cast over the required distance and to anchor the bait in position, a compromise may have to be made between aerodynamics and anchorage. If you are fishing on a slope, a flat-sided weight will not roll out of position, so that you can use a semi-fixed leger rig or a free-running set-up (note that the semi-fixed leger rig will probably hook more fish, but gives no indication when fish are investigating the bait). Whichever rig you chose, try to ensure that any fish that breaks free is not left attached to a heavy weight and a long length of line.

Having laid a bed of bait in an area that you feel is likely to contain carp, chosen a rig to present the bait and set up your rod-rest, which should be equipped with a pair of audible alarms and a butt bite-indicator bobbin of some type, you now need to cast your bait into that precise area of the swim. To do this, line up your line with an object on the far bank or else use a marker float as described above. When you have cast the bait into position, carefully tighten the line until the bobbin is suspended beneath the rod. You should now put the reel into bait-runner mode, either allow it to backwind or open the bale arm and place the line in a line clip. Failure to adopt such precautions may result in the rod being lost or the line being broken. (On heavily fished waters, carp may become wary of tight lines in the water, and if this appears to be the case, clip a back lead on to the line at the tip of the rod to sink the line onto the lakebed.)

The trap having been set, you must now await a result. Because of the low densities of fish present, and their distance from you, you are likely to experience long periods of inactivity between bites. But part of the joy of carp angling is anticipating action while you are waiting in a comfortable chair, scanning the water for signs of fish. (And a lakeside can be a haven for a wide range of other creatures, too: birds are often prolific, and you may

see deer, foxes and other such wild creatures around some waters, while the lake itself will probably contain frogs and toads that can be heard croaking in springtime as they search for mates.) If you are expecting to spend a long time beside a lake, you will need to erect a bivvy or shelter of some sort to protect you from inclement weather, and will also need cooking facilities. Many young people enjoy the camping aspect of carp angling as much as the fishing, and there may also be a strong social aspect to the sport. The downside of spending long periods of time beside a lake with bait and food is that it can encourage rats to frequent the area, which spread such diseases as Weil's disease, a flu-like illness that can be fatal. Hygiene is therefore very important, and it is advisable to carry antiseptic wipes with which to clean your hands before handling food.

Once you have caught a carp, it's crucial to take care when handling and unhooking it, and an unhooking mat is essential to prevent the fish being damaged as it flaps about. The fish should be unhooked gently with forceps and weighed in a sling. If it is worthy of being photographed, this should be done with the minimum of delay. The fish should then be held carefully in the water until it is strong enough to swim off powerfully. It often helps to place the carp in a specially designed sack

before photographing it, which enables you to set up your tripod and prepare your camera while the fish is safely recuperating in the water. If you do this, however, ensure that you secure the sack to the bank with a bank stick and retaining cord.

OPPOSITE PAGE The long-session angler sleeps in a bivvy, relying upon audible bite alarms to wake him when the quarry takes the bait.

RIGHT A fine common carp in excess of twenty pounds.

Tempting predators with lures

ABOVE A selection of surface lures.

The joy of lure-fishing is that it is an active method of angling that requires the angler's constant involvement. It is also a very useful way of locating predatory fish because even when they fail to take the lure, they will often follow it into the bank or side of the boat, thereby boosting the angler's confidence, but not always bending his or her rod (it is likely that they can see the angler and are consequently suspicious of the lure). Although these fish can sometimes be enticed, lure-caught fish are generally hooked on their initial strike at the lure or not at all.

Lure-anglers need to consider many issues as they set about deceiving the predators that they are seeking. Different lures have been designed with particular predatory species in mind, so anglers should ensure that they have a selection of the appropriate lures. The venue being fished will also influence the lures needed: if the water is shallow, for example, those that can be fished within a few feet of the surface will be required; conversely, if the water is deep, lures that can sink or swim in deep water are more likely to work. Above all, the lure must stimulate the quarry's interest, which it is more likely to do if placed close to the fish.

Having selected the lure, the angler should then cast it out, either as near to the fish as possible or beyond where they are lying, before retrieving it in a way that mimics an injured fish, or any creature that resembles a source of food for the predator. Many successful lures do not look like any particular species of fish, and I therefore suspect that the reaction that they provoke in predatory fish is due to their shape, or the movement that is imparted to them by the angler, rather than the details of their appearance. (And beware of lures that are designed to attract anglers rather than fish.)

I have sometimes used lures in conjunction with baits to catch predators. If a pike has repeatedly followed a lure without taking it, dropping a dead bait into its lair will often bring a result, for instance. Lures are also useful for searching water from a boat, and I have found that drifting along, continually casting lures until a pike is caught or seen, is a good way of discovering concentrations of fish, at which point you can drop anchor and cast out a dead bait to await the predator's attention. On the subject of dead baits, I should mention the tactic of wobbling them. Do this by mounting a dead bait on either a specially designed mount or a pair of treble hooks. Then cast out the bait and retrieve it carefully, as you would a lure, imparting movement to the bait in an attempt to imitate a sick or injured fish.

Such baits can also be trolled behind the boat, covering vast areas of water.

Although I have concentrated on pike in this section because they readily attack lures, making them ideal targets for the lure-angler, many other species can also be tempted by artificial lures. Perch and chub, for instance, can be fished for using small lures, including plastic worms and grubs, on ultra-light tackle.

I have based this section on lure-fishing on my experiences in the United Kingdom. I am, however, conscious that the origin of most lures is North America, where they are used to great effect in the pursuit of that prime sporting fish, the freshwater bass. I have caught a few of these fish from lakes in Canada using floating plugs, and was highly impressed by their aggressive strikes at the lure as it was twitched close to weed beds or structures. In the vast lakes of the north, American lure-anglers also seek pike and the mighty muskellunge.

Finally, lure-fishing is the ideal angling method for travelling anglers with limited time. A lure rod, accessories and a few lures are easily packed, and there is no need to collect bait. All that anglers need to do is to obtain permission to fish, clip a lure to their lines and start searching the water. (For more details on the roving angler, see pages 442 to 445.)

BELOW Pollock are often tempted using lures. Note the large eyes typical of a night-feeding predator.

Experimenting with lures

Armed with a few lures, a rod, reel, net and a few other essentials, it's a good idea to experiment with lure-fishing by roaming along a bank, casting here and there. Good lure-anglers should be confident that a fish is likely to take the lure every time that one is cast, but when you are fishing a venue whose features do not obviously hold fish, you will need to adopt a searching casting pattern. To do this, stand at the water's edge, imagine that you are positioned at the centre of a clock face, facing 12 o'clock, and then search the water between 9 and 3 o'clock. Try not to be too mechanical in your approach, and cast with inspiration, not like a robot. Indeed, I recommend casting to different points of the 'clock' at random because this approach is more likely to surprise a fish when a lure lands near it. (Although I do not know whether a fish is more likely to take a lure that approaches it gradually or suddenly, I suspect that its sudden appearance is more likely to provoke a fish to lurch instinctively towards it.)

ABOVE The angler wanders along the bank, casting into promising areas.

In most venues, there are features or areas — such as weed beds, sunken trees or areas that incorporate changes in the contours of the bottom — that will probably hold large concentrations of fish, and these are the areas on which you should concentrate your efforts because they provide ambush points for predatory fish. Always be on the lookout for signs of predatory fish attacking their prey, such as showers of small fish leaping from the water or a large swirling pattern within the water.

Remember that if you have previous experience of a venue, that will greatly influence where you concentrate your efforts, areas that have proved productive in the past always being worth a few extra casts.

Fishing a canal for pike

We will now fish a weedy canal that contains a healthy population of pike, toothy predators that, being suckers for a well-presented lure, are the lure-angler's ideal target. They lurk waiting in their lairs within the weedy waters until a victim presents itself, whereupon they accelerate to engulf it.

Tackle required

- Polarising glasses to reduce surface glare.
- A 7½ ft (2.3m) lure rod.
- An ABU bait-casting multiplier reel.
- 50lb (22.7kg) bs braided line.
- 28lb (12.7kg) bs wire trace.
- A swivel.
- Snap links.
- Various lures (see below).
- A landing net.
- Unhooking gear.
- Scales for weighing your quarry.
- A carry bag

Starting off in a relatively weed-free area, select a lure that casts easily, both to warm you up and encourage the line to work freely from the spool. As you get into the casting rhythm, you should start to feel at one with your rod and reel. The rod should feel like an extension of your arm as you relax and make each cast, sending the lure

ABOVE The retrieve imparts movement to the lure.

RIGHT Bait-casting reel and bull dawg lure.

probing into every promising-looking spot.

As you move along the canal, you may come to areas of dense weed that you suspect hold fish. If so, select a lure that is unlikely to become snagged, cast it as close as possible to the weeds and retrieve it carefully, so that it flutters

and vibrates in the water. Although you could carry a huge selection of lures to cover every conceivable situation, this is not really practical when wandering along a canal bank. (It is a different matter when you're fishing from a boat and don't have to carry them yourself, however, when you will furthermore be fishing a larger area of water and will consequently be facing a wider range of potential situations.) Instead, it's best to carry a limited range of lures, such as the following, from which to make your selection.

• Super-shad rap: this floating plug casts well and can provoke savage strikes from pike lying several feet below the water's surface. The lure dives to a depth of around 6ft (1.8m), depending on the retrieve, and is best fished using a stop-start retrieve. I often cast it out over weeds, allow it to rest briefly after it has landed and then start to retrieve it briskly, pausing to allow it to float over weeds or obstacles.

LEFT The boat angler has access to far more water than the bank angler.

BELOW A take could come at any moment as the angler retrieves the lure.

• Spinner bait: although this odd-shaped lure does not cast particularly well, it has the big advantage of bouncing off most snags, which means that it can be cast into reed beds and at the edge of lily beds without the risk of losing it. It tends to work well with a steady retrieve. It is an excellent lure for finding fish, but not the best hooking lure; a stinger hook can be added to improve its hook-up rate, but note that this will affect the lure's snag-resistant qualities. It comes in a range of colours, with which you can experiment to match the prevailing conditions.

• Jake: this lure always gives me confidence as it wiggles enticingly along on the retrieve. Fish it in a manner similar to the super-shad rap (see above).

• Bull dawg: this soft rubber lure sinks slowly in the water and can be retrieved quickly, slowly or in a series of jerks. It is a good lure to choose when searching deeper swims and provokes positive takes (which can prove troublesome when a pike totally engulfs the lure, however).

• Spoon: this lure is both easy to cast and can cover a lot of water. Extra life can be imparted by pausing the retrieve and allowing the spoon to flutter enticingly downwards for a moment.

• Surface lure: as its name suggests, a surface lure is fished on the surface of the water. As it is brought back across the surface, it splutters and splashes and creates a wake, thereby attracting the attention of the pike below, which attack it with explosive takes that really get the angler's heart racing. During the summer, when weed growth has covered large expanses of water, these lures are the angler's only chance of tempting a fish.

The clarity of the water will greatly influence the colour of the lure that you should select. Although many anglers believe that a big, bright lure that gives off plenty of vibrations is needed in dirty water, I have found that dark lures sometimes work equally well. I tend to use large lures of around 6in (15.2cm) in length for most of my pike fishing, having found that small lures both provoke fewer takes and are difficult to remove from the pike's jaws. Each

venue is different, however, and large lures may be inappropriate in small venues.

Apart from its pattern, action and colour, you will need to consider many other factors when selecting a lure, such as its size and weight, whether it floats or sinks and so on. All of these criteria need to be pondered and matched not only to the prevailing conditions but, more difficult still, to your quarry's preferences. Remember that each swim

ABOVE The crazy crawler surface lure in action.

fished may need a different lure, making good-quality snap links essential for quick and easy lure changes.

Having eventually dropped the right lure into a pike's lair, you will feel the rod's tip being wrenched over as the angry pike shakes its head in an attempt to free itself from the lure's hooks. Keep the rod held upright and the line

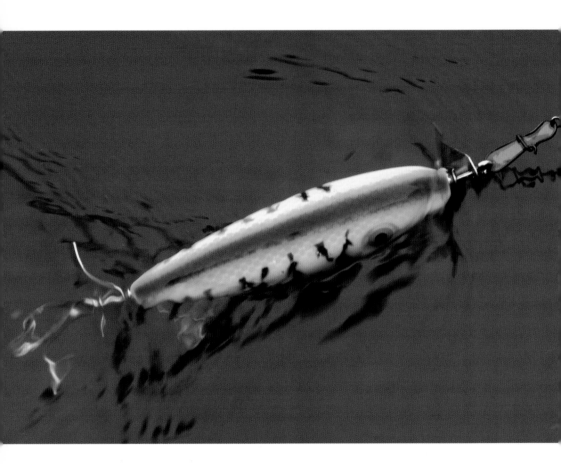

ABOVE Surface lures create a tempting wake upon the surface. This lure has a small propeller at nose and tail.

tight as you allow the rod to absorb the fish's lunges. Give line if you have to, but be firm and keep the fish out of the weeds if possible.

When the fish has been played out, you can either land it by hand or with a landing net. Take care if you are landing it by hand, however, because dealing with an angry pike attached to a treble hook is no joke, believe me. I once impaled my hand on a large treble hook while unhooking a Nile perch, and it was not a sight for the squeamish. If this happens to you, you will need a good pair of snips with which to cut the hook's shank before seeking medical attention. Smaller pike are probably best landed by hand because this method avoids the danger of the hooks becoming entangled in the mesh of a landing net. Larger pike are usually netted, with care being taken to prevent the hooks from catching in the net. Once landed, the pike should be laid on a patch of soft grass or an unhooking mat and handled firmly, but carefully. Remove the hooks from the pike using a pair of long-nosed pliers or forceps, but if the hooks are deeply imbedded, you may need a pair of side-cutters with which to cut through their shanks. Remember that the fish's welfare is paramount at all times, and that it should be released as quickly as possible after you have unhooked it (you may have to support it carefully until it has fully recovered and is able to swim away).

When you have covered all of the prime spots along the canal, you may wish to return to areas that showed promise earlier. If a big pike followed the lure earlier in the day, but failed to take it, for instance, a return visit to that spot could prove fruitful.

You should catch several pike with your lures over a day's fishing. Being a wandering angler, you should also see far more than the static angler. I am often surprised to see other species of fish as I am casting my lures, such as large carp and bream swimming under the rod tip, seemingly unaware of my presence, although they are unapproachable on those days when I have actually targeted them. (I was once told a tale about the fish in a pond within a golf course. Being used to them, the fish would take little notice of the golfers as they strode around the pool, but when an angler approached with his rod and kit, the same fish melted away as though they sensed danger!)

Tempting freshwater predators with live and dead baits

Because predatory fish prey on other fish, you will clearly have to use either a fish bait or an artificial lure to catch them. When trying to locate predatory fish, features that provide cover for the predator and its prey are the first place to look; find a large shoal of bait fish, and predators will generally be close at hand. The methods used for locating fish in gravel pits and large still waters apply equally to predatory fish, too, so

ABOVE Dead baiting on large reservoir in winter.

BELOW Mackerel make superb dead baits.

that drop offs, weed beds and variations in the contours of the bottom are all worth exploring.

In theory, live fish are the ultimate baits for predators, and they will indeed out-fish dead baits in many situations. Apart from ethical issues, there are certain barriers that prevent their use, however. Live baits are banned in many freshwater areas to prevent the potential spread of disease, for example, and it is illegal to transport live baits from venue to venue in the United Kingdom.

ABOVE This fine pike took a trout live bait.

Most of the pike landed in UK waters are tempted with live or dead baits, while those in the United States and Canada are fished with artificial lures. And although I am sure that an American pike would snap up a mackerel dead bait with the same relish as its English counterpart, it is always advisable to accept that local anglers know best and consequently to emulate their methods.

LEFT Pike : the ultimate freshwater predator.

Although groundbaiting is not used extensively in freshwater-predator fishing, its use can pay dividends, either by drawing bait fish or by introducing fishy particles into the swim, both of which in turn attract predators. Using a feeder stuffed with minced fish or cotton wool soaked in fish oil and flavours can also improve catches (and dead baits can similarly be made more attractive to pike and other predators by being injected with oils and flavours). Generally, however, pike anglers fish live or dead baits in their favoured swims without using groundbait.

Dead baits have a big advantage over live baits in that they can be cast considerable distances from the shore. Although a live bait can be drifted out over the water for long distances using specialist tackle, this is only effective if the wind is blowing in the right direction. If it is permitted, boat anglers can, however, use live baits to search the water, a successful method often being to troll live baits suspended beneath floats slowly along, behind a boat powered either by oars or an electric motor, over the heads of the lurking pike. Indeed, when fishing on large waters, a boat gives the angler a distinct advantage, namely the freedom to explore areas out of the shore angler's reach – just pull up the anchor, and you're on the move.

Pike anglers traditionally attach their baits with treble hooks, and variations on the famous Jardine snap tackle (named for Alfred Jardine, one of the greatest pike anglers of all time, who died in 1910) still prevail. The simple and effective snap tackle consists of two treble hooks mounted on a wire trace,

and remember that when fishing for pike or any species with sharp teeth, a wire trace is essential if you are to avoid both losing a fish and condemning it to a slow death through its throat having been sealed by the hooks. Anglers fishing for predators like catfish generally use large, single hooks to hold their baits, while perch and smaller predators require scaled-down tackle in

BELOW A specimen pike from a canal.

keeping with their size. Smaller hooks and lighter lines can be used, but if pike are present, it would be prudent to use a wire trace.

It's vital that your tackle includes an effective bite indicator for predators if you are to avoid deep-hooking a fish, which can injure it. Floats provide good visual indications of bites, particularly when distance-casting is not required when fishing from boats. When legering from the shoreline, some form of drop-off indicator will be necessary, in which the bobbin drops free as the fish moves off with the bait, leaving no resistance as the line is allowed to flow freely from the open spool or bait-runner. The drop-off alarm can be used in conjunction with an audible alarm, which allows your attention to wander away from your rods during long periods of inactivity.

Finally, on receiving a run from any predator, remember that it is again essential to set your hooks early to avoiding deep-hooking the fish (see pages 410 to 412).

Catching still-water trout

Still-water trout fisheries can be divided into three broad categories: small commercial trout fisheries; stocked reservoirs and lakes; and wild fisheries.

Small commercial trout fisheries

Small commercial trout fisheries are often stocked with trout that have grown to quite large sizes. In many instances, the trout are reared on site and the lake stocked on a put-and-take basis. Although they are generally expensive to fish, they provide anglers with good sport.

LEFT A lake nestles between mountains, providing stunning scenery for still-water fishing.

BELOW Trout being fed in the stew pond of a commercial fishery.

Small commercial trout fisheries are in many respects ideal for the beginner. They are relatively easy to tempt fish from, for example, while their generally small size makes them far less daunting angling prospects than larger waters. The only problem with starting your angling career at such waters is that the average size of the trout is often more than 2lb (907g), which means that if you progress to reservoirs or wild fisheries, you may be disappointed by the smaller-sized fish that they contain.

Stocked reservoirs and lakes

Stocked reservoirs and lakes offer the angler a far greater challenge than small commercial trout fisheries. The trout with which they are stocked are usually rainbow trout, which are cheaper to rear and grow to a worthwhile size far faster than brown trout.

Such waters are likely to be far larger than small commercial trout fisheries, and, as a result, the trout tend to become naturalised to some extent

and start to feed on natural foods like aquatic insects. As a result, the angler's choice of fly pattern becomes more important, and catching these fish will be harder work. Indeed, these fish often make up for their smaller size by fighting harder and tasting superior to more recent stocks of fish.

OPPOSITE PAGE TOP A large trout puts a healthy curve in the rod.

OPPOSITE PAGE BOTTOM Casting a fly for reservoir trout.

BELOW A fine rainbow and selection of successful fly patterns.

Wild fisheries

Truly wild trout fisheries are scarce, but the fishing that they offer is to be savoured. The trout are often brown trout, which have a beauty that makes them well worth catching. In many highland lakes and tarns, they are small, but plentiful, and rise to take small flies with pleasing regularity.

In some large natural lakes, huge brown trout, commonly referred to as 'ferox', lurk in the depths, where they can be caught using a deeply trolled lure or bait.

Fishing for rainbow trout in a small still water

We will now consider ways of catching trout and the tactics at our disposal. We will start by fishing a small still water stocked with rainbow trout averaging 2 to 3lb (907g to 1.4kg) in weight, but also holding a good number weighing more than 10lb (4.5kg). The water is clear and has depths averaging around 5ft (1.5m). The fly life is abundant during warm weather and the trout occasionally rise freely.

Tackle required

- Polarising glasses.
- A 9½ ft (2.9m) long fly rod, matched to a weight-forward (WF) 7 floating line.
- A 6lb (2.7kg) bs leader.
- A variety of nymphs, lures and flies.
- A landing net.
- A priest.
- Line-clippers.
- Fly floatant
- A spare reel or spool loaded with a WF 7 sinking line.
- A 7ft (2.1m) long brook rod – a lightweight rod for use on small streams.

- A WF 5 floating line.
- A 4lb (1.8kg) bs leader.
- A variety of nymphs and dry flies.
- A marrow spoon (optional).
- A trout bass (a traditional reed bag).

Note that the second light rod with line and leader specified in the list of tackle above will give you the option of angling with a more sporting outfit (and this is the outfit that I use on most of my visits to the particular small water that I'm using as an example). Being light, it is a joy to use and provides great sport when the trout are hooked. Such an outfit is, however, more difficult to cast in strong winds, and needs careful handling when large fish are hooked.

Assessing the situation

Having arrived at the fishery and purchased your day ticket, it is a good idea to ask for a little advice on flies. Fishery owners are generally very helpful, and will usually suggest suitable patterns of fly to try, and there will often be a well-stocked tackle room

selling them, too.

On approaching the water, you will need to decide where to start your day's fishing. Because the stock density is high, it should not be too difficult to locate the fish, but note that some spots will yield fish more regularly than others. The beginner would probably be wise to select a position on the bank that offers trouble-free casting. Try to avoid standing near trees and, if possible, try to position yourself so that the wind is either behind you or is blowing from left to right, if you are right-handed, or from right to left, if you are left-handed.

Always wear a pair of polarising glasses. These serve two purposes: firstly, they help you to see into the

ABOVE Fishery owners can be relied upon for sound advice.

BELOW Polarising glasses give valuable protection to the eyes.

water by removing the surface glare; and, secondly, they provide your eyes with valuable protection from the fly on the end of your line. (On the subject of

ABOVE Anglers concentrate on presenting their offerings.

danger from flies, always approach other fly-anglers with care; a discreet cough or word of greeting will alert them to your presence. Although all anglers should be on the lookout for others while casting, the reality is that we forget about everyone else as we concentrate on the fish in front of us, so always beware of an angler's back cast!)

Which fly and leader to use?

Having selected a spot to fish, your next decision will be which fly and leader to use. If you are going to try a small nymph, a light, unobtrusive leader will be required to enhance its presentation. If you are going to use a lure, you can use a heavier leader, the fish probably having less time to inspect the lure; the lure will also encourage savage takes that can snap a light leader. My choice for 90 per cent of my small-water trout fishing is nymphs or dry flies.

Some anglers carry a huge range of patterns to cover any preferences that the trout may have, but a dozen patterns will generally catch you your quota of fish on most days. On many occasions, all that the change of fly accomplishes is boosting the angler's confidence, although this is an important factor in successful angling because a confident angler will always fish in a more effective manner. Indeed, I would almost go so far as to say that how a fly is fished can be more important than the pattern. Although each angler would probably give you a different list of their top six fly

ABOVE A gold-head nymph has successfully deceived.

patterns, and you will develop your own preferences in time, my own top six nymphs are: the pheasant-tail nymph; the black buzzer; the Montana nymph; the damsel-fly nymph; the gold-head hare's-ear nymph; and the mayfly nymph. (Note that it's advisable to keep them in different sizes.) My top six dry flies are: the black gnat; the grey duster; Greenwell's glory; the daddy-longlegs; the mayfly; and the coch-y-bundi. My favourite traditional wet flies are: the black n peacock spider; the bloody

butcher; the march brown; and the mallard and claret.

Consider the following issues when choosing a fly. Which flies regularly catch fish at that fishery? At what depth are the fish feeding? (Look for signs of rising fish or fish bulging just beneath the water's surface.) Are there any live flies on the water? (Look into the windward margins of the water for clues.) Which flies are the anglers around you using? To elaborate, if the

ABOVE The angler in the background has obviously made a wise choice of fly.

weather is cold, the fish are likely to be deeper in the water; if it is warm, they may be higher in the water. If the fish are splashing as they rise, a dry fly may be appropriate. If the fish are near the surface, a small, light nymph or buzzer (the aquatic stage of an insect that emerges as a fly) will probably be more successful. For deeper-feeding fish, use a long leader and a weighted nymph.

Casting and retrieving

Whichever fly pattern you start with, keep your eyes on the water and look out for signs of feeding fish. When angling, no two days are ever the same, and you will also see that the trout's behaviour changes over the course of a day. All will be quiet around the lake, with no one seeing any action, for example, when you suddenly notice that all of the anglers around the lake have

LEFT Suddenly the angler's rod bends as the trout come on the feed.

BELOW Watch the tip of the line carefully.

LEFT Concentration is the key.

bent rods as a result of the fish switching into feeding mode for a short, frantic spell.

Let's assume that there is little sign of activity on the surface. Cast out your line and allow the fly to sink slowly to the depth that you want to fish. Always watch the tip of the line and be prepared to strike firmly if you see it twitch. Trout sometimes take the fly as it sinks into the water, and are frequently attracted by the plopping noise that it makes as it enters the water.

When the fly or nymph has eventually sunk to the correct depth, start to make your retrieve. This should usually be slow, albeit with the occasional twitch to add life to the fly or nymph (try to imagine how a live aquatic insect would move in the water and imitate that). Keep watching the tip of the line and be prepared to tighten the line as soon as you sense that a fish has taken the fly. Concentration is the key because by the time you feel a tug, it may be too late, the fish having discovered the deception. My favourite

OPPOSITE PAGE A sinking line disappears into the water.

RIGHT, FROM TOP TO BOTTOM The figure-of-eight retrieve. The angler slowly retrieves, coiling the line into the palm of his hand.

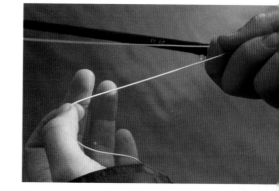

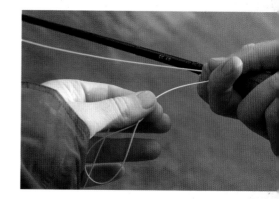

retrieve is a figure of eight as I finger the line into loose coils in my hand. Be aware of your fly at all times, and of where it is. As you lift it slowly from the water in preparation for the next cast, peer into the water because you may see trout following the fly, and a little twitch of the line will then sometimes provoke a reaction.

Make each cast with hope and confidence. If your confidence is starting to seep away, however, it may be time either to change the fly or to adopt a speedier, or slower, retrieve (the possible permutations are endless). If you feel that your concentration is starting to slip, stop and have a drink and a five-minute break while you think

about what may bring you success. Look around, relax, breathe in the fresh air and watch the birds as they swoop down onto the water.

Hold on a minute, birds swooping down onto the water. Why? Are they feeding on some hatching insects? Yes, perhaps they are. Would a couple of small buzzers, fished just below the surface, do the trick? Having found inspiration, modify the leader, attach a dropper (a short length of line that is used to attach a second fly), tie a buzzer to the line and lightly grease the leader to within a couple of centimetres of the buzzer. Cast out the buzzer and allow it to drift in the breeze as you retrieve it

very slowly. Suddenly there is a bulge in the water, the line shoots forward and a flick of your wrist connects it with a fish. As you are holding the rod high to absorb the pressure of the trout's frantic efforts to shed the hook, the reel screams as the trout heads off on a run for the far side of the lake. Keep calm and keep applying moderate pressure to the line. When the fish stops running, apply more pressure and try to retrieve the line. You can do this by drawing in the line by hand and allowing it to coil on the ground or else by winding the line onto the reel. (If the fish is large, I prefer to wind the line on to the reel, thereby reducing the risk of it becoming entangled with any debris on the bank, but there is really no right or wrong way.)

When the fish is lying on its side with its mouth open, draw it towards you, into the landing net that you are holding. (Be prepared for the fish to make a last-minute plunge for freedom.) If you are intending to keep the fish for the table, dispatch it with a priest.

If you want, you could now use a marrow spoon to discover what the fish had eaten before being captured. Then place the fish in a trout bass (a traditional

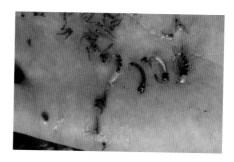

ABOVE Buzzers and the nymphs they imitate.

BOTTOM LEFT A marrow spoon is used to examine the trout's stomach contents.

BOTTOM RIGHT This provides vital clues as to what imitation he should try.

reed bag) and either store it out of the sun or lower it into the cool water to maintain its freshness. Having enjoyed your taste of success, you can now continue fishing with renewed confidence.

BELOW A fine limit bag taken from a large reservoir.

Most fisheries offer a choice of permit specifying a bag limit (that is, a total number of fish caught) based on the price paid. I have noticed that some anglers can become obsessed with reaching their limit, but it really shouldn't matter. Enjoy your day; enjoy

casting your fly; and enjoy anticipating the take. We all like to go home with a heavy bag digging into our shoulder, but don't let greed tarnish your enjoyment of your day. When angling on small still waters, I often find that I catch my bag of fish too quickly and end up at home cutting the lawn, when I would rather be fishing!

After returning home, you will have the task of cleaning the fish to prepare it for eating. Thereafter, there is something rather satisfying about sitting down to enjoy a freshly grilled trout and glass of wine after a day spent beside the lake.

ABOVE The full tail on this rainbow trout gave the angler an exhilarating battle.

BELOW At the end of the day enjoy your catch with a glass of wine.

Alternative tactics

On those days when no fish can be tempted using the methods outlined above, you could try a few alternative tactics.

A lure or traditional wet fly fished fairly fast and near the surface will sometimes trigger an attack from a trout. (On some occasions, a bow wave can be seen behind the fly as the trout closes in on the lure.) It may be exciting, but this type of fishing is not particularly satisfying because the trout has been antagonised rather than deceived, although it may at least mean that you go home with something after a slow day.

Another ploy is to switch to a sinking line and search for trout near the bottom. One particularly effective method is to select a fly termed a 'booby', an extremely buoyant creation that should be fished on a very short leader of 17¾ to 23½in (45 to 60cm). Let the sinking line sink to the bottom of the lake, then begin the retrieve with very short pulls of a few centimetres at a time. Between each twitch, pause for a few seconds and watch the line as it leaves the rod's tip. Be prepared to strike at any movement because takes vary from discreet nudges to vicious, arm-wrenching pulls. Although this method is frowned upon by the angling purist, who likens it to bait fishing, it is really no different from fishing a nymph slowly near the surface.

The tactics that I have discussed here will catch you a trout on most days, but the difficulty lies in deciding on the appropriate tactic for the day in question. Getting it right is the satisfying part.

Fishing for trout in larger waters

Fishing large lakes or reservoirs gives anglers the opportunity to enjoy good sport at a reasonable price. You will generally have to work harder for your fish than when fishing at small commercial fisheries.

Although much of the advice given above for fishing for trout in a small still water applies to larger waters, too, I recommend using a slightly heavier outfit, both to enable longer casts and to withstand strong winds better.

When fishing a large reservoir, I generally carry two rods made up ready to fish: a heavier outfit with a lure and sinking line; and a lighter outfit with a floating line and a team of nymphs or dry flies. As you become more experienced, you will be able to invest in a wider range of specialist tools, but you will be able to catch plenty of fish with these outfits to start with.

LEFT Deceived with a gold-head buzzer.

Tackle required

A 9½ to 10½ ft (2.9 to 3.2m) long fly rod matched to a weight-forward (WF) 8 or 9 sinking line and a floating line of the same weight and taper.

- A 9½ ft (2.9m) long fly rod matched to a WF 7 floating line.
- A 6lb (2.7kg) bs leader.
- A variety of nymphs, lures and flies.
- A landing net.
- A priest.
- Line clippers.
- A fly floatant.

Assessing the situation

Large waters require greater fish-locating skills than small waters. And because vast expanses of water may be devoid of fish, it's important to give careful thought to where you are going to start your day. If a boat is available, this will obviously give you access to far more water, but then boat-fishing brings its own problems and does not guarantee success. In fact, I would advise beginners to stick to dry land until they have fully mastered their casting skills.

So where will the trout be? Well, although trout are nomadic by nature, they still haunt areas that hold food, so scan the water looking for features like weed beds, feeder streams and any structures that may provide the fish with food or shelter, and try to ascertain where the water is deep or shallow. Any barren areas surrounding the lake or reservoir tend to signify less insect life and fry for the trout to hunt down.

The wind has a great deal of influence on trout in large still waters, and it is often helpful to start your search for them on the windward shore. You may find them close to the shore, feeding on hatching insects and food that has been carried there by wind-driven currents. Casting into the wind demands great effort and will undoubtedly cause the beginner's line to become tangled, but moving to a sheltered area will often bring little gain because the trout will be further out. If you observe the surface of the water, you should see wind lanes, areas of calmer water that carry food for the trout, and these are the spots to aim for.

Angling tactics

If you can see the trout feeding near to the water's surface, a floating line is probably the best choice to start with. You could fish a team of three flies, with a leaded nymph on the point, or end of leader, a lighter fly above and a small lure or bushy fly on the top dropper (which is a hook-length off the main leader). The possible permutations are many, and there is room for much experimentation. Ideally, try to cast across the wind and allow the line to drift around in a curve. Watch the tip of the line where the leader sinks into the water. Concentrate hard, and be prepared to pull the hook home at the slightest sign of any interest in your flies. Be warned, however, that although a team of flies may prove effective, it may be more trouble than it is worth for a beginner who has not yet fully mastered the art of tangle-free casting.

Early in the season, the fish are likely to be deep down in the cold water, reluctant to approach the surface. This is when the sinking line, with its ability to deliver the fly to deep-lying fish, comes into its own. Using larger lures may pay dividends, too, with black and white being the first coloured patterns to try. I generally recommend fishing a lure with a slow retrieve. Many takes come as a savage tug that electrifies the angler, others as a mere tightening of the line. The take of a fish is, perhaps, angling's defining moment, when all of those hours of searching for a successful deceit are finally rewarded. The actual landing of the fish is a triumph, but almost an anticlimax in comparison to the thrill of the take.

The sinking line can be used throughout the season. During hot, sunny weather, trout often seek out deep water with a high oxygen level, for example, making a lure fished deep the only tactic likely to succeed.

At times, trout feed voraciously on fry, and can sometimes be caught on lures tied to imitate this food source, particularly the lake or reservoir's larger residents, which frequently come into the margins of the water in pursuit of the fry.

I must emphasise the importance of observing the water for signs of trout. Search the water carefully, casting a variety of fly patterns, using different retrieves and varying the depth, and you will eventually find the correct combination. Remember, too, that each fly is designed to be fished in a specific manner. Each year sees the introduction of a new batch of creations invented by imaginative fly-dressers, and methods also evolve as innovations creep into the sport. Site bobbins would have been considered unsporting at one time, for example, but are now widely used on still waters and some rivers. (A site bobbin is a piece of highly visible, buoyant material that is fixed between the fly line and leader. When a trout takes the fly, the bobbin disappears – like a float – whereupon, with a flick of the wrist, the angler connects with a trout that may otherwise have gone undetected.)

As I mentioned previously, a boat

usually a bushy type of pattern, is often grabbed by trout as it is allowed to create a wake on the surface before being lifted off for the next cast. Because it is traditionally used on the lochs of Scotland and Ireland, this method of fishing is frequently called 'loch style'.

When fishing from an anchored boat, you can, of course, use similar tactics to those used when angling from the bank. If you are fishing from a boat, remember always to show consideration to anglers who are fishing from the shore or from other boats by keeping a good distance away and remaining aware of how fast you are drifting.

Because fly-fishing is considered the most enjoyable and sporting way of angling for trout, I have discussed only this angling method. And although normal coarse-fishing techniques can be employed when fishing for trout on waters that allow it, I do not find such fishing particularly rewarding. On some large, wild lakes, lochs and loughs, the mighty ferox trout can be tempted by trolling plugs or spoons in the depths, for instance.

ABOVE Afloat in search of reservoir trout.

gives the angler the opportunity to cover a lot of water, and drifting with the wind is an effective method of boat-fishing. If the wind is strong, a drogue (effectively a parachute in the water behind the boat) must be used to slow the speed of the drift. A team of flies is then cast into the water in front of the moving boat, being retrieved to the side of the boat and lifted slowly from the water. The top fly, which is often referred to as the 'bob fly' and is

Salmon fishing

Although salmon spend much of their lives in the sea, they are generally referred to as a freshwater species. They start out in life by emerging from gravel spawning grounds (redds) in rivers many miles from the sea. The immature salmon, called parr, live in the river for a couple of years. At this stage in their lives, they closely resemble small, brown trout and are often caught by trout anglers. After this period, they undergo a physiological change that prepares them for life in salt water, being transformed into silvery smolts, which resemble the adult fish. The smolts travel downstream and then make their way out to sea. They face numerous perils on their journey, and are preyed upon by many predators, ranging from seals and sea birds to fish. Those smolts that survive reap a harvest of food from the ocean's rich feeding grounds, and a diet of herring, squid, plankton, sand eel and a variety of other ocean creatures enables them to pile on weight at a rate of up to thirty times their body weight within a year. At some point after this first year at sea the fish – now called salmon – migrate back to the river of their birth. (Salmon that return to the river after only one or two years are referred to as grilse). They travel upstream to spawn on the same redds from which they themselves hatched to ensure the propagation of another generation of silver travellers before returning to the sea. The Atlantic salmon occasionally survives to return to the river to spawn for a second, or even third, time. The Pacific varieties travel to their spawning grounds, spawn and then die, however, after which their rotting carcasses

LEFT Admiring a fine Atlantic salmon.

RIGHT Searching the river for the salmon on its return journey.

NEXT PAGE These rivers are often very beautiful.

ABOVE A bar of shimmering silver.

enrich the river environment for future generations. It is an amazing life cycle.

The angler seeks the salmon on its journey upstream, endeavouring to tempt it with a selection of baits, flies and lures. The strange thing is that the salmon does not feed in fresh water and therefore, in theory, has no need to take any food into its mouth, prompting the question, 'Why do salmon take the bait if they don't need food?' No one really knows the answer, but, believe me, salmon take baits and lures with determination on occasions, although there are admittedly times when they totally ignore everything being offered to them. I have dangled

worms over salmons' snouts for over half an hour with no response, only for them suddenly to engulf the bait in a breathtaking display of sheer aggression.

Salmon are caught on flies, baits and spinners, although the strict rules governing many waters often limit the methods permissible, many to fly-fishing only. Anglers could once keep most of the salmon that they caught, but in today's climate of dwindling stocks conservation is paramount, and a system of catch and release is becoming widespread, with strict limits on fish for the table being enforced elsewhere.

Considered by many anglers to be the ultimate freshwater prize, this mighty fish is undoubtedly the king of the river, and deserves the utmost respect. And by telling you how I landed my first salmon, I hope to give you a few ideas about how to set about catching this species of fish.

My first salmon

Salmon. The name immediately conjures up a picture in the angler's mind: many regard it as a fish that is pursued by the privileged few; others consider it a charismatic creature, whose remarkable life cycle lends it a romantic air. The rivers in which salmon run are generally set within areas of outstanding natural beauty, thus adding to the enjoyment of their pursuit.

It is many years since I caught my first salmon, an 8lb (3.6kg) bar of shimmering silver, freshly arrived in the river from the sea and adorned with sea lice. Even so, I can recall the moment when that salmon took my spinner as if it happened only yesterday.

It is strange how one can try so hard to achieve something, but when one actually does, it seems so easy. I had been casting spinners into a local river in the hope of catching salmon for several years. Having learned where they lay, I cast my lure into these places over and over again, trying to remember all of the words of advice that I had read in books and magazines. Eventually, after several seasons of failure, I turned my attention to another local river, which was totally

BELOW The lure is cast repeatedly into the pool.

different in character to the first. This river was a spate river, with crystal-clear water, except for those magical periods following the rain. Then, as it fined down following the spate, silver salmon would surge upstream. Because you could at least occasionally see salmon in its waters, this river gave me a big psychological boost.

I started a concerted campaign to make a catch at the season's start, in March, visiting the river two or three times a week regardless of the weather and river conditions. Salmon do not generally start to run up this river until mid-April, so I was unlikely to make a catch during that first month. Still, I began to learn where not to cast if I

wanted to keep my expensive spinners, and enjoyed the onset of spring, seeing the first vivid-green leaves emerge, the dippers and wagtails bobbing along and the river tumbling over moss-covered rocks. I also watched the local anglers peering expectantly into the water, noted where they placed each cast and chatted to them, too, eagerly logging each snippet of information in my mind.

At first I was puzzled by the invisibility of the salmon, although it seemed that other anglers could see them clearly. Surely a fish weighing 7 or 8lb (3.2 to 3.6kg) should be easy enough to spot in clear, shallow water? Then, as time went by, experience and my Polaroid glasses helped me to discern shapes in the water more clearly. Although the salmon still blended perfectly into the river's shimmering currents, I started to detect the shadows, tails and shapes of fish. I realised that the fish lay up in the same spots time and time again, and that if you stood and peered at these spots, the

LEFT Hoping for a fleeting glimpse.

RIGHT The spinner is flicked into every likely lie.

ever-changing water surface would occasionally flatten, providing a window into the river below. And a fleeting glimpse is enough to alert the angler to the presence of the quarry, whereupon a bait or lure can be carefully presented to trick the enigmatic fish.

ABOVE A tense moment as the battle nears its conclusion.

There are, of course, many occasions when anglers cannot see the fish that they are seeking, when they may cast a lure into a likely lie in the hope of provoking a response. I caught my first salmon doing just that. I flicked the spinner across the pool, as I had done thousands of time before, but this time, as the spinner hit the water, there was an eruption of spray, the rod slammed around into a curve and a silver bar came leaping into the air. I cannot say that I played the fish in a calm and patient manner. Amazed by its speed and power, my legs shook with excitement as the salmon dashed crazily up and down the river before me, parrying its every turn with my rod, thereby preventing it from escaping up- or downstream. (If the fish had managed to move below me, I would not have been able to follow it due to a steep, overhanging rock face.) Finally, after a couple of minutes, I managed to get the tailor that I was using around the wrist of the salmon's tail.

I dispatched the fish quickly, with a slight feeling of remorse, and then sat trembling beside my prize. Its flanks gleamed and shimmered blue and silver, in my eyes far surpassing the sparkle and beauty of the finest jewels. A few sea lice clung to its flanks, an indication that it had been in the river for less than forty-eight hours. It had probably arrived from the sea on the previous night's tide. And after travelling back to the river of its birth, following a couple of years living far out in the ocean, it had succumbed to a shiny bar of metal adorned with a treble hook.

I have landed many salmon since that first one, but have never forgotten the excitement of that particular take.

'In search of that moment.'

Indeed, it is the take — that split second when the deception is complete — that gives anglers the greatest pleasure. Many hours are spent in search of that moment, which, I guess, is the essence of angling.

The basics of salmon fishing

As salmon forge their way upstream on their journey from the sea, they frequently stop to rest. These resting points are called 'lies', and it is here that the angler should present the offering to the salmon.

Baits, including worms and prawns, are often used, but check that bait fishing is allowed, as some fisheries ban baits. Sufficient weight needs to be added to the line to sink the bait, yet not so much that it cannot bounce downstream with the current. The bait is then cast upstream and allowed to trundle back down, past the fish. The

ABOVE Trundling a worm downstream.

BELOW A promising stretch of river.

rod is gripped throughout, and the line held carefully between the fingers, feeling for the moment when a salmon takes the bait, which may take the form of a gentle nudge or a savage pull. Many angling textbooks tell you that the angler will feel the salmon gently take the bait and slowly engulf it, after which the waiting angler sets the hook. In reality, the angler bounces the weight along the bottom, gently lifts the rod to keep the bait moving and then suddenly finds a salmon on the end of the line.

When offering a fly or spinner, the normal approach is to cast it down and across the stream, starting at the top of a pool or likely stretch of river. To send it to the taking depth, a sinking line may be required if you are using a fly, or a weight should be added to the trace if you are using a spinner. The fly or spinner is allowed to sink slightly, the line is then tightened and the fly or spinner allowed to swing around in the current, travelling, it is hoped, over the heads of the resting salmon.

After each cast, the angler takes a step downstream and recasts, so covering a vast amount of water in a day's fishing. The fly or spinner should be fished at a speed that appeals to the salmon, which, as a general rule, is as slowly as possible. Try not to become too robotic, however: a cast upstream and rapid retrieve downstream, with the current, to ensure that the spinner is working will sometimes provoke a response from a hitherto unresponsive salmon. Indeed, salmon are unpredictable creatures, and a lure may have passed through a pool full of salmon many times without eliciting a response, when, for no apparent reason, a fish suddenly attacks it with gusto.

BELOW As a general rule fish the lure slowly.

A river

The timeless quality of a river's perpetual journey.

As I fish, I often reflect on the timeless quality of a river's perpetual flow towards the sea. Like the Earth's throbbing veins, rivers flow on seemingly forever (or at least until humankind's abuse bleeds them dry).

Each river has a character of its own, which changes from its source to the sea. And each section of a river has its own inhabitants. We have visited the upper reaches of a river and fished for trout.

We have discussed casting a line for sea trout and the silver salmon that migrate up our cleaner rivers. Now we will move on to fishing the mid- to lower reaches of a river for such coarse fish as roach, chub and barbel. All of these fish are primarily angled for with a baited hook, although an artificial lure or fly may occasionally prove successful.

Assessing the situation

Cast a line into water that is devoid of fish, and you will be fishless, so, as with all venues, the first hurdle to cross when fishing a river is locating the fish. You must therefore learn to read the water, and a river is in many ways far easier to read than other types of water as it twists and turns through the landscape, its rippling surface providing clues about what lies beneath. If the water is clear, and you are wearing polarising glasses, you will, of course, soon be able to see where best to cast your baited hook. And if you peer into the depths and give your eyes time to focus, you may even spot the very fish that you are seeking, or at least the shapes and shadows of your quarry.

What are the factors that determine a fish's location in the river? The answer to this question is food, flow, security, depth and the consistency of the riverbed. Let's look at each in turn and then imagine a swim in a river that is likely to provide them all.

In rivers, some food is brought to fish via a flow that washes it downstream, as though it were on a conveyor belt. Other food is either growing or trapped in certain locations, so that the fish may need to root about in the bottom, weed or sediment to seek it out. Fish are therefore likely to be found where food is to be found, or where the flow will bring it to them.

If the flow is too fast, the fish will have to expend valuable energy on maintaining their position. And because fish are reluctant to waste energy, they will instead seek a position that they can comfortably maintain, often just out of the main flow. If you study a river's surface, you will be able to observe the currents' influence on it. A point worth remembering is that the currents that are visible to us on a river's surface may differ considerably from those nearer the riverbed, however, so that it is quite possible that a turbulent surface conceals tranquil depths. Note that on the edge of the main current is what is termed the 'crease', and it is here that fish will often position themselves.

The fish in the river will have been pursued by predators throughout their lives. Predatory fish, otters, herons, cormorants, kingfishers and anglers all prey on them, and the fish will therefore seek to hide from these creatures, or at least escape to nearby cover when danger threatens. This is why any form of sheltering structure will attract fish, such as boulders, weeds, fallen trees and even discarded rubbish like shopping trolleys. (And anglers are reluctant to fish too close to these areas for fear of losing their tackle.)

Turbulent surfaces may conceal
tranquil depths.

The river's surface hides many secrets.

The water's depth is also a great influence on the location of fish. Deeper water provides fish with greater security, making it worth seeking out any such areas, which include the inside curves of bends that have been scoured out by the current, waterfalls or weirs and areas where the ever-flowing river has dug out deep pits. By contrast, fish are easy prey for predators when in shallow water, which is why the angler will generally find these areas unyielding during daylight hours.

The consistency of the riverbed will vary from muddy, sandy and gravelly to rocky, and the substances at each extreme – mud and rock – are generally the least productive for the angler,

ABOVE A barbel is displayed in the evening sunlight.

probably because there is little flow in muddy areas, while rocky areas have resulted from a constant scouring by the river's strongest currents. The river's scaly inhabitants seem to find sand and gravel more attractive.

The time of day and condition of the water also have an influence on where the fish may be located. The cover of darkness certainly encourages many species to feed with less caution, and the river's fish will often come out of hiding during the hours of darkness to feed in areas that were unsafe during the day. This is why shallow areas that were devoid of fish in the sunshine will often hold fish in the dead of night. Coloured water brought about by a spate will also encourage the fish to feed with vigour. In this instance, timing is of great importance to the angler, however, because during the initial stages of the spate, high levels of ammonia and turbidity will often sour the water, putting the fish off their feed. This is one reason why a river yields more fish as its level begins to fall following a spate.

An angler who lives near to a river and is able to keep a close eye on it clearly has a distinct advantage over visiting anglers, who often have to make the best of the conditions that prevail during their visit. If you are one of the latter, a short-cut to determining the fishes' location is either to ask an experienced local angler or to hire a guide to show you the best spots and methods. In my angling career, I have been fortunate enough to have formed friendships with anglers who live near famous rivers. Their help has enabled me to land many fish that I would have struggled to locate alone. Each river has

swims that look perfect, yet fail to live up to their promise, and the local angler's advice will frequently save you many hours of wasted fishing in these time-absorbing swims. A local angler may even show you exactly where to cast your bait, and in some instances, a couple of feet can make all the difference between a good and a bad day's sport.

Having established the factors that are likely to influence the location of the fish that we are seeking, now let's take a look at the best methods with which to catch them. To a large extent, the species that we are targeting will determine the methods and tackle that should be used. Bottom-feeding fish need to be targeted with a bait on the bottom, for instance, while mid-water species will respond better to a bait suspended beneath a float. A degree of flexibility is required if the angler is to get the best from each situation, however.

The angling methods used on a river will, to some extent, be variations on those used on still waters, the most influential factor being water flow. Although you can greatly influence the

LEFT Discussing tactics beside a weir pool.

movement of the river's inhabitants by means of the sensible application of such bait as loose feed and groundbait, if you are intending to keep fish in a certain area, it is important to ensure that the bait doesn't all wash downstream, where the fish will follow. This is why hemp seed is a particularly good attractor when targeting bottom-feeding fish like barbel: the tiny seeds sink quickly into the bottom's silt and gravel, encouraging the fish to root about in search of every last grain. Light baits, such as maggots and casters, should be introduced well upstream or in a feeder anchored to the bottom.

Feeder-fishing

The swimfeeder is an extremely useful tactic to use on rivers, and has produced excellent catches for me over the years. The block-end feeder is traditionally used in conjunction with maggots, which can be supplemented with hemp seed, casters or chopped worm. The feeder needs to be heavy enough just to hold its position on the riverbed, and some designs enable leads to be clipped to them to achieve this aim. Use a feeder rod that incorporates a fine tip that will clearly show up any bites.

Choose a swim that either has a proven track record or is judged to meet the criteria for success, preferably one that is gravel-bottomed, of a moderate depth and either adjacent to, or slightly upstream from, the cover that holds the fish. It is essential to position the feeder correctly, and it should ideally be cast either opposite the angler's position on the bank or slightly upstream.

The feeder having sunk to the bottom, immediately allow the line to pull freely from the spool of the reel, forming a downstream bow in the line. Place the rod on a rod-rest, with its tip at an angle to the river and pointing downstream. If the current is strong, you will need to keep the rod tip high to reduce the current's drag on the line. The line should be tensioned so that a curve is formed in the quiver tip. If the correct weight has been chosen, the feeder should now remain on the bottom.

At the start of the session, the angler should refill and recast the feeder into the same position every few minutes to ensure that plenty of feed enters the swim. It's therefore vital to ensure that you carry a large quantity of bait to the riverside to build up the swim successfully. The fish, it is hoped, will be stimulated by the constant trickle of bait, and will follow the trail to the feeder, beneath which is a hook baited with maggots. When the fish takes the bait, the quiver tip will announce the success of the angler's trickery by either pulling around or springing straight back as the feeder is dislodged from the bottom, allowing the line to fall slack. The length of the hook link can be critical, and I generally start with around 18in (45.7cm) and then increase or decrease the length as necessary as the day progresses. If the angler is experienced, a second rod can be used and the bait fished with a plain lead downstream from the feeder's position. Different bait can also be fished from this rod, thereby perhaps tempting fish that may be wary of the feeder.

LEFT Gazing at a pair of rod tips on a glorious summer's day.

The traditional block-end feeder can work extremely well, but is by no means the only method that you can employ. Many specialist anglers have adapted carp-fishing tactics to tempt river species, including the carp that seem to have become abundant in the world's rivers. The rigs and set-ups used on still waters can be modified to suit many river situations, too, as long as you remember to make allowances for that ever-present flow.

The open-end or cage feeder, filled with a compressed groundbait mixture, is also widely used on rivers, being cast out in much the same way as the block-end feeder. (Specialist groundbaits can be purchased that are full of feed-inducing ingredients, but the angler can always use a cheap old favourite like mashed bread.) When the feeder hits the riverbed, its contents burst forth and drift downstream, enticing fish into the vicinity. Roach and bream are particularly susceptible to this approach, which works especially well in slow-moving rivers when targeting bream.

Legering

There are many occasions when a straightforward leger rig will tempt fish. The swim being fished will determine the position of the bait, and a leger rig can be fished upstream, downstream or across a river, depending on any obstructions on the bank side and the location of the fish.

A variation on legering bait is to roll the bait along the bottom while holding the rod. This tactic is widely used when fishing baits for salmon, but is also productive in many other situations. Select a bait that is instantly attractive to fish, a large lobworm, chunk of luncheon meat or bread flake being ideal. Using the minimum of weight necessary to keep the bait on the riverbed, hold the line between your fingers, feeling for the pull of a fish, as you encourage the bait to trundle downstream through the swim in search of its residents. This method covers a great deal of water and is an ideal way of getting to know the water that you are fishing. A large number of swims can be explored in this way during a day at the riverside, and if you are unencumbered by a heavy load you can wander over a large area.

Float-fishing

If the fish are positioned some way above the riverbed or are actively searching for food, presenting moving bait beneath a float could prove an effective way of catching them. Some species, such as grayling, tend to shoal in particular areas, and can provide hectic sport when located and fished for with a float. Float-fishing in flowing water, which is often referred to as 'trotting', is a delightful angling method, but demands a degree of finesse if it is to be successful.

Float-fishing requires a stretch of river of reasonably uniform depth and moderate flow. Match a long rod measuring up to 15ft (4.6m) in length to a centre-pin or fixed-spool reel. Use a light line treated with line floatant to help you to control the float, which should be a buoyant type, such as a chubber or stick float (bouyant floats that can support the bait and tackle without submerging easily. Having ascertained the water depth by careful plumbing, fix the top and bottom of the float to the line with float-rubbers (short rubber sleeves that fix the float to the line). I ensure that the bait just clears the bottom to start with.

Stand at the upstream end of the swim and introduce a few tasty free offerings into the area of water where you are intending to trot the float. Now flick out the float and allow it to float downstream, carefully checking the line to ensure that it is tight. When the current starts to create a bow in the line, respond by 'mending the line', that is, by sweeping the rod upstream to lift the line from the water, thereby correcting the drag that is threatening to pull the float off course. If the float is pulled under by a fish, react immediately, before a wary fish ejects the bait. At intervals, you could hold the float back, allowing the bait to flutter upward in the water for a moment before letting it resume its journey.

When the float has reached the bottom of the swim, retrieve it, refill it with bait and repeat the process after introducing a few loose offerings into the water to build up the fishes' confidence. If bites are not forthcoming, you could fine-tune the set-up, perhaps by adjusting the depth of the float or repositioning the split shot. (If the flow is fast, the split shot will need to be near the hook bait, but if the current is slow, it may be better to fish them shirt-button style – that is so that they are evenly spaced.)

If you are fishing an eddy or a slow-moving swim, you could use a waggler float in much the same way as in a lake. (A waggler float is a float that is fished bottom end only.)

Shore fishing

Shore fishing offers the angler a tremendous array of species to catch from numerous locations throughout the seasons. For many people, the great attraction of sea angling is the unpredictability of the sea, and with thousands of species swimming freely in its waters, it is impossible to be absolutely sure what will take the bait next. Although a 'chuck it and chance it' approach is unlikely to give consistent results, it is, however, possible to target certain species.

You will first have to decide which species you intend to catch. Because most sea fish are migratory to some extent, and will only be within casting range at certain times of the year, targeting the species of fish that are prevalent along the coastline during a particular season is a realistic approach. Carrying out a little research at fishing-tackle shops, angling clubs and tourist information centres should give you a good idea of where to go and when.

The single biggest differential between saltwater and freshwater fishing is the tidal cycle. Not only does this have a great deal of influence on the movement and feeding patterns of most species of fish, it also determines whether the angler can reach certain fish-holding areas. (While we're on the subject of the tidal cycle, a word of warning: always be aware of the state of the tide and avoid becoming cut off by a rising tide. A lack of this basic knowledge results in many people being drowned each year, so always plan an escape route, and if there is a gulley behind you that is likely to be filled by the tide, keep a close eye on it and leave your position before it becomes full.) The weather, the clarity and depth of the water, the season, the nature of the seabed and your angling ability are all further factors that will influence your success as a shore angler.

Try not to be intimidated by the vastness of the sea, but instead think of it as though it were a lake or river. You will be fishing the margins of the sea, which thankfully attract plenty of fish. Remember that fish are motivated by

RIGHT Who knows what will take the bait next?

two major urges: to feed and to reproduce. Reproducing fish being less inclined to feed, your first task should therefore be to locate the food that your target fish feed upon.

Now let's look at different shore-angling venues.

BELOW An apparently rocky beach may have sand below the tide line.

NEXT PAGE Hopes rise as the tide floods.

Beaches

There are many types of beach, each with its own characteristics. The tides and weather sculpt and mould each beach, which continues to evolve, year in year out. Although nature generally carves a beach slowly, over thousands of years, a sandy beach can become rocky overnight if a violent storm rips the sandy covering from its rocky bones.

The consistency of a beach varies according to the tidal cycle, too. Low tide may reveal sand, for instance, while large pebbles or rocks may abound at high water. The careful study of a beach will give clues about the type of fish that may be swimming off it.

The gradient of the beach will have some bearing on the distance that you will need to cast your bait. In general, a gradually sloping beach will require you to cast your bait a considerable distance in order to reach the deeper water. By contrast, deep water will be within easy casting range on a steeply shelved beach. Water depth is not, however, a vital indication of fishes' whereabouts. Fish will venture into shallow water to feed if they feel safe, and often at night, and large predators will also follow their prey inshore. The best time to fish from many beaches is after dark, when the need to cast long distances is greatly reduced because the fish frequently come within easy casting range. If the water is heavily coloured, they may also venture close to the beach during the day.

Beaches that contain plenty of weeds and rocks will be visited by many species of fish to feed on the plentiful food that is hidden in these areas. Because such features provide cover from predators, too, the fish will also feel confident about swimming into shallow waters.

Before fishing any beach venue, try to learn as much about it as you can. If possible, study it at low water. Look for any features that may attract fish, such as gullies that may trap food or act as highways for travelling fish; patches of seaweed or shingle; streams and rivers that flow onto the beach; and worm casts that may indicate areas where fish expect to find food. As well as noting these potential aids to fish location, look for any snags that may ensnare your tackle. You will find it helpful to line up all of these features with some point above the high-water mark, and it is also advisable to take a photograph of the beach at low water from a high vantage point, so that you have an idea of what lies beneath the surface when the tide comes in.

Be warned that weed can represent a hazard to the beach angler. After storms, large amounts of loose weed

can accumulate on the beach, making fishing almost impossible because bits of weed tend to catch on the line, snagging the leader knot and pulling the bait out of position. It's therefore important to keep your eyes peeled for weed, and, if it is really bad, to seek an alternative venue.

Before fishing a beach, seek the advice of local anglers. And if an angling competition is being held there, try to visit the beach either during the match or afterwards to try to discover which areas yielded fish and which baits and methods proved successful. Don't assume that the organisers arranged for the competition to take place when the tide was in its optimum state, however, because other factors may have affected their choice of time.

A beach session

We will be fishing a sandy beach that yields several varieties of ray. The water is always coloured at this venue, the result of strong tides and the huge amounts of silt in the area. The beach can only be fished for a couple of hours each side of low water, and then only at spring tides (the highest tides, which occur at, or near, the new and full moon). At low water, it is possible to cast baits into a deep channel to reach the fish that often feed readily during daylight, the coloured water making them feel secure.

Tackle required

- Waders.
- Two 12ft (3.7m) long beachcasters.
- A tripod rod-rest.
- A 6oz (170g) grip lead.
- Two multiplier reels, loaded with 15 to 20lb (6.8 to 9kg) bs line.
- Paternoster rigs.
- A pennel rig consisting of 3/0 and 4/0 hooks.
- Sand eel baits.
- Scissors for trimming line and bait.
- Elastic for securing bait to the hook.
- Weights.
- A drink and snack to sustain you.

You will need to wear waders, both to negotiate the many gullies that crisscross the venue and to enable you to wade into the water and grab any fish that you may hook. We will be fishing a pair of beachcasters on a stable tripod rod-rest. A grip lead (which has wires that grip the seabed) of around 6oz is required to carry out the bait and anchor it into position. We will be using a simple paternoster rig and pennel hook set-up, incorporating a bait clip to enhance the casting distance by reducing air resistance. The bait that we will be using is sand eel, a small fish that frequents sandy beaches and provides food for a vast number of predatory fish and sea birds.

BELOW The shore angler at sunset.

The rod arches over as the hook is set.

Having arrived at the beach well before low water and set up your tackle, you can commence fishing once you have walked out to within casting range of the gulley. Cast out the baits up tide and allow them to sink to the bottom, so that slack line is immediately pulled from the reel, forming a bow that pulls the grip wires into the seabed, anchoring the bait. Place the rod in the rod-rest and tension the line until the rod is slightly bent. Loosen the reel's drag and set the ratchet to allow line to be taken if a fish moves off with the bait.

Repeat this procedure for the second rod, to which you could attach a different bait or rig to help you to build up a picture of what works best at the venue. If a particular set-up works well, both rods can subsequently be set up with the same successful bait or rig.

With the rods now poised on the rod-rest, their tips will move to the rhythm of the sea as waves and currents pull at the line. Observe the rod tips carefully to acertain such normal movements.

Out at sea, your trap is set, the bait and hook being attached to a line that will transmit any movement to you via the rod's tip. You will usually receive a clear indication of a fish having taken the bait because the rod's tip will move sharply, and out of synch with the waves and tidal pull. A bite may be transmitted by a series of rattles, or, if it is a good one, the rod's tip may be dragged seaward as the fish purposefully moves off with the bait. Another indication could be the line falling slack as the weight's anchor wires lose their grip on the seabed through a fish engulfing the bait. In any case, when you are confident that a fish has been hooked, pick up the rod, take up any slack and pull the hook home.

If the rods' tips fail to register any activity after fifteen minutes, reel in the baits and examine them. If a bait looks untouched, you can leave it out in the sea for a further five minutes next time. Remember always to use fresh bait to ensure that the bait's juices are as attractive to fish as possible. It is also bad practice to leave bait in the water for long periods. In any case, if crabs or small fish are numerous, the bait will be reduced to nothing within a very short time, and there is no point in fishing with bare hooks. Keep the sand eel baits in a cool box or the shade until they are needed, and never leave bait in the sun, which will quickly render it mushy and unusable.

Throughout the session, continue the process of casting and rebaiting. You could try making casts of different distances to search out the fish. It sometimes pays to cast out a big bait that will continue to emit a scent trail for a considerable period of time. If a cast is made at low tide, you can leave such a bait in situ and walk back up the beach with the advancing tide, paying out line as you walk in this way. It is possible to position bait well beyond casting range.

It may be that you catch several dogfish, which have constantly been grabbing the baits with which you intended to hook more worthy species. When the rod's tip nods, indicating that one of these scavengers has discovered the bait, and you are sure that the bait is in its mouth, reel it in. Be careful when unhooking it, however, as its sandpaper-like skin can inflict a nasty graze that is liable to become infected. You may not have targeted them, but dogfish at least provide a little action on an otherwise quiet day, and are often welcome catches during competitions.

As the tide starts to flood, my companion gets a more decisive bite, so that his rod arches over and the line is pulled from the reel. He picks up the rod and tightens the line to the fish. The ray attempts to hold its position, using the tide to push itself on to the sandy bottom. Steady pressure gets the fish moving, however, and soon a ray is being held aloft and admired before being carefully unhooked and released so that it can grow a little bigger.

On this beach, as on many others, the productive period is relatively short, with most fish being caught during the first hour of the flood tide. When you think that this period is over, pack up your tackle and pick up any litter to take home with you. Any unused bait can either also be taken home and frozen for use as groundbait or fed to the seagulls.

RIGHT A small-eyed ray is admired before it is returned.

Nighttime on the beach

Angler's hours are not always sociable
hours, and the keen angler may want to
visit the beach when others are fast
asleep in their beds. This is because
many fish are, to a large extent,
nocturnal, and will come close inshore
to feed under cover of the night. On
beaches, this is far more apparent than
from deep rock marks, where fish can
still be caught in daylight. A beach that
is swarming with swimmers and surfers
will not be safe to fish in daylight, and
probably wouldn't produce any fish

ABOVE Conger eels can be caught close inshore
after dark.

anyway, but the situation changes after
sunset.

If you are intending to fish after
dark, you will need a light of some type,
and I recommend a headlight for a
shallow beach with clear water. Try to
prevent it from shining into the water,
however, because the bright light will
alarm certain light-sensitive fish,
especially bass and some other species
that come into very shallow water. If

possible, only use the light for baiting up. If the beach is steeply shelved and the water coloured, you could use a lantern. Pressure lamps fuelled by paraffin or unleaded petrol are used by many anglers, and give a good light around base camp. The best all-round light for the night angler is, however, the headlight, which can be purchased with rechargeable batteries that last for many hours and directs light to wherever the angler wants to see, leaving his or her hands free.

Remember that the temperature will drop considerably after dark, even during the summer months, so always make sure that you have adequately warm clothing and a hot drink. Cold anglers do not fish well, and certainly don't derive maximum enjoyment from a session!

Fishing a beach after sunset is a magical experience. The sound of the surf is magnified as your hearing takes over as your primary sense. Thousands of stars can often be seen twinkling high in the night sky, as shooting stars streak across the heavens. Insects swarm about on the sand, while wild creatures, such as foxes, prowl the shoreline in search of food (and many anglers have lost their catch or bait to a wily fox sneaking up to steal an easy meal). As dawn approaches, a chill always seems to precede the rising sun, signalling a prime time for fish to come to feed.

Harbours, piers, breakwaters and jetties

Stationing yourself at a harbour, pier, breakwater or jetty can often prove fruitful.

Harbours

Harbours around the world hold a wide variety of fish, many of which can be targeted using the methods covered in the section above on beaches. Watery environments within the harbour are likely to be affected by human activities, with large amounts of waste, fish-market scraps, bread from harbour-side cafés and so on all finding their way into the water. And it may sound distasteful, but when raw sewage enters the sea, it provides rich pickings for fish that are scavenging for food.

Grey mullet are one of the species that seems to thrive in many such areas throughout the world, and can provide exciting sport for the angler. They, and other species that frequent harbours, can be caught using light tackle similar to that used to catch medium-sized freshwater species on lakes and rivers. You can attract fish into your vicinity

ABOVE A fine catch of grey mullet.

LEFT This angler float fishes for mullet whilst a second rod is fished at distance for plaice on the seabed.

with groundbait. Place some bread or fish guts in an onion sack or old net and lower it into the water beside the harbour wall. The continual movement of the water will send a stream of particles down tide, hopefully drawing fish into the area. Having been attracted by the groundbait, the fish will, with luck, take a small piece of bread flake or fish flesh suspended beneath a small float. You may have to experiment to find the correct depth at which to suspend the bait, and may sometimes find using a sliding float advantageous.

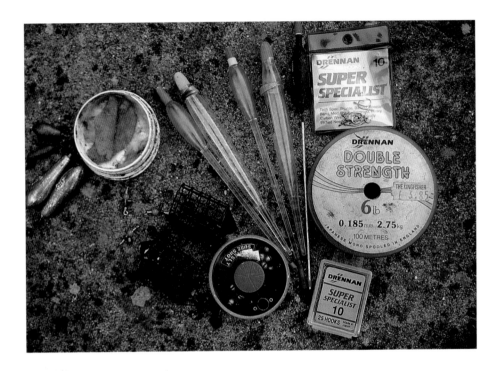

ABOVE A selection of terminal tackle used for mullet fishing. Leger weights, line floatant, floats, cage feeders, hooks and trace line.

Before starting to fish, consider how you are going to land a catch. If there is no access to the water's edge to enable you to net a fish, you will need to use a drop net. This consists of a net within a frame attached to a rope that you can lower into the water from your vantage point high above, drawing the exhausted fish carefully over the net before hauling it up to you.

Grey mullet can also be caught using a paternoster rig fished in conjunction with a quiver-tip rod. The rig can be fished with a plain weight or a feeder packed with mashed or liquidised bread. (Liquidised bread is an excellent groundbait that is easily prepared by placing some fresh, sliced bread in a blender and transforming it into fine crumbs. It can then either be thrown into the water, moulded around a method feeder or pushed into a cage feeder.) Remember that you will need to introduce bait to the water regularly to keep fish in the area and feeding.

Because they often house an abundance of small, easy-to-catch fish, harbours are ideal venues for young anglers. Indeed, many children start off on the road to sea angling by catching crabs with hand-held lines beside harbour walls. Harbours also tend to be sheltered from the elements, which means that it is unlikely that any big waves will sweep the angler away. Even so, caution should still be exercised whenever there is deep water nearby.

When fishing in harbours, or, indeed in any area, be aware of the people around you. Be warned that your line may become entangled in any yachts or dinghies that are sailing in the harbour. Keep an eye open for swimmers, and, when casting, look behind you. Never leave any discarded bait or litter behind you, and do not cut up bait on benches. Many venues have been lost to anglers as the result of some of their number's thoughtless actions. The lady in the white dress is seldom amused when she sits on a bit of smelly bait; the dog-owner is distressed when his beloved dog picks up a bit of bait containing a sharp hook. So do not give anglers a bad name, and keep and leave the venue tidy.

Piers, breakwaters and jetties

Piers, breakwaters and jetties are often extremely productive venues for the angler. Easily accessible, they can provide excellent fishing for many species of fish. Their most noticeable advantage is that they can give access to deep water that is unreachable from the natural shoreline.

The base of such structures should never be overlooked because large fish, such as conger, often lurk in the hidden recesses beneath, feeding on the smaller fish that shelter and feed within. The area away from the structure could well be barren and fishless, however, and the angler's instinct to launch bait as far as possible would be wrong in such instances, so keep an open mind and listen to any local advice that you may be given. Certain sides of the structure may fish better on the flood or ebb, so do not assume that high water is always the best time to fish. As when fishing on the beach or rocks, nighttime is a prime time to catch larger specimens, and if you are targeting these species, make sure that your tackle is equal to landing them. Remember, too, that heavy monofilament or wire may be needed to prevent the trace from being bitten off by toothy predators. Also ensure that you have the means with which to reach hooked fish, be they steps, a drop net or a gaff.

A wide variety of methods can be used to good effect to catch fish from these structures, depending on the species targeted. Float-fishing beneath lights at night is often productive, the fish being attracted to such situations and coming very close to the surface. I can remember catching grey mullet on floating bread crust beneath harbour lights many years ago, and although I have never repeated my feat at any similar venue, I feel sure that this method must work elsewhere. I also know of a bridge that can yield large catches of bass if you fish a white fly directly beneath its floodlights. An open

and resourceful mind can contribute to many a successful session, so always keep an eye open for any opportunities that may present themselves.

Many pelagic species of fish (fish that inhabit the mid- and upper waters) can be found around piers, breakwaters and jetties, and can provide great sport when fished for with a bait presented beneath a float. A brightly coloured float bobbing about on the water surface provides a fascinating focus point, and the excitement that it evokes when it suddenly plunges out of sight often enthralls young anglers, who may not have the patience of their elders.

To fish a sliding float rig, you will need a lightweight rod measuring around 10 to 12ft (3 to 3.7m) in length, a carp rod or spinning rod being the ideal choice. Match this to a fixed-spool reel and a line of around 10lb (4.5kg) breaking strain. Set up a sliding float rig (see page 120) and select an appropriately sized hook for the bait being used. For a sliver of mackerel skin, for instance, select a size 2 fine-wire hook. Cut a long, thin strip from the bait that will flutter enticingly in the tide, resembling a small, injured fish. Set the stop knot so that the bait will be fished at the depth at which you think the fish are swimming. Cast out carefully, stopping the tackle momentarily before it hits the water to straighten the rig. The float should cock within a few seconds and then sit primed on the surface. Keep a tight line to the float, and, if it sinks, reel the fish in and raise the rod smartly to set the hook.

Because piers, breakwaters and jetties are easily accessible, they are visited by many anglers and are consequently sociable venues from which to fish, making them ideal for the angler who enjoys mixing with others and telling yarns of past triumphs and disasters. Their accessibility makes them suitable for anglers with disabilities, too. (Sadly, some piers and breakwaters have been lost over the years due to lack of funding, depriving such anglers of access to their sport.) Like harbours, they are also ideal venues for the young angler. There is seldom a need for distance-casting, and they furthermore provide a comparatively safe platform from which

to fish during severe weather, when many rock marks and beaches become totally unfishable. (Note that local advice on weather conditions should always be sought, however, and that you should never take chances with the sea. If it is really rough, it is often better to go home and remain dry and safe.)

Rock fishing

Rock marks provide extremely useful platforms from which to cast a line. Like all venues, they vary greatly, there being no such thing as a typical rock mark. Some will give you access to

A rocky foreshore full of potential.

deeper water than you would be able to reach from a beach, thereby allowing you to get closer to your quarry, while many actually flank beaches, enabling the angler to cast out into the low-water zone at high water. Many other rock marks enable bait to be launched into the mysterious zone that lies beneath the low-water mark.

It is vital that you understand the danger of rising tides and the risk of being cut off, and that you always remain aware of the tide and state of the sea. Make sure that your position is well above any larger-than-average waves that may surge up the rocks because if the rock mark is exposed to ocean swells, large waves can sweep in with no warning and toss the unfortunate angler into a watery grave.

On the subject of safety, it's essential to wear stout footwear with a good grip when clambering around on rocks. Try to avoid carrying too much tackle because some rock marks demand long walks and have tricky descents that are

LEFT This rock promontory give access to deep water.

best attempted with free hands. Keep an eye on the weather, too: some rock marks that are easily accessible in dry weather become treacherous when it rains or when spray drenches the rocks. It is inadvisable to fish alone on rock marks, especially at night, but if you must, always tell someone where you are going and carry a mobile phone in case of emergency.

Many rock marks are very productive venues that yield a wide variety of species through the use of many different angling methods. The tackle that you choose to use should depend on the type of fish that you intend to catch. For bottom-dwelling species, you could use the beachcasters that we used on the beach (see page 340). If the ground that you are fishing over is particularly rough and likely to snag your end rig, it may, however, be necessary to use a heavier main line in conjunction with a rotten bottom (a length of weaker line) tied to the weight, so that if the weight snags on something, this weak link will break first, thereby ensuring that the only loss is the weight, and not the main rig and

any fish. Note, however, that it is unsafe to use a direct rotten bottom when casting over a long distance because the weight could break away as the cast is being made, potentially injuring someone. To avoid this happening, you need to use some form of release mechanism, such as an 'S'-shaped link, to take the shock of the cast, which will then unclip itself when the weight hits the seabed, leaving only the rotten

ABOVE Rock fishing in calm waters

RIGHT Looking for new marks on a steep rugged coastline.

bottom attached. When fishing rough ground, the pulley rig can also be useful because the weight is pulled clear of snags when retrieving a fish.

Local knowledge is invaluable when deciding which species of fish to target

from rock marks in different seasons. The nature of the seabed will, to a large extent, determine what you are likely to catch. Many species live among rocky gullies, kelp and weed, and if you want to extract these fish from such terrain, you will need strong tackle and a no-nonsense approach. Some species, such as wrasse, necessitate you holding the rod if you are to detect their bites. When a fish is judged to have taken the bait, you must strike and apply heavy pressure to raise the fish from the bottom and away from its sanctuary. It is difficult to cover the way in which you should deal with each species of fish that you are likely to encounter, so I must instead encourage you to think carefully about the species that you are seeking and how to approach it. For example, a big conger eel living amid a rocky haven will take bait quite gently, so that

hooking it will require patience. Strike too early, and you may not hook the fish. Leave too much time, and the conger will probably snag the tackle. It is only when you believe that the bait is well inside the conger's mouth that you stand any chance of landing the fish, and even then you will have to exert as much effort as your tackle will withstand.

The advice that I have given may have left you thinking that rock fishing is all about brute force, but not finesse. This is certainly true when you are targeting large fish in tackle-busting terrain, and I

ABOVE A tricky descent that requires a rope and stout footwear.

RIGHT Rugged terrain will require strong tackle.

have seen many fish lost due to the angler's reluctance to use the tools of the trade correctly. If a fish gets its head down and locates a rocky haven, you will almost certainly lose it. Although a fish may be released from a snag if you allow the line to fall slack, enabling the fish to swim free if you are lucky, you will usually be forced to pull to break the

When it comes to angling methods, the rock angler has many options, including the standard bottom-fishing approach used by the beach angler. Float-fishing from rock marks can be highly effective, for instance, and gives the angler the chance to cover a wide range of depths. The light-tackle approach that I outlined in the harbour section (see page 345) can also be extremely productive.

Lure-fishing from rocks is highly rewarding at certain times of the year, especially if the water is clear enough. Rocks and beds of seaweed provide havens for many fish, and because predatory fish launch strikes on their prey in these areas, the lure-angler can entice them by passing the lure as close as possible to their lairs. Lures that sink down to the taking depth can cover deep water, and after casting out, you

line, and the feeling of disappointment that you experience when the line breaks and falls limp is sickening.

Much of the advice that I gave about water clarity and conditions in the beach section (see page 334) applies just as much to rock marks, but also note that the deeper water offered by rocks is often fruitful in calm weather and clear-water conditions.

ABOVE LEFT A plump winter cod.

RIGHT An 18lb (8kg) cod caught from a deep water rock mark.

NEXT PAGE The angler enjoys the wait with a fine backdrop.

should count until the lure is near to the seabed before starting the retrieve. By varying the countdown, you search various depths until taking fish are found, it becomes easy to get the lure into this taking zone cast after cast. Avoid losing expensive lures by starting the retrieve before the tackle becomes snagged.

Shallow water also yields plenty of good fish to lures. This terrain is best covered using floating plugs that work within around 3ft (1m) of the surface. It is possible to fish these lures over weeds and rocks that you would be unable to cover using any other method. In some instances, surface lures can be used to stimulate aggressive takes from predators in very shallow water. This type of fishing sets the pulse racing as large fish erupt from the water to smash into the lure, often at close range.

LEFT Preparing to cast a lure in the fading light.

RIGHT Dusk and dawn are peak periods for the lure angler as he casts from the rocks.

ABOVE Every sunset is to be savoured.

LEFT A rocky headland as the light fades.

(When fishing in clear, shallow water like this, you'll find a pair of Polaroid glasses invaluable for detecting fish that follow the lure to the water's edge and then turn away at the last second.)

Lure-fishing from the shore is often at its most productive at dusk and dawn, when predatory fish often seem to go on a feeding spree. In some areas, fish can even be taken after dark using lures. The best colour of lure to use after dark is said to be black, probably because all that the fish sees is a silhouette against the night sky.

Estuary fishing

The geological features and location of an estuary – the zone where a river meets the sea – determine its character, as well as the species of fish that you are likely to encounter. When I think about my local estuary in England, for example, my mind conjures up a vision of muddy banks, flounder during the autumn and winter and mullet and bass during the summer. Because these species can all be caught on relatively light tackle, the estuary often provides good sport.

Estuaries are often protected from strong winds by the adjacent landmass, and a natural sand bar may also have evolved at the mouth, which shelters the waters within from the ocean's fury. Manmade structures guard the mouth of some estuaries, too, providing shelter for a fleet of boats. There is usually a certain merging of salt- and freshwater angling techniques within many estuary locations, which makes some dedicated sea anglers reluctant to visit such venues except when inclement weather means that they are the only places that it is practical to visit.

Estuaries can be divided into three broad categories: shallow estuaries, deep-water estuaries and little and large estuaries.

Shallow estuaries

As the tides follow their daily routine of ebb and flood, the shallow estuary undergoes a major transformation. At low tide, mud and sand may dominate, with birds feeding on the rich diversity

of marine life that lives here. Anglers can also reap rewards by harvesting crabs and worms for bait.

The river flows down a central channel, which consists of brackish water, the salinity changing as the river travels towards the sea and merges with its salt.

The arrival of the incoming tide brings a feeling of promise as it pushes in twice each day, bringing with it a fresh influx of fish in search of food from a rich larder. Anglers who place their baits or lures wisely may therefore be richly rewarded. The baits used by anglers are often natural baits that have been harvested from this very same zone at low water. Flatfish, such as flounder, are prime targets for the estuary angler, and are easily tempted using the baits that are favoured locally impaled on light, fine-wire hooks. I must emphasise using baits that are favoured locally because different estuaries seem to contain fish with varying tastes. In my local estuary, for instance, the flounder eagerly devour bunches of harbour ragworm, a bait that may seldom receives a bite in other

estuaries, where the flounder may instead have a strong preference for peeler crab. This is one of the reasons why it is important always to try to glean information from local anglers.

Do not assume that the flood tide will always be the most productive time for fishing because the ebb tide can sometimes be far more so. Fish drop back into the main channels as the tide drops, and may become concentrated in small areas. The central channel also holds fish at low water, providing good sport for the angler who is targeting certain species.

Shallow estuaries are greatly influenced by the rivers that feed them. After periods of heavy rain inland, the water will be murky and choked with the detritus and debris that has been swept down the river by floods. Such estuaries will often yield a rich crop of fish as they fine down following a spate. (You may be better off fishing elsewhere during the spate itself, however.)

The species of fish found in a

LEFT Flounder fishing in a shallow estuary.

shallow estuary vary from its source to its mouth, where it meets the sea, and the angling methods used will therefore need to be adapted accordingly. At the mouth of the estuary, the tactics employed will usually be no different from those used by the beach angler (see pages 338 to 341).

One of my favourite methods is fly-fishing for shoals of bass as they move into the estuary, providing great sport on a hot summer day, when the sky is blue and the water clear. An outfit similar to that used for fishing reservoir trout (see pages 278 to 301) is ideal, although I recommend that you use a non-corrosive fly reel because salt water will play havoc with any susceptible tackle. Tie the flies onto stainless-steel hooks so that they emulate fry. Cast the lure ahead of the shoals of bass as they hunt in the shallow water, then strip it back to provoke savage strikes from the spiky silver fish. (A word of warning: take care not to injure yourself on the spines on the fins and gill covers as you

The weedy rocks exposed here at low water attract large shoals of grey mullet at high water.

unhook the bass prior to their release.)

Grey mullet are prolific in many estuaries. There are two main species of grey mullet swimming in British waters: the thick-lipped and the thin-lipped mullet, each necessitating a different angling approach. Thick-lipped mullet should be targeted with light freshwater tackle, the most popular bait being bread, either float-fished or legered in conjunction with groundbait. Thin-lipped mullet are often targeted with a spinner whose treble hook has been replaced with a small, single hook and baited with harbour ragworm. The spinner is then cast out and retrieved through the mullet shoals. Interestingly, these fish will often totally ignore the offering for long periods of time before suddenly switching into a feeding frenzy, lashing at the baited lure with relish.

Deep-water estuaries

When the rise and fall of the tide is not as pronounced as in shallow estuaries, and steep-sided hills lead to the sea, estuaries may have a different character. Some have dense woods that grow right down to the water level, and the water

may also contain very deep channels
that provide homes for many species of
fish. The saline content of these
estuaries may make them suitable for
open-sea fish to dwell in, and large,
predatory species of ray and conger will
frequently also be available to the angler,
in addition to the fish that are common
to shallow estuaries. The tactics used for
beach fishing (see pages 334 to 335) or
rock fishing (see pages 353 to 367)
should therefore be used as appropriate.

Harbours (see pages 345 to 351)
and marinas are frequently housed
within deep-water estuaries, providing a
sheltered habitat, while the hills that
surround such estuaries also provide
welcome shelter from strong winds.
This makes them ideal venues for
anglers on days when the open sea is
out of bounds due to inclement
weather. It's nevertheless important to
ensure that you don't come into
conflict with other water-users. Large
ships, as well as yachts and dinghies, use
the deep water within these sheltered
havens, providing an interesting
spectacle for the anglers quietly
observing their comings and goings

from the sidelines. Sometimes, however,
the presence of jet skis and speedboats
can prevent anglers from pursuing their
sport, in which case the sensible
solution is to rise early and cast a line
when all is peaceful.

Little and large estuaries

Each and every stream or river that
trickles into the sea has its own
characteristics, and may attract a variety
of fish species. And although some of

LEFT This River emerges beneath the bridge into a short estuary in southwest Ireland. As an angler it's impossible to cross without wondering what fish have passed upstream into the river system.

BELOW Looking down from the bridge.

these estuaries are very short, they often prove real angling hotspots. Migratory species, such as freshwater eels, congregate in many small estuaries, in turn attracting predators that can be targeted by the angler. Sea trout and salmon will also run into quite small rivers in some areas, especially when swimming from a larger expanse of water. In some regions, these migratory visitors can be tempted using flies or spinners.

At the other end of the scale are the vast estuaries at the mouths of such rivers as the mighty Amazon in South America, the Congo in Africa and the Fraser in Canada. These enormous channels of water, which often measure several miles across, can hold huge species of fish, the catching of which requires specialist tackle and knowledge.

Saltwater boat-fishing

Taking to a boat gives anglers the opportunity to present baits to a wide variety of species, many of which are seldom encountered from the shore. Boat-fishing can also be an extremely exciting branch of angling that provides catches that are usually far larger in size than those made from the shoreline. Be warned, however, that you should not set out to sea in your own boat unless you are very experienced and have a full understanding of the relevant safety and

maritime protocol. When boat-fishing, the angler's success mainly depends on the skill of the skipper of the boat, who will locate the fish and position the boat to enable the angler to gain access to the fish; if the skipper gets it wrong, the angler will fail to make a catch. The best way to start off your saltwater boat-fishing career is therefore to book a trip on a charter boat with an experienced skipper. Before setting out to sea, ensure that the boat is fully

LEFT A fleet of charter boats head out to sea.

ABOVE With a rush of white water behind the boat we head for the off-shore marks.

licensed and insured.

Most modern charter boats are equipped with a wide range of sophisticated equipment to assist in the location of likely fish habitats and, indeed, fish. Wrecks and other significant fish havens can be pinpointed by co-ordinates programmed into computerised navigation systems like the Global Positioning System (GPS), enabling productive marks to be successfully revisited (and many such locations are closely guarded secrets). Fish-finders use sonic pulses to provide inside information, including water depth, and can even showing images of fish in the waters beneath the boat. In this way, I have often seen huge shoals of fish above wrecks and reefs that have shown no interest in the baits or lure being offered, illustrating how fish sometimes refuse to feed, which, if we couldn't see them with our own eyes, would lead us to believe that they weren't there.

Many angling clubs regularly organise boat trips, which is an ideal way to become involved with boat-fishing. Your fellow members will give you advice, and club officials will generally choose to venture out in tides that are likely to be productive. Good boats have reputations that have been earned through the seasons and are

RIGHT The screen of a modern fish finder.

BELOW Anglers on the quay head prepare to board their charter boat.

booked up well in advance, the owners often giving first choice to clubs that are regular customers. Six anglers is an adequate number on an average-sized charter boat, so when booking a trip, ensure that the boat won't be overcrowded. Too many anglers lead to tangled lines and frustration, making it far better to pay a little more per head for a trouble-free and enjoyable day.

The main factor that will determine your enjoyment of boat-fishing is your own seaworthiness, that is, whether you suffer from seasickness. I have been stricken with seasickness on several occasions, on both rough and calm days, and, believe me, it is not a pleasant experience. Travel bands and seasickness tablets generally, but not always, ensure that I have a good day afloat, so the only advice that I can give you is to take the necessary remedies and make sure that you set sail on a full stomach because there is little worse than being seasick on an empty stomach.

I will now outline a few boat excursions to illustrate the methods that can be adopted when boat-fishing.

A day offshore

When fishing baits on the seabed from an anchored boat, there is a choice of two basic methods: up-tiding or down-tiding.

Up-tiding

The up-tiding technique first became popular in shallow waters with strong tides, anglers finding that bait fished away from the boat caught significantly more fish. (It is thought that the vibrations emitted from the hull of the boat can scare away fish in the immediate vicinity.)

Anglers use rods measuring 9 to 10ft (2.7 to 3m) in length and multiplier reels. A grip weight is used, and the baited rig cast up-tide, away from the boat. The weight is allowed to sink to the seabed and plenty of line is paid out into the tide. When a bow is

OPPOSITE PAGE The rod bends into a fish far below.

BELOW The Global Positioning System gives the skipper the exact position of the boat – invaluable if mist or fog descends.

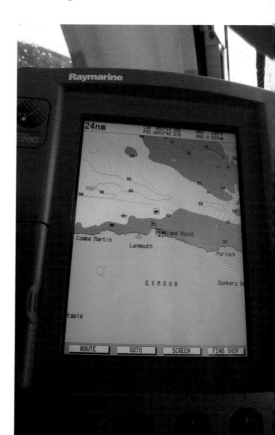

formed in the line, the reel is engaged. The rod's tip will pull over and the weight's grip wires will, it is hoped, anchor it firmly into the seabed. When a fish takes the bait, the rod's tip will nod and the line will then often fall slack as the weight is dislodged. The angler will have to wind the line onto the reel until the weight of the fish is felt, after which

ABOVE Casting a baited rig up-tide.

the fish should be carefully played to the side of the boat.

The great advantage of up-tiding is that it enables the use of relatively light gear, thus providing the angler with more sport.

Down-tiding

In down-tiding, bait is lowered from the side of the boat with sufficient weight to take it to the seabed and keep it there. The stronger the tide, the heavier the weight needed to hold the bait to the bottom, although a line with a relatively thin diameter, such as braid or wire, sometimes enables the use of lighter weights.

Tackle

- A 9½ ft (2.9m) long up-tide rod.
- A 20lb (9kg) bs line.
- A grip lead.
- A 80 to 100lb (36 to 45.4kg) bs trace.
- A 7ft (2.1m) long, 20lb (9kg) class boat rod.
- Multiplier reels.
- A 20lb (9kg) bs line.
- A 6oz to 2lb (170 to 907g) lead weight.
- An appropriate trace line.

This trip is in search of bottom-feeding fish in a strong tidal run, with water measuring perhaps 40 to 60ft (12.2 to 18.3m) in depth. I am one of a party of anglers who have met up in preparation for a day at sea. As always, we seem to have far too much gear with us as we make our way to the boat moored in the harbour. The skipper welcomes us aboard and discusses the plans for the day. We are going to fish a gravel bank about 1 mile (1.6km) offshore, where we can expect to catch a wide variety of species, including ray, cod and various small members of the shark family. We therefore set off feeling very optimistic.

Most of the party have elected to use up-tiding tactics and start to tackle up as the boat steams out to the mark that we are going to fish. Some anglers at the stern have elected to use two rods, one an up-tide rod and the other a down-tide rod, an option that, when employed at the stern, lessens the risk of entanglement with other lines. Many anglers consider the stern to be the prime position on a boat, especially when down-tiding, and a well-organised party

of anglers will try to ensure that those at the stern use lighter weights than those at the bow to ensure that all of the baits are being fished well apart. There are few things that are more frustrating to a boat-angler than trying to play a fish that has become entangled with a fellow angler's line.

The skipper studies the seabed contours on his echo-sounder before positioning the boat and lowering the anchor. As soon as he declares 'lines in', we anglers can cast or lower our baits into the water. It is essential that we listen carefully to the skipper's

instructions throughout the day: he is the boss for reasons of safety, and generally knows best regarding fish-catching tactics. Good skippers will work hard to try to locate fish for their anglers, and skippers and anglers will ideally work together as a team in trying to get the best out of a day afloat.

Succulent baits are prepared and attached to hooks in the hope of tempting specimens from the gravel bank below. Because a strong tide is running, the anglers using down-tide rods are forced to use a weight weighing more than 1lb (453g) to ensure that it reaches the bottom. The up-tide rigs are cast well up tide and allowed to sink to the bottom, a substantial length of line being paid out to enable the grip wires to grip into the seabed. The rods are then either held or propped on a rod-rest to await the attention of a hungry fish below.

A period of anticipation follows as each angler wonders what the day will bring. When it happens, the first bite of the day boosts the confidence of all on board, the next few bites bringing a succession of lesser spotted dogfish into the boat. Although these ravenous members of the shark family reach pest proportions at certain times of year, when they grab baits intended for worthier quarry, their bites keep the angler interested on quiet days, while competition anglers are pleased to catch any fish that counts towards their total number of points.

LEFT This fine blonde ray used its wings to give strong resistance in the tide.

After half an hour or so, a rod tip signals that a more substantial fish has taken a bait. The angler takes up the bow of line from the grip weight until he can feel the weight of the fish. He then applies pressure to ensure that the hook is set. The tide pull means that he has a long struggle ahead before he can get the fish to the side of the boat, and must carefully judge how much strain the tackle can apply to the fish without risking breakage. Patience and a little muscle eventually prevail, and the sight of a fine, blonde ray rewards the angler. The captor proudly displays his fish for the camera before releasing it to help to preserve stocks. (Conservation is of paramount importance to anglers in these days of diminishing stocks. And while anglers endeavoured to fill their freezers in years gone by, today they return a large number of fish to the sea, although the occasional fish is dispatched perfectly legitimately to provide a healthy

ABOVE Spurdog are members of the shark family.

RIGHT This cod took a whole squid bait fished up-tide.

meal for its captor and his or her friends and family.)

As the day progresses, several species come into the boat: the cod, thornback ray, small-eyed ray, blonde ray, spur dog and dogfish have all provided a good day's sport. For his part, the skipper has kept the anglers supplied with tea, coffee, encouragement and advice throughout the day. (It bears repeating: the key to a good day's boat-fishing is a good skipper!)

Boat-anglers target a huge range of species, each of which determines a different approach: if it has sharp teeth, a wire trace may be required, for instance. Heavy tackle is needed to ensure that anglers have a good chance of landing large, powerful specimens, as well as when the bottom is particularly rough, and anglers fishing over wrecks and reefs can expect heavy tackle losses.

BELOW Good sport continues throughout the day.

Drifting

Drifting with the wind and tide can sometimes cover more ground and, as a result, more fish, than angling from an anchored boat. Drifting also enables lighter tackle to be used, providing anglers with greater sport from the fish that they hook. I have spent many days adrift at sea in search of various species (and note that the tackle chosen should be determined by the species being sought).

Once again, the skipper's skill will determine how successful anglers are during their day adrift.

Drifting for flatfish with light tackle

Flatfish, such as plaice, can be found on sandbanks in areas like the famous Skerries off the coast of southern England. Anglers catch these tasty flatfish on the light carp and spinning rods that are more often employed for freshwater angling. A line of around 10lb (4.5kg) bs is used with a weight of around 2oz (57g). A long trace measuring more than 10ft (3m) in length is commonly employed, to the end of which is attached a small, fine-

BELOW Plaice provide good sport and a delicious meal at the end of the day.

LEFT Pollock from a rocky reef.

wire hook (2 to 2/0), loaded with the preferred local bait. Peeler crab, lugworm and ragworm are generally the baits that are most often used, a long, thin strip of squid often being added to enhance the bait's attractiveness. Flatfish are very inquisitive, and anglers have found that beads, sequins and spoons often draw them to the baited hook.

When fishing for flatfish, the basic technique is to lower the rig to the seabed and then to hold the rod. The angler can feel the weight as it bounces across the sandy ridges, sending up flurries of sand that attract the attention of the flatfish. A flatfish will then, with luck, follow in the wake of the weight and grab the bait. On feeling increased resistance, the angler should pay out plenty of line (which may go against the normal instinct to tighten the line on feeling a bite) to enable the flatfish to swallow the bait. When the angler judges that sufficient time has passed, the line is tightened and the fish played to the surface.

Drifting over wrecks and reefs

The offshore wrecks of sunken ships and rocky reefs provide havens for large numbers of fish species, many of which, such as bass and pollock, are predatory, and can be tempted by artificial lures, usually imitation sand eels like jelly worms.

The skipper has to be careful to start the drift at the up-tide side of the mark, whereupon the anglers lower their lures, which are fished on long traces, until they feel them bump on the bottom. The lures are then carefully retrieved. When it comes, the take may be preceded by a series of taps as the fish snaps at the tail of the lure; the reel should then be wound until the fish hooks itself, after which the angler should hang on and ensure that the reel drag has been set correctly. Too tight, and the line will break; too loose, and the fish will find sanctuary in the wreck or reef.

Rather than a lure, a live sand eel, launce or long sliver of fish can sometimes entice a finicky feeder, as can a change of lure size or colour. (Lure colour is a puzzling subject: because many scientists believe that

ABOVE Fresh mackerel baits come aboard.

colours are undetectable at the depths that lures are often fished, a lure's colour should be irrelevant, yet the experience of many anglers and skippers contradicts this assumption. Always be prepared to experiment with lure colours throughout the day and to react to any discoveries that you or your colleagues may make.)

Anglers also catch such bait fish as mackerel on the drift, using strings of artificial lures like feathers. A string may consist of up to six lures, so that large numbers of shoal fish can be caught quickly. Such fishing is often practised on the way to a venue as a means of filling the bait box for the day ahead with prime, fresh bait. And although it is not really a part of the day's sport, there is some pleasure to be derived from swinging a string of gleaming mackerel aboard.

For general reef or wreck fishing using lures, a 20lb (9kg) class boat rod or up-tider will suffice. Match this to a multiplier reel and a 15 to 20lb (6.8 to 9kg) bs monofilament or 30 to 50lb (13.6 to 22.7kg) bs braided line. The trace should generally be long, and

should consist of a clear monofilament of 25 to 50lb (11.3 to 22.7kg) bs.

Rough-ground drifting

I have done a lot of rough-ground drifting as a secondary method while shark fishing. The tackle generally consists of an up-tide rod and matching multiplier reel. The end tackle is simple and comprises a trace of heavy monofilament tipped with a wire trace if necessary; the weight is tied to a short rotten bottom to ensure that any tackle losses are kept to a minimum. The bait is lowered to the bottom and then reeled up a few turns to keep it clear of the seabed. The angler holds the rod while waiting for action. When bites come, they are generally fierce, the fish hooking itself as it rushes up from the bottom to grab the bait.

A large range of species can be taken using such tactics, ray and dogfish being the exception, however, because they seldom swim up from the bottom to secure the bait.

Shark fishing

Shark fishing is not for the faint-hearted: sharks are big, dangerous fish, and should only be targeted when the boat is in the hands of an experienced skipper.

Shark fishing is a waiting game. You can spend hours, and sometimes days, drifting with the wind and tide, watching and waiting for a glimpse of a fin or dark shape in the rubby-dubby trail. The scream of the ratchet, when it comes, sets the heart racing. Angling for pollock, tope and other species with drifted baits helps to pass the time, and the shark rods are almost forgotten when the action becomes hectic. Mackerel are often taken, and sometimes cooked fresh from the sea and eaten off the bone, a crispy delicacy that you savour as you drift on in hope. The cry of the gulls in the air and the monotonous sound of the sea gently caressing the drifting boat encourages you to snooze and daydream.

Porbeagle shark.

I shall now tell you about a day's sharking that I experienced. This was my second year of making shark-fishing trips. The previous year, I had been out three times, the first two trips being uneventful. On the third trip, I brought a porbeagle weighing around 50lb (22.7kg) to the side of the boat; seven sharks had visited the side of the boat that day, mine being the smallest! My success had been enough to make me want to try again. This year, my first two trips had been cancelled due to rough weather, the curse of boat-anglers worldwide. This time, however, the weather was good, although the summer was coming to an end.

Four of us had hired a boat. (When shark fishing, it is normal to limit the numbers on board. This reduces the risk of tangles and gives the anglers more of a chance of hooking a shark, although the reduced numbers means that the cost of the trip is substantially higher than if there were more anglers on board.) We had an hour and a half of steaming ahead of us before reaching the shark grounds, during which we sat, occasionally chatting, but mainly anticipating the day ahead. Then the waiting was over and the boat's engines were silenced. Onion sacks full of fish bits, bran and pilchard oil were lowered over the side to dangle in the clear water beside the boat. An oily slick

soon spread out into the ocean. Mackerel baits were impaled on big, strong 12/0 hooks attached to 400lb (181kg) bs wire traces before being lowered and suspended at varying depths beneath brightly coloured cistern floats.

'How deep do you set the bait, then?' asked John, who was on his first shark-fishing trip. 'Depends on the day', I replied, while demonstrating how to set the depth of the bait beneath the float using a matchstick and piece of electrical sleeving. 'What the . . .!' John exclaimed, '. . . I think I have a take!' The line was wrenched from John's grasp and pulled powerfully from the reel. John waited for a moment or two and then endeavoured to set the hook. The heavy rod locked over and an unseen mass of muscle powered away. Sadly, the hook pulled free within a few seconds.

A moment later, Jason's reel screamed out, and then he, too, was locked in battle. Twenty minutes passed before the beaten shark was beside the boat, ready for tagging and releasing. These few moments are always tense. Such a large, powerful fish must not

ABOVE A big Porbeagle battles for freedom.

RIGHT Shark fishing is not for the faint-hearted.

messed with, not least because a careless moment with a tangled trace could easily drag an angler overboard or cut off a finger or two. It is imperative that everyone on the boat works as a team and follows the skipper's directions carefully. The shark having been admired by all on board, the trace was then cut as close as possible to the hook and the fish was allowed to swim

LEFT Tense moments as the angler decides when to set the hook.

BELOW Cutting up fish for the rubby dubby.
BELOW RIGHT The rubby dubby bag dangles at the side of the boat.

strongly away. Within a minute or two, another reel screamed out, and Paul was battling with an angry predator that gave him a good workout lasting over twenty minutes.

As the day progressed, we fished several drifts, and eventually I was the only angler without a shark. Then, with sharks circling all around the boat, a particularly big beast circled my float. Seconds later, the line started to pour from the reel and the float bobbed. I held the rod, adrenaline rushing through my veins. The shark moved away, but I waited until I felt that the bait was well within those fearsome

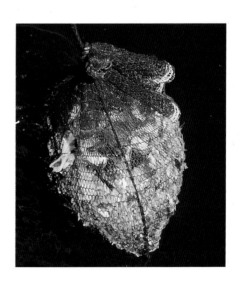

jaws. I engaged the clutch, allowed the
line to pull tight, then cranked the reel
hard, leaning back on the rod with all
my might. The shark responded and set
off for the horizon. I leaned back as the
rod arched over and the line ripped
from the reel. This felt good! Then a
slack line . . . I went from ecstasy to
dejection in the space of thirty seconds.
I reeled in a ragged mackerel – the
hook had pulled free. 'Not your day',
observed one of my fellow anglers.

ABOVE A Porbeagle is brought to the side of the
boat before being released.

The day ended with seven sharks
having been brought to the side of the
boat. Fifteen fish were hooked, two sadly
broke free and six came off the hook.
What a day it had been! Although I
hadn't caught a shark, I had shared a
fabulous day with a bunch of good
friends, three of whom had caught their

first shark on their first shark-fishing trip.

Three days later, I was drifting in hope again. The sun shone, the gulls cried, the mackerel tasted good. But the orange cisterns sat in an oily slick and the reels were silent. Maybe next time.

Trolling

Trolling is the trailing of real or artificial baits behind a boat. Many anglers' first experience of sea angling will have been trolling a string of mackerel feathers behind a boat with a hand line. Years later, if they are lucky, they may find themselves trolling much larger lures for large, predatory game fish in the world's tropical oceans. Luxurious boats and tropical oceans were once the playgrounds of the rich and famous, but in these times of more general affluence, increasing numbers of anglers are able to experience the thrill of fishing these areas of deep, blue water, most of which are only a few hours away from an airport.

Mighty game fish, such as sailfish, marlin, tuna and barracuda, patrol these waters, and lures intended to entice them are trolled behind well-equipped boats at what is sometimes considerable speeds. Several rods are generally used, with the baits being spread out using outriggers. The baits or lures skip across the water's surface, giving the impression of a shoal of bait fish, which, it is hoped, will attract the attention of the predators as they swim the ocean depths in search of prey. Although this form of fishing can become rather tedious on account of the long periods of inactivity that the angler often endures, when a fish is sighted or the ratchet screams, adrenaline rushes through the veins and the hours, or days, of waiting are instantly forgotten.

Powerful rods and reels are used for trolling, while heavyweight lines of up to 130lb (59kg) bs are used to subdue the fish. With battles frequently lasting for hours, the angler may end up exhausted and sometimes beaten. Some anglers regard trolling as the ultimate in angling, the marlin being considered the pinnacle of achievement in the eyes of many. I have not yet fished for marlin, but if I ever do, I know that I will only succeed with the help of an experienced skipper.

Hooking and landing fish

When the deception has been successful and the fish has taken the bait or lure, the angler must set the hook and bring the fish to the water's edge. I will assume that you have selected your tackle wisely and that it is therefore adequate to the task of landing the species of fish that you have targeted.

The actual setting of the hook depends, to a large extent, on the terminal tackle that is being used. In some instances, an efficient set-up will already have hooked the fish, and you may have been notified of this by the rod's tip or bite indicator. Even if the fish has been hooked, it is still standard practice to pull the hook home, however. (I am reluctant to use the word 'strike' in this context because all that you often have to do is to pick up the rod, tighten the line by winding the reel handle, lift the rod until you feel resistance and then apply steady pressure and make gains on the line until the fish is ready for landing.)

If you have not used a self-hooking set-up, you must set the hook before the fish ejects the bait. Do this by ensuring that the line is tight and then quickly raising the rod to drive the hook into the fish's mouth (this is called a 'strike'). The force required will be in proportion to the tackle being used and how far your quarry is from you. When free-lining or float-fishing, it will almost always be necessary to strike. If you are fishing with light tackle, a harsh strike would break the line, however, which is why only a flick of the wrist is needed when using light lines. If there is a long length of line between the fish and you, you will need to increase the force exerted accordingly to take up the slack and stretch.

A good way to illustrate these principles would be to tie a heavy weight to the end of a monofilament line (which has a degree of stretch, unlike braided lines) and apply pressure on a short line; the weight will either move easily or the line will break. If you were then to extend the distance between you and the weight to, perhaps, 165ft (50m), it is unlikely that you would be

LEFT Playing a fish with skilled application of rod, line and reel.

able to move the weight or break the line easily. To illustrate these principles further, consider the following two extreme situations. Firstly, an angler fishing for roach with a 1lb (453g) bs line will need to strike with great care to avoid breaking the line. Secondly, an angler fishing for shark with a 50lb (22.7kg) bs line and big hook will need to strike with all of his might to drive the hook into the shark's mouth, which is packed with teeth and gristle. When the angler is sure that the bait is within the shark's jaws, he should frantically wind the reel until the line is tight and he feels the weight of the fish. He should then lean back on the rod, continuing to crank the reel handle. On feeling the full weight of the fish, he should lower the rod, while continuing to keep a tight line by cranking the reel handle, repeating the process. He should then hold on tight as the angry shark tries to put distance between itself and the angler. This is the next stage of

LEFT Bent rod and waiting net.

RIGHT Applying heavy pressure to keep a barbel out of a weedy summer haven in mid-stream.

the process: the fish is now hooked and will need to be played out until it has been subdued enough to bring to the water's edge.

You must use the rod, reel and line to exert pressure on the fish. If the fish is small, it can easily be reeled in and lifted from the water. If the fish is large or powerful, however, it will need to be played carefully to avoid the line breaking or the hook being pulled from its hold. All reels have some form of clutch that can release a line under pressure, and the clutch will need to be set so that the line can be pulled from the reel at a pressure less than that of the line's breaking strain. A setting of

BELOW The angler applies extra pressure on the spools lip using his fingers.

RIGHT The long rod used here helps to keep the line clear of the rocks.

25 per cent of the line's breaking strain is a realistic starting point, although, in practice, the setting is generally ascertained simply by testing the clutch by pulling the line against the setting until it feels right.

The rod acts as a shock absorber, helping to prevent the line from breaking and the hook from losing its hold. Keep the rod at an angle in relation to the fish to absorb the lunges that the fish makes as it shakes its head in an attempt to free itself from the hook. If the fish is large and powerful, be prepared to allow it to swim away (or 'run'), taking line from the clutch as it does so. When it stops its run, you will need to retrieve the line by pumping the fish towards you. Do this by raising the rod to the 12 o'clock position, and then lowering it to 2 o'clock retrieving the line as you lower the rod. Each time you lift the rod, you will recover more line. Note that failing to pump the fish in this way will put undue strain on the reel. And under no circumstances continue to wind the handle of a fixed-spool reel while the clutch is giving out line because this would twist the line, leading to tangles.

The angler tires a fish by applying pressure and pulling the fish off-

LEFT My son does battle with a large carp.

BELOW A mighty Nile perch shakes its head in an attempt to loosen the hooks.

LEFT Extracting the hook from a specimen barbel.

balance, and this process of playing a fish can take a long time, depending on the tackle being used and the size of the fish. Most fish will be landed in under five minutes, while a big fish, such as a mighty tuna or marlin, could take hours to land. I play fish as hard as my tackle permits in the belief that many fish are lost through an angler's lack of confidence during the fight. If fish are played too gently, they can either find snags or the hook hold can wear until the hook pulls free, for instance. Although only experience will perfect your fish-playing skills, you should seldom lose a fish if you have a

correctly set clutch, enough line and a correctly matched rod.

When the fish begins to tire, it will start to roll on its side and its mouth will begin to open. It is now almost ready to be landed. If you are using a net, immerse it in the water and bring the fish over it. Never make quick stabs at the fish because this will alarm it, prompting it to surge away in a bid for freedom. (As a precautionary measure to counter these last-minute escape attempts, it is advisable to slacken the clutch slightly when the fish is on a

ABOVE Angler and shark do battle. In some cases the angler feels he is played!

short line.) When the fish is within the net's arms, lift the net smoothly and carefully lift the fish from the water, supporting the net as you do so to avoid damaging the fish.

If you are not using a net, there are several other ways of landing fish that are too heavy to be swung into your hand, although because each species of fish demands a slightly different approach, it is impossible to give you

exact advice. It may be possible to land the fish either by grabbing it firmly across its back or by slipping your fingers carefully into its gill covers and then lifting it, for example. Some species can alternatively be grabbed by the wrist of the tail, the salmon being a good example. If the shoreline is gently shelved, you could carefully bring the fish to the edge and beach it. Large fish that are destined to be eaten can be landed using a gaff hook, which should ideally be inserted under the chin, or otherwise anywhere that will give you the best purchase, just behind the head generally being the best target. Any fish landed in this way should be dispatched quickly using a priest.

You should now carry the fish to a safe place to unhook it. If you are intending to return the fish to the water, avoid handling it with dry hands. Instead, either wet your hands or hold the fish with a damp cloth to avoid removing its protective slime and mucus.

LEFT This battle with an unseen giant ended in disappointment when the fish found a submerged tree and transferred the lure to its trunk.

BELOW Care must be taken when removing the hooks from big fish like this Nile perch.

Lay it on a soft surface such as an unhooking mat and kneel beside it, artery forceps or another form of unhooking tool at the ready.

Unhooking procedures vary slightly according to the species of fish. If the hook is visible in the corner of the mouth, it may be possible to grip the hook shank firmly and then push the hook free. If the fish has been hooked in the mouth or throat, however, you

will need to use a pair of forceps or long-nosed pliers or else a disgorger to grip the hook firmly and extract it by means of a combination of pushing, pulling and twisting. (Be very careful to avoid injuring yourself if the fish has a fearsome set of teeth.) If the hook is out of sight, you will have to cut the trace as close as possible to the hook in the hope that the fish's internal digestive juices will dissolve the hook. Large fish, such as shark, are often best treated in this way in any case to avoid injuring both the angler and the fish. (And note that using bronzed hooks rather than their stainless-steel counterparts will help to improve the survival rate of big game fish.)

RIGHT A large carp is safely in the net.

Chapter 3

Natural factors

Nature is complex, fascinating and, at times, unpredictable, and the angler has to adapt to it, which, I feel, is one of angling's greatest attractions. Sometimes we are able to pick and choose when and where we fish, but at other times we have no option but to make the best of a less than ideal situation and use our skill to succeed. Indeed, the angler who stays at home waiting for the sun to shine will catch far fewer fish than the angler who optimistically sets out to fish, rain or shine.

Because angling is totally governed by the laws of nature, when we set out to catch fish, our success or failure will be determined by our ability to adapt to these natural factors, although the environment in which we are fishing will obviously also have an influence on how much they affect our chances.

So what exactly are these natural factors that so affect our sport? The first that springs to mind is the weather, followed by the seasons, the lunar cycle, tides, migrations, spawning, light values and time of day, abundance of natural food and geographical features. Many of these factors are interwoven, in that they have either a direct effect on, or parallel relationship with, each other.

I am not a scientist, but have, over the years, built up my own opinions on nature's influences and how they affect my day by the water. These opinions are, without doubt, influenced heavily by the writings of other anglers, and you, too, will in time develop your own opinions and cast out accordingly.

So let's discuss each factor separately and try to increase our awareness of the natural world, as well as how it affects the fish that we seek and our chances of connecting with them.

ABOVE Changing light values often encourage the fish to feed.

This diagram gives some idea of how natural factors are linked.

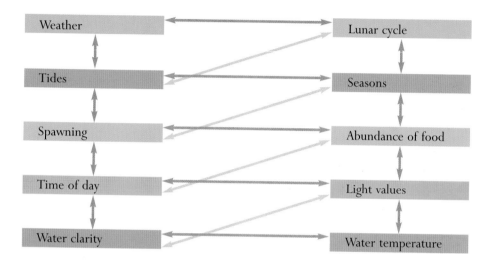

The Seasons

The natural seasons of spring, summer, autumn and winter affect the weather patterns to varying extents depending on where you are, and the angler must learn to adapt to this.

The life cycle of a fish is dictated by the seasonal patterns, its biological clock running in time with them. I mention how fish migrate as a result of their need to spawn and feed. This fish behaviour has evolved over millions of years and is nature's way of ensuring the survival of each species. It is no coincidence that many fish spawn in the winter or spring, ensuring that their fry have an abundance of food throughout the summer months as well as lush weed growth to give a degree of protection from predators.

There are fishing seasons that have been laid down by regulatory bodies in order to help protect fish during spawning. Anglers should always check with the local authority to determine the 'rod-and-line' season for the fish they seek.

The weather

The weather has a huge effect on every day that we spend beside the water. Good fishing weather is not always perfect picnic weather, but as long as you are correctly attired (see pages 94 to 98) and there is a chance of catching fish, you will probably enjoy your day, whatever the weather.

In this technological age, weather forecasts have become increasingly reliable, with satellite imagery helping to remove much of the guesswork. And although forecasters will never be able to predict exactly how the weather will

ABOVE Winter's frozen river.

RIGHT Calm autumn waters flow seaward through wooded banks.

be – clouds may mean rain or snow, for example, but how much? – I would nevertheless recommend always studying the forecast carefully before venturing forth. If you are planning a trip days in advance, the weather forecast can also help you to decide the best venue at which to try your luck, and thus also the species that you will be targeting and the tackle required.

Wind

Over the long term, the prevailing wind direction will affect the geographical structure of a coastline or the tree growth around a lake to a certain extent. A windward shore may suffer from bank erosion, for instance, while a sheltered shore will be more able to support the weed growth that harbours insect life.

In the short term, a strong wind may stir up sediment in a lake, encouraging some species of fish to feed more confidently on the food that has been dislodged, but such clouded water may, on the other hand, deter species like trout from taking an artificial fly. On the open coast, a strong wind will whip up the waves and surf. Shore fishing may benefit from the turbulence thus created, with such fish as bass hunting for food in the white water and cod and large, predatory fish coming close inshore to feast on the wealth of crustacea and worm life that has been ripped from its home. (Note that having an intimate knowledge of your local coastline will ensure that you can always find a sheltered mark in all but the severest of gales.)

The rough seas that create the coloured water conditions suitable for bait-fishing may well render lure-fishing a waste of time, however. In fact, rough sea is the boat-angler's worst nightmare: if it is too rough, it will, at worst, be unsafe to venture out, but if it is safe enough to take to sea, the conditions may make the experience an uncomfortable one. Charter-boat skippers often have a difficult decision to make when deciding if a trip should go ahead or be cancelled. Although a trip should always be cancelled if

RIGHT Waves surge upon a rocky shore.

anglers' safety is likely to be compromised, deciding whether anglers will be uncomfortable can be difficult. A cancelled trip means a loss of earnings for the skipper, and anglers will therefore often be asked to decide whether they wish to proceed, which is not always easy.

The wind is measured on the Beaufort scale, which ranges from 0 to 12.

Scale	Range of wind speed (knots)	Description	Sea state	Wave height
0	0–1	Calm	Mirror-like	4in (10cm)
1	1–3	Light	Ripples	4in (10cm)
2	4–6	Light breeze	Wavelets	7in (18cm)
3	7–10	Gentle breeze	Larger wavelets	2ft (60cm)
4	11–16	Moderate breeze	Small waves; 'white horses'	3ft (91cm
5	17–21	Fresh breeze	Moderate waves	6ft (1.8m)
6	22–27	Strong breeze	Large waves	9 to10ft (2.7 to 3m)
7	28–33	Near gale	Heaped waves	13ft (4m)
8	34–40	Gale	High waves	18ft (5.5m)
9	41–47	Strong gale	High waves; dense spray	23ft (7m)
10	48–55	Storm	Very high waves; white water	29ft (8.8m)
11	56–63	Violent storm	Exceptionally high waves	37ft (11.2m)
12	64+	Hurricane	Air filled with foam; sea white, with driving spray	50ft (15.2m)

In terms of fishing in the open sea, a force 6 wind and above is likely to make angling difficult, and when it comes to boat trips, any trip into the open sea is likely to be cancelled. In some areas, steep cliffs, sea lochs, estuaries and large harbours will give sufficient protection for the trip to be enjoyed, despite the strong winds.

Freshwater angling is less affected by strong winds, except when fishing on large, open expanses of water like reservoirs or lakes, when fishing from a boat can become either impossible or dangerous.

The wind can have a profound effect on the location of fish, particularly in large expanses of fresh water, where the water at the surface tends to be warmer. When this body of water pushes into the shoreline, it is forced downwards, creating an area of warmer water that can stimulate insects to hatch, in turn attracting feeding fish. This area of water is also likely to have a higher oxygen level, which can again stimulate piscine activity. Any insects and other sources of food for fish that are caught on the water's surface will drift towards the windward shore, too, providing rich picking for the lake's inhabitants.

Having pointed you in the direction of the windward shore, I should now point out that this is not always the place to head for. Casting into a strong wind is extremely difficult for a start, and the angler on the windward shore may suffer during colder weather, when the cold water at the surface creates a band of cold air. The angler will also find that a wind from behind enables longer casts, or, in some circumstances, the opportunity to drift out baits and cover areas that are not normally reachable by conventional means.

By contrast, a gentle breeze will, as a rule, enhance any day on, or beside, the water. Dead-calm water seldom results in good catches, however.

Wind direction also seems to have a profound effect on the behaviour of fish, particularly in the open sea. There is a fisherman's rhyme that declares, 'When the wind is in the east, fish bite least, and when the wind is in the west, fish bite best'. In the area in which I live, this maxim seems to apply to many species of fish, although not all of them. The wind-direction factor seems to vary greatly, according to local geography, but I have noticed that around the coast that I fish, westerly winds stir up the sea, creating conditions that encourage fish to swim close inshore; easterly winds tend to have the opposite effect, however. Cod and bass certainly seem to feed far better when there is a westerly wind, yet, perhaps strangely, shark feeding off the coastline are more likely to be caught when there is an easterly wind. One of my angling companions attributes this phenomenon to the way that the boat drifts offshore. I have a different theory, however, and believe the reason to lie in barometric pressure. It is often said that pike feed better during rising, or high, pressure, while other species, such as carp, feed more during low, or falling, pressure. Easterly winds often coincide with areas of high pressure, and westerly winds with areas of low pressure. Because both the pike and shark are predators, the link seems logical to me, but I'm sure that other people have different theories.

Rain

Having discussed the wind and barometric pressure, the next element of the weather to consider is rain. Rain's most dramatic influence on angling is its effect on rivers. A lack of rain will lead to low, clear rivers from which it can be extremely difficult to extract fish. Heavy rain, on the other hand, can herald a thick, muddy torrent that is equally difficult for the angler to cope with, and that can sometimes lead to extremely dangerous conditions. Indeed, some rivers can rise at such a frightening speed that they prevent escape, with many anglers being swept to their deaths each year. So be cautious! Beware of steep banks that may become impossible to negotiate following heavy rain, and also beware of wading out too far in a rising river.

The sweet smell of fresh water encourages salmon and migratory fish to run into rising rivers. As a general rule, however, the best time to visit a river is as it fines down following a spate, when the water's enhanced oxygen levels and reduced clarity (which makes fish feel secure) and the abundance of food being swept downstream by the strengthened currents cause most species of fish to feed well.

The onset of rain also stimulates fish into action in lakes and ponds. I have often found that fish in these bodies of water come to feed directly following a heavy shower, perhaps because the change in conditions causes a sudden influx of oxygenated water or hatching insects.

The sea is relatively unaffected by rain, except when the waters of rain-swollen estuaries rush into it. Being rivers, estuaries tend to fish far better when the water level recedes and the water starts to clear. Be warned, however, that the large amounts of debris that may be swept down the estuary by a flood can make fishing difficult. If a piece of debris becomes entangled with the line, for instance, its weight can pull the terminal tackle from its position on the estuary bed, at times making it hard for the angler to retrieve it.

When fishing from rocks, also be warned that rain will often render them extremely slippery, in which case proceed with caution and do not attempt to make any steep descents to isolated marks.

BELOW Reflections on calm waters.

Sunshine

Sunshine provides light and warms the water. Dawn and dusk are the key periods when many species of fish feed, possibly because these are times when aquatic insects become more active. As the fish rise to the surface, they may be attacked from below by predatory fish. Predators use the reduced light levels (see also light values on pages 433 to 436) that prevail at sunrise and sunset both as camouflage and to enhance their upward-looking vision as they prepare to attack.

If I could stipulate the weather for a day's fishing, it would undoubtedly be dry and bright, with the occasional cloud

and a light breeze from the west. In reality, however, we have to adapt to whatever the weather throws at us, which I suppose, is one of the joys of angling.

ABOVE Bright waters are a joy to fish.

BELOW Winter ice lines the river bank.

The lunar cycle

The moon seems to have a big influence on piscine behaviour beyond its obvious link with the tides (see below). A full moon and a clear sky will result in a night that is not especially dark, which does not encourage nocturnal species of fish to feed confidently, for example, as I have found when fishing from rock marks for conger eel; when the moon disappears behind clouds, however, they immediately commence feeding.

When I visited Alderney, one of the Channel Islands in the English Channel, with a party of anglers, we all struggled to catch fish. The local anglers later told us that they did not bother fishing during full moons because they had so little success, and, lesson learned, we vowed to check the lunar cycle before our next visit. Indeed, some anglers keep detailed records of the lunar cycle and their fishing sessions in an attempt to highlight the days and nights that will prove the most productive.

A full moon rises over a distant hill as anglers contemplate the night ahead.

Tides

The tidal cycle has a major impact on sea anglers (but not freshwater anglers), dictating where they can fish and at what time. Before setting out to fish in salt water, it is therefore essential to study a tide table.

Tides are caused by the gravitational pull of the moon and sun. The largest movement of water occurs during spring tides, when the sun and moon are in alignment, so that their individual effects are reinforced. When the sun is at a right angle to the Earth, smaller tides, called neap tides, occur.

In most parts of the world, there are two tides on each lunar day. And because a lunar day lasts for 24 hours, 50 minutes and 28 seconds, the tides occur approximately 50 minutes later each lunar day.

In my experience, the best tides to fish vary greatly, depending on the location, venue and species being sought. Many sea anglers feel more confident when fishing during spring tides, however, believing that the additional movement stimulates fish to feed.

Migrations

The world's waters form a vast migratory network for many of its species of fish. While some fish are territorial, or confined in location, others travel enormous distances, driven primarily by the need to breed or feed. It is no use fishing for fish that are not there, which is why anglers who are fishing for migratory fish must have some knowledge of their migratory pattern if they are to cast their line into a section of their journey.

When many anglers think of migratory fish, salmon automatically spring to mind. Salmon move into river systems from the sea on their way to their spawning redds many miles upstream. They do not all enter these systems at once, however, nature having instead ensured that their arrival is staggered over a period of several months so that if a natural disaster strikes, the species will survive. Local data accumulated over many years should reveal a pattern (although note that this may be affected by tides and rainfall) showing that the first of the season's fish usually enter a river system within a few days or weeks of the same date each year. If you want to catch salmon, you will therefore need to access this information and plan your trip accordingly.

Fish migrate throughout the seasons in the world's oceans, and anglers around the world try to ambush the fish as they pass by. The water temperature and presence of food influence the course of many of these migrations. The English coast, for example, sees an influx of mackerel each summer, generally starting during the month of May. These fish prey upon vast shoals of sand eel and whitebait and are in turn hunted by larger predators, such as bass, shark and tope. So find the mackerel, and you will have located their hunters.

Spawning

Although breeding and migration are closely linked, the fish that spawn in enclosed waters are not migratory species. Many of the species that spawn in shallow areas of lakes become targets for anglers before and afterwards. Pike, for example, move into shallow areas of water in preparation for spawning at a time when they are at their heaviest, giving anglers the chance to increase their personal bests by several pounds or kilos. It is usually up to the individual angler to decide whether it is right to target spawning fish, but a close season, a period of the year when it is prohibited to catch certain fish, is sometimes imposed to protect fish stocks during what can be a vulnerable time for them. Yet many coarse fish, such as carp, seldom feed during the act of spawning, making the benefits of a close season questionable, as they are otherwise engaged, although a break

from anglers certainly gives vegetation a chance to recover and birds a chance to breed undisturbed. After the rigours of spawning, fish will certainly feed hard to rebuild their strength.

Coarse fish normally breed during the springtime, when the water temperature starts to climb and their hatched-out fry consequently have rich sources of daphnia and other insect life to feed upon.

Most game fish spawn during the late autumn or winter, when the water temperature is at its lowest, and a strict close season generally ensures that they are undisturbed at this time. In the United Kingdom, rainbow trout are normally infertile, which is why no such close season is enforced to protect them, although individual fisheries may nevertheless impose their own.

Note that spawning fish can attract the attention of predators that can themselves be targeted by the wily angler.

LEFT This salmon river will be closed to anglers during the winter spawning period.

Light values and time of day

Weather conditions, the time of day and water clarity all have an effect on the light values within the waters that we fish, and light values in turn seem to have a profound effect on how fish feed, with many species feeding particularly well at dawn and dusk. It is therefore imperative that you know the light values that are likely to suit the species that you are targeting.

Many predatory fish, in particular, seem to feed better after dark and are seldom caught during the hours of daylight. Conger eels, for instance, appear especially reluctant to feed in bright conditions, except in deep water, where the light values are lower. Armed with this knowledge, you may conclude that it is best to fish for conger either at night or in deep water, from a boat, during the day. Yet there are always exceptions to general rules like these. I recall fishing from a rock mark on a

LEFT A summer dawn will often provide the best chance of the day.

bright, sunny day several years ago, close to a young angler who was lowering his fish bait directly into the water at his feet. 'Hey, mister,' he exclaimed, 'there's a massive eel down here'. I walked over to where he stood, and, sure enough, saw a conger weighing perhaps 20lb (9kg) approaching the bait. The eel was easily observed in the bright sunlight and crystal-clear water as it sidled up to the bait and slowly engulfed it. The boy attempted to extract the beast from its home, but as his rod bent and the conger thrashed angrily on the surface, his line parted with a crack. That boy will never forget the experience, and I will never forget the conger that fed on a hot, sunny day in less than 6ft (1.8m) of clear water.

I could give you many such examples of fish doing what they shouldn't to illustrate the point that nature's rules are not rigid. There are, however, certain general guidelines that can be followed with some confidence, although there is always a chance that the unexpected will happen.

Species of fish that feed predominantly by day feed by sight, while fish that feed by night, or in coloured water, use their keen sense of smell to detect food. Many fish also have sensors along their lateral line that can detect the vibrations given off by their prey. Each species has evolved to suit its particular niche: a fish with big eyes, for instance, is perfectly suited to sight-feeding in low light. In fresh water, the feeding habits of various species seem to vary from venue to venue, with the season, water temperature and water clarity all contributing to their preferences. Carp, for example, feed almost exclusively at night at some venues, but more during daylight hours at others.

The angling methods that we use are also influenced by light values. Artificial lures generally work better in clear water during daylight hours, for instance. Sea trout, however, can be caught when fly-fishing at night using lures, probably because they can see the lure's silhouette as it passes overhead and attack that. (This theory appears to be confirmed by the fact that black lures are among the most effective, and black plugs also work well when targeting sea bass after dark in some areas.)

Small changes in light values can often trigger a feeding spell in fish. I have often sat awaiting a bite on a

Temperature

On a global scale water temperature affects where each species of fish is to be located. On a more local scale water temperature affects the way fish behave and feed.

Many species of fish will show a reduction in activity as their body metabolism slows down with a decline in temperature. Some species will enter a state of semi-hibernation during cold winter periods. When the water temperature suddenly rises a feeding spree sometimes follows that can be a productive time for the angler.

Many anglers carry a thermometer to the waterside. This can help to decide what species of fish to target. For example, it is widely accepted that barbel are reluctant to feed at a temperature much below 5°C (40°F) whilst chub will continue to feed even as ice lines the river bank.

ABOVE Winter sunshine shimmers on the water.

cloudy day, when the breaking of the sun through the clouds has coincided with a bite. Conversely, the passing of a cloud over the sun on a bright and sunny day can have the same result. Light values are therefore very relevant to the angler's chances of catching fish, and remember that each species has its own preference, which can vary from one location to another.

An abundance of natural food

Because locating food is a major driving force in a fish's life, if you position the right bait where a fish expects to find food, you should catch it.

It is important that you know what sort of food your quarry is seeking if you are to deceive it. Predatory fish chasing sand eel in the open sea are best located by finding the sand eel and then casting an appropriate imitation, for example. Note that bait fish can sometimes be located by observing flocks of seabirds: when they start diving into the water in a feeding frenzy, it can be assumed that predatory fish are also launching an attack beneath the waves. (Indeed, witnessing the savagery of nature while out on a boat can be awe-inspiring. Imagine seeing seabirds plunging into the sea from high in the sky, and mackerel and bass attacking from beneath, while their prey erupt from the sea in cascades of silver and spray, and watching dolphins emerging gracefully from the water at the edge of this feeding frenzy, with the sinister fin of a shark occasionally cutting the water's surface.)

Sea anglers should be able to locate potentially food-rich areas by walking along the shoreline when the tide is out. The presence of marine worms will be betrayed by their casts or tiny burrows in the mud or sand, for instance; rocks and weeds will shelter crabs and other creatures on which fish prey; and gullies and indentations will trap food as it is washed along by the tide. Casting near any of these areas should yield fish.

In lakes and rivers, fish may feed on hatching insects, which means that you should locate the hatching areas in order to find the fish (remember to take the water temperature, wind direction and other influential natural factors into account, too). Fish could also be grazing on beds of tiny bloodworm on the bottom of the lake, which could cause a problem, however, in that the fish may become so preoccupied with this source of food that they refuse other offerings.

Geographical features

Each species of fish is perfectly matched to the environment in which it lives, and the geographical make-up of the land adjacent to, and beneath, the water will give clues as to what sort of species you can expect to catch there. In addition, each species favours a particular habitat, as determined by its needs, and looking at the species will usually provide a clue as to where it is best suited.

A flatfish, for example, which dwells on areas of sand or mud, is coloured in a way that camouflages it from predators above as it lies on the sand, as well as from its own prey. Its eyes protrude from its body, enabling it to look up and around. Its flat shape is perfectly suited to its lifestyle, helping it to maintain its position on the seabed as the currents wash by.

The pike relies on ambush to trap its prey. Its green-mottled flanks blend in perfectly with the weed beds in which it waits before accelerating to devour its unfortunate victim.

RIGHT A dramatic geographic landscape, which the angler must interpret.

The silver salmon's streamlined shape and powerful muscles help it to forge upstream, over waterfalls and through powerful currents.

The shark's powerful body is designed continually to roam the open seas in search of prey. Its amazing sense of smell and sensors enable it to detect an injured fish from an incredible distance.

With its long, snake-like body, the conger eel is perfectly designed for lurking among rocks and kelp.

A river meanders quietly to the sea through a varied landscape.

Chapter 4

The roving rod

Exploring new territory is, perhaps, one of angling's greatest pleasures. The first cast that you make into new water is always accompanied by an air of optimism and an anticipation of as yet unexperienced delights. If the trip has been planned well in advance, and a considerable journey has been made, the greater the feeling of expectation. And sometimes the water will live up to these expectations, with rods bending and reels screaming as the prize struggles for freedom. More often, however, the angler will first have to adapt to the new venue and learn a few new tricks.

Preparation is of the utmost importance before travelling away from home. You will need to know which species you are likely to catch, what the local angling methods are, where to buy permits, licences and so on. And although this book covers many of the environments that you are likely to encounter, helping you to make an educated guess about local fishing

methods and so on, you really should do your own research. Note that if the trip involves air travel and you want to avoid incurring hefty excess-luggage charges, you may have to make compromises regarding the tackle that you are taking. Indeed, it may be worth hiring tackle on arrival at your destination, especially if your own is unsuitable for the task ahead.

Now let's look at the preparations that may be required for a serious angling holiday and then put together a tackle bag suitable for a quick cast should the opportunity arise when you are away from home.

LEFT The path to the water is full of optimism.

ABOVE The world of angling is vast.

Angling holidays

You may have been inspired to make an angling trip to an unknown destination by your fellow anglers, the pages of a book or magazine or a television programme. You may already be picturing yourself holding a big fish that you have caught easily, in which case, be warned that the reality will seldom be as you imagined. There may be big fish at your destination, but will they be easy to catch? Perhaps, but only if you are in the right place at the right time with the right bait. Angling's fundamentals are the same wherever

ABOVE Saltwater shallows offer superb sport for the fly-fisher.

RIGHT Make sure you have the right lures before you arrive.

you are in the world, so always try to keep your expectations realistic.

I have not travelled widely throughout the world in search of fish, but know of several anglers who have. They have succeeded either by carrying out plenty of research or by hiring experienced guides to assist in their quest. Before embarking on any voyage, it is therefore essential to know as much as possible about the species of fish that you are targeting, and you'll find your local library a rich source of information, as well as the World Wide Web.

Package angling holidays are an easy option that offer a very good chance of success, provided that you are a reasonably competent angler. Several years ago, I visited Lake Nasser, in Egypt, on an angling safari. It proved to be a fascinating excursion in search of the legendary Nile perch, a predatory species of freshwater fish that grows to

weights in excess of 400lb (181kg), with perch weighing more than 100lb (45kg) being relatively common captures.

Before embarking on this trip, I read all that I could on the subject of Lake Nasser and its Nile perch. I wrote letters to leading anglers who had visited the lake and went along to see slide shows given by such anglers. From this research, I was able to put together a list of the tackle that I needed for the trip, much of which I already possessed.

I still needed to purchase a few items, however, including a selection of appropriate lures, to which replacement hooks had to be fitted to ensure that they had the strength to withstand the enormous power of my quarry.

When travelling to a far-off

LEFT The shoreline of Egypt's Lake Nasser.

BELOW Our guide prepares fresh Nile perch for the evening meal.

destination, you must make sure that you have adequate spare tackle. If your reel were to pack up and you had no spare, for instance, all of your efforts would be wasted, as would also be the case if you were to run out of line or lose all of your hooks or lures. The question of how many lures and so on to take can only really be ascertained by seeking the advice of anglers who have already visited the water, however.

The big advantage of going on an organised angling package holiday is that guides will take you to the fish. Without their local knowledge, it would take far too long to locate your target species yourself, given a holiday's limited time. My experience in Egypt was extremely rewarding, with a large number of Nile perch falling to our lures, the best pulling the scales to 83lb (37.6kg). And our success was largely due to the skill of our guides, who took us to the Nile-perch hotspots that had been discovered through the constant exploration of this massive lake.

Visits to foreign lands in search of big fish are always exciting, but when you look back on them, it is not always the fish that stand out in your memory. The people whom you met and the environments that you visited frequently remain permanently etched on your mind, along with the memory of wild waters – often in remote and beautiful

TOP RIGHT A massive shore-caught Nile perch.

BOTTOM RIGHT A Nile perch of 83lb (37kg) is carefully returned to ensure future sport.

BELOW Stout footwear was essential as we fished from a steep rocky shoreline.

locations – that hold large fish. When I look back on my trip to Egypt and Lake Nasser, the black, star-studded night sky and sounds made by thousands of frogs and insects echoing through the balmy air linger in my mind, while the memory of waking at first light one morning to hear the eerie cry of a jackal drifting across the vast water comes flooding back. All in all, I would advise trying to catch big fish in a foreign land at least once in your life if you have the chance.

If you are away from home – perhaps on business or a family holiday –

Opportunistic angling

opportunities to fish may come your way. It is therefore advisable to travel prepared and to carry out a bit of research before leaving to help you to decide which bits of kit to take. Although you probably won't be able to carry all of the gear that you ideally need, you can nevertheless take enough to enable you to catch fish.

Telescopic rods or travel rods in several sections can easily be packed, and, when teamed with a suitable reel and a tackle box full of sundry items, will enable you to catch fish anywhere in the world. If I had to choose a rod to pack, it would be a spinning rod measuring around 10ft (3m) in length. I would match this with a fixed-spool reel loaded with a 12lb (5.4kg) bs line, and would also pack a spare spool loaded with a 6lb (2.7) bs line to give me a greater choice of tactics. In addition, a few hooks, swivels, weights, floats and spinners will cover many situations.

A couple of examples of my own opportunistic angling spring to mind. I

once visited Toronto, in Canada, with my wife. Before we set off, I purchased a telescopic rod to stow in my suitcase in case the opportunity to have a dabble came along. I also sent away for a tourist leaflet on fishing in the area to give me an idea of what to expect. This also gave me information on where to obtain permits and licenses A small river only a five-minute walk away from where we were staying was said to contain carp and a small type of catfish.

The morning after we arrived, I set off with a rod in my hand and a tin of sweet corn in my bag. Although the river was set in a wooded suburban area, the strange birdsong that filled the air gave it a far more exotic atmosphere. I set up a float rig and tied a size 8 hook to my 8lb (3.6kg) bs line before wandering along the riverbank and tossing a handful of sweet corn into promising-looking areas. I eventually spotted movement in the water. On my first cast, the float settled and was pulled under, and soon a small catfish was swinging into my hand. (It may have been small, but adding a new species to my list of captures is always satisfying.)

LEFT Casting under the midday sun.

A few yards further downstream, I saw a cloud of mud rise in the water. As soon as I glimpsed a bronze, scaly back, I threw some sweet corn into position and waited tensely. The float trembled and then started to move slowly before disappearing hearteningly from sight. A flick of the wrist was then followed by a well-bent rod and I was the image of the contented angler the world over. I admired the common carp that I'd caught, which weighed around 8lb (3.6kg), before lowering her back into her home surroundings. Finally, I packed my kit away secure in the knowledge that Canadian carp have identical tastes to British carp. (The strange thing, however, is that while British anglers love carp, they are classed as vermin in Canada.)

I used my little telescopic rod several times on that holiday to tempt large-mouth bass, pumpkinseed and northern pike. It has since accompanied me on several family holidays, and has been used to catch a range of species from various venues.

Wherever you travel, there will be opportunities to catch fish, and you can enjoy short bursts of great fun if you seize the chance. Catching fish from new locations is always satisfying, and another great advantage of taking a fishing rod with you is that it often helps you to make contact with fellow anglers. I have frequently wandered along a seafront or river and struck up conversations with total strangers. A fishing rod tends to break down many superficial barriers, encouraging anglers to talk freely among themselves so that they are soon chatting merrily away as though they have been friends for years. Indeed, angling is a wonderful medium for making a wide range of friends, and an interest in angling can bridge differences of generation, nationality, religion and class.

RIGHT Setting off on an Egyptian fishing safari.

Match fishing

Successful match anglers have a fiercely competitive streak, their aim being to catch more than anyone else and to win prizes, trophies and cash. Such anglers compete at all levels, ranging from small, club-based competitions to international matches in which they represent their countries.

Dedicated match anglers devote their lives to the sport, spending vast amounts of money on bait, tackle and travel. A lucky few will make it big and will earn enough from the sport to pay their bills, be it with their winnings or lucrative sponsorships.

Competitions

Angling competitions are held throughout the world. The competition formats vary in structure within the different disciplines, and the methods, boundaries and so on may also be restricted to give all of the competitors a fair chance. Every competing angler needs to be fully aware of the rules before starting out.

LEFT Anglers deep in concentration, determined to out-fish their fellow competitors.

Some anglers believe match fishing to be contrary to the true spirit of angling, believing that fishing against fellow anglers, often for financial gain, brings out the worst in people. In my opinion, however, there is room for all types in the angling world. Competitions are certainly the basis for a lot of social intercourse between anglers, and friendly rivalry is, on the whole, a healthy part of the scene. (Unsavoury incidents, such as cheating, admittedly sometimes occur when money is involved, but I find it hard to comprehend why people cheat, for they are actually cheating only themselves.)

Now let's look at several types of match formats and the rules that commonly apply.

Coarse matches

Coarse angling has historically had a strong competitive element. During the industrial age, many major industries' employees would often be members of large angling clubs that organised competitions at weekends, when coaches and trains would take anglers to canals and rivers to fish against either each other or rival clubs. These matches were very much social occasions, with anglers meeting up at the end of the day for a pint or two before travelling home to their families and another week in the factory or mine. Although times have changed, the general match-fishing format survives. Anglers arrive at the venue an hour or two before the start and pay an entry fee, which is often divided, half going towards the prize money and half boosting the club's income. In addition, anglers enter a pool, in effect placing a bet on themselves to win the competition. The pool money is divided in various ways, depending on the number of competitors. In a small competition, the winner may take home all of the pool money. In a larger match, anglers will probably be divided up into sections – each section typically containing ten anglers – giving each a better chance of winning a prize. (It is unlikely that the fish will be distributed evenly along the length of water being fished, so if you are in a poor section, you are unlikely to win the match; you may, however, win your section.)

After paying your entry fee and pool money, there will be a draw for your peg (swim). Each peg is numbered, and you will receive a slip of paper giving you access to your swim for the day. If you have done your homework, you should have walked the match length and learnt about each section and which methods are likely to succeed. (If possible, visit the venue before the match and either have a practice session or watch a weigh-in to see what is caught. Chat to local anglers and glean as much information from them as possible. Local tackle shops are always worth a visit, too, and their staff are usually eager to help, especially if they think that you will spend money in the shop.)

Having arrived at your swim, it is now time to tackle up and get ready to fish. Ensure that you know all of the rules. You will generally be able to plumb the depth before the start of the match, but check the rules in case they forbid this. Introducing groundbait or

RIGHT Match fishing is a sociable affair.

loose feed to the swim is normally against the rules.

The match will often start at 10.00am and finish five hours later, at 3.00pm. The start and finish will be signalled by a blast of a whistle or horn. For the duration of the match, you will have to try to extract as many fish as possible from the water ahead of you (and remember that you can only catch the fish in front of you). If you have a good peg and have read the water correctly, you may end up a winner, with a bulging keepnet (a net that you suspend in the water to keep the fish that you have caught alive). You will have to make many decisions throughout the match, and may have to alter your tactics. The most important decision is often whether to build up a bag weight (the total weight of your catch) consisting of lots of small fish or of less numerous, but larger fish. The anglers on either side of you can influence the tactics that you adopt: if it is halfway through the match and you are trailing behind your neighbours, for instance, you may decide to go all out for that one big fish to beat their net of tiddlers.

In team events, it is likely that each member of a team will be in a different section and will be awarded points for his or her placing within that section. For example, if there are ten anglers in each section, the winner will receive ten points, the runner-up, nine points; the angler who comes third, eight points and so on. It is therefore possible that no anglers in the winning team will have won their sections, but that their points total was the highest because all caught fish. (Being a member of a team is often quite stressful in that you are under pressure not to let the team down.)

It takes a lot of dedication to reach the top in coarse angling. Today, matches are sponsored and the prize money can run into the thousands; teams wear matching outfits and their tackle is provided by their sponsors. It's a far cry from the coach loads of anglers who once went out for a sociable day by the river and enjoyed a pie and beer afterwards.

LEFT Concentrate hard, for a missed bite could win or lose the match.

Competitive trout fishing

Trout-fishing competitions are predominantly fly-fishing only, almost always take place on still waters – with anglers fishing either from a boat or the shore – and are likely to be bag-weight contests. Fly-fishing methods are restricted in some competitions, with, perhaps, a maximum size of fly being stipulated. Some boat competitions are loch-style only, with anglers drifting in the breeze and casting a team of small, traditional flies in front of the boat.

Trout-fishing competitions are not generally pegged, but often have sections. The anglers draw numbers from a hat and move off from the draw point in numerical order. In common with all angling competitions, there are rigorously maintained start and finish times. In small still-water competitions, anglers are often pegged, but a rotating system is implemented to ensure that all have an equal chance. Each angler fishes for perhaps thirty minutes in a swim before moving on to the next, which has been vacated by another competitor, who has similarly moved on.

Unwanted trout that are brought to the scales are often donated to a residential home or similar good cause. Limit bags are generally stipulated, in line with normal fishery rules.

Some large, prestigious competition results are widely distributed. If they are good, they reflect well on the fishery that hosted the competition, thereby enticing new visitors, which is why stock levels are sometimes increased immediately before a competition.

Sea-angling matches

Sea-angling matches are generally fished on a large venue that provides the competitors with plenty of room. They can be either fixed-venue or roving events. In a roving competition, the anglers can fish anywhere along a designated coastline, or even within a county. Most competitions are fished according to national rules, as laid down by the sport's governing body. The match venue should ideally be uniform throughout, giving all of the competitors a fair chance of success.

Although some competitions are pegged, most are not, with the anglers simply paying their entry and pool monies before selecting any unoccupied pitch on the beach that they feel looks promising. (Because the best spots are taken first, competitors should try to arrive as early as possible. When the rules permit it, it is standard practice to erect a rod-rest tripod to reserve a pitch.)

Sea-angling competitions used to be predominantly bag-weight contests, but now that conservation has become so important, other formats are increasing in popularity. The catch-and-release system is often practised, with the fish being measured and then returned to the sea once its length has been verified by a steward. (A steward is a club official or nominated person who ensures that the rules are followed and any cheats eliminated.) Points systems are often implemented according to varying criteria, such as length or species of fish, too. Many clubs also hold best-specimen competitions, in which fish are judged against a local specimen list. Each species has a target weight, and the weights of all the fish measured are given as percentages of this optimum weight. Species competitions are also popular with some clubs, and particularly with boat-anglers. The anglers receive points for each species of fish landed, the winner being the angler who has landed the most species. Points are sometimes awarded to different species according to their status: a dogfish or pouting would, for example, be worth one point, a bass, five points and so on.

Chapter 5

Safety

Statistically, angling is rated as a dangerous sport, which is why I feel that we should take a look at the hazards and risks that anglers face and the measures that we can take to minimise them.

My dictionary defines a hazard as 'exposure or vulnerability to injury, loss etc', and a risk as the 'probability of incurring accident or loss'. To clarify these definitions, I would like to quote an example that I was once given during a training course: 'A can of petrol with no top is a hazard. The risk is that someone will light a match near that open top', the result of which would clearly be a nasty accident. And a dictionary definition of an accident is 'an unforeseen event, or one without an apparent cause', which means that foresight and awareness are the keys to avoiding accidents.

Fishing in deep water

The danger of falling into the water is the risk most often associated with angling, and although it is possible to drown in only inches of water, the greatest risks are incurred when fishing in deep water. It is therefore important to heed the following advice.

• Wear suitable footwear, with a good grip, and tread carefully.

• Be on the look-out for slippery weeds and rocks, especially following rain.

• Remember that steep banks can become muddy slides that are impossible to negotiate safely after it has rained.

• Be aware that the banks of a river or lake may suffer from erosion and have overhangs that could collapse onto anyone standing at the edge, precipitating them into the water.

• If you can't swim, learn how to.

• If the conditions render it necessary, wear a buoyancy device. Flotation suits and waistcoats have saved many anglers' lives.

• When fishing in salt water, be aware of the state of the tide.

• Constantly watch the state of the sea and keep an eye on incoming waves.

• On a river, look out for rising water levels. Heavy rain upstream may cause a river to rise rapidly. If you are fishing the lower tidal reaches of a river, also be aware of the incursion of the tide; some stretches are not obviously tidal, and if it is unexpected, the sudden influx of water that occurs before high water can be quite alarming.

Wading

If your day involves wading, do not wade too deep and be aware of the current. Also remember the following tips.

• Ensure that the soles of your waders or footwear have a good grip.

• Always make sure that you can escape from the point to which you are wading. (If you are wading downstream to a promontory, for example, the current may prevent you from returning via the same route.)

• Be aware of the bottom and use a wading stick to probe it for holes or sudden changes of contour. (The handle of a landing net is a good substitute for a wading stick.)

• When wading next to deep water, always wear a self-inflating life jacket.

• If you are wading in the sea, be aware of the rising tide and make allowances for waves that are larger than average.

• If you fall in wearing waders, keep calm and allow your legs to float to the surface because the air within the waders will help to keep you afloat. Try to drift downstream feet first, and to climb out when you reach shallower water. If you are in the sea, try to manoeuvre yourself to the shore. Be warned that if you panic, lower your legs and raise your arms, your waders will fill with water, you will disappear beneath the surface and may then drown!

Boat-angling

Before getting on to a charter boat, check that the skipper is licensed and insured. Take note of the following advice, too.

• If you are going out in your own boat, ensure that it is suitable for the water on which you going to float.

• Ensure that the boat is kitted out with such necessary safety equipment as life rafts, life jackets, communication equipment, a compass, flares, oars, a sump pump or bailer, an anchor and a rope.

BELOW Life jackets are essential items for boat anglers.

ABOVE All sea-angling boats should carry flares to raise the alarm if things go wrong.

- Listen to the shipping forecast.
- Avoid setting out in fog or mist.
- Know the area that you are navigating.
- Study the tide times and be aware of local conditions and potential areas of danger, such as tide races, submerged rocks, sandbanks, lobster pots, floating debris, nets, mooring ropes and so on.
- On a small boat, wear a life jacket at all times.
- Always let somebody know where you are intending to fish to ensure that a search can be mounted in the right area should you fail to return on time. If you are going to be late back home because the fishing is good (or the pub beckons on the way), let someone know that you are safely on dry land.

Fish hooks

It is almost inevitable that accidents will occur through fish hooks becoming embedded in your fingers or hands. If a hook becomes imbedded beneath the barb, it will be necessary to cut the shank before attempting to remove the hook. In most instances, it is wise to seek medical attention.

The most hazardous hooks are, without doubt, the treble hooks that are attached to many lures. A flailing treble can easily catch the hand if the fish makes a last-minute shake of the head, so great care must be taken when attempting to land such fish as pike by hand. Note that although gloves can offer a degree of protection, they also have the potential to make matters worse if the hook penetrates both glove and flesh.

Also heed the following advice.

• When fly-fishing, always wear eye protection and a hat because a gust of wind or mistimed cast can result in a hook becoming embedded in the face or head.

• Before casting, always look out for other people in the vicinity.

• Discard hooks responsibly to avoid injuring both humans and wildlife.

Lines

Remember that fishing lines pose a serious risk to wildlife if they are discarded, as well as the following tips.

• If the end tackle becomes snagged in the bottom, pull for a break with great care. Ideally, wrap the line around a piece of wood because if it is wrapped around the hand, it can easily cut deeply into the flesh. Strong, thin-diameter braided lines are particularly dangerous in this respect.

• Some brands of monofilament line are very stretchy, so if your terminal tackle becomes snagged at close range, never look towards the snag while attempting to pull the tackle free because the line can catapult the weight and hook towards you at a surprisingly high velocity.

Casting

As well as ensuring that the immediate
vicinity is clear before casting out (and
if you are fishing in a public area, pay
particular attention to passers-by), note
the following advice.

• Make sure that there are no boats or
other water-users within your casting
range.

• Use adequate shock leaders for
casting, as well as reliable links between
all items of terminal tackle.

BELOW Shock leaders are essential when powerful
casts are being made.

Dangerous fish

Certain fish that we seek to catch can cause us harm if we do not treat them with respect. Shark, pike, barracuda, conger and other fish with sharp teeth are particularly dangerous, which is why you should avoid coming into close contact with such species and should take great care when extracting hooks from them (see pages 411 to 412). In addition, heed the following warnings.

• Large, powerful fish have the potential to cause injury as they struggle to escape, so keep well clear of sharks or congers, in particular, as they thrash about in the close confines of a boat. Indeed, think carefully before bringing them into a boat, and ensure that the deck is free of clutter if you do.

BELOW Pike have a fine set of teeth and need treating with respect.

RIGHT Only experienced anglers should attempt to remove the hooks from a shark.

BELOW Hold a dogfish safely with the tail firmly against its body, and avoiding rasping contact with its sandpaper-like skin.

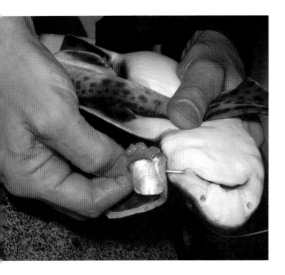

• Many members of the shark family have abrasive, sandpaper-like skin, so handle them firmly, but with care because if their skin comes into contact with your own, it may result in a graze that will be very prone to infection.

• Some species of fish, particularly members of the bass family, have spikes on their fins, tails and gill covers. Before handling such fish, be aware of where these spikes are situated, and wear a pair of gloves to avoid being injured.

• There are several species of poisonous fish throughout the world, the poison generally being housed within spikes. In British waters, the weaver is particularly dangerous, and has inflicted pain on many unwary bathers after their bare feet have trodden upon them as they lie buried in the sand.

Miscellaneous advice

Many of the hazards that anglers face are common in our lives, and not solely confined to the world of angling, so take care when you are fishing. Losing sight of the rising tide, the crumbling riverbank beneath your feet or the high-voltage power lines above your head is so easy when you are absorbed in the quest for fish. Remember that an accident will, at best, spoil a day's fishing, and, at worst, your life! Here are some final safety tips.

• Carry a small first-aid kit containing plasters, antiseptic wipes, ointments and creams with which to treat minor wounds and insect bites.

• Personal hygiene is important to reduce the risk of infection and disease, so clean and cover any cuts or grazes. Remember that the rat population of many waters can transmit Weil's disease (which is potentially fatal) via their urine.

• Unless you apply adequate protection to your skin in the summer, you may easily succumb to sunburn, so slop on sunscreen and wear a hat to ward off sunstroke. Always carry lots of liquids to prevent yourself from becoming dehydrated.

• If possible, do not fish alone, but if you do, ensure that someone knows where you have gone and when you expect to return. Take a mobile phone with you because it will provide a vital link to help if an accident occurs.

• Check the weather forecast before setting out. Try to avoid fishing during electrical storms because carbon-fibre rods are particularly good conductors of electricity, making a fatal lightning strike possible.

• Overhead power lines pose a serious risk to anglers who are misguided enough to fish near them. Long, carbon-fibre poles have inadvertently touched power lines on numerous occasions, resulting in death! Fishing lines similarly have the potential to transmit electricity throughout their length to the unfortunate angler.

• When digging for bait on remote mud flats or sandbanks, be aware of the possibility of mist or fog obscuring your escape route. If the area in which you are digging is prone to these conditions, carry a compass.

• The most dangerous aspect of many trips to the waterside is the journey back. If you have been out all night, remember the dangers inherent in driving when tired, and never drive if you are in danger of falling asleep at the wheel.

Chapter 6

Angling photography

In years gone by, a large specimen fish often ended up in a glass case, to be admired on a mantelpiece or wall. Many old public houses still display these antiquities, and they remain objects of fascination to anglers. The art of taxidermy is now rarely practised, however, hence the value of these relics from a bygone age. Today, anglers tend to preserve the memory of their angling triumphs, and the images of a successful day's fishing, on film, thereby allowing fish to be returned to the water unharmed.

Although I am not an expert photographer, over the years I have learnt by trial and error to take reasonable photographs of the fish that I catch, as well as of my angling friends and their captures. It is always nice to be able to look back on significant days spent at the water's edge, and to share those moments with fellow anglers when they visit your home. And with luck, your photographs will inspire your angling colleagues to accompany you on some new escapade in search of fish.

A wide variety of cameras are available. In this picture we have a 35mm compact, a small digital camera and single-lens reflex (SLR) complete with flash.

Choosing a camera

There is a bewildering array of cameras to choose from, most of which are capable of delivering good results. There are several basic formats, notably conventional, 35mm film cameras and digital cameras.

Before buying a camera, consider your options carefully, seek advice from a reputable dealer and buy the best that you can afford. Remember that it will be exposed to the elements, and that cameras and water – particularly salt water – do not make a happy combination. You should also prevent your camera from coming into contact with sand, mud, fish slime and bait.

Conventional cameras

Available as compact or single-lens reflex (SLR) models, each of these 35mm cameras has its advantages.

Compact cameras are the ideal size to fit into the side compartment of an angling bag. They are simple to use, and generally have an automatic shooting mode – perfect when asking a passer-by to take a photograph of you and the fish that you have just landed.

SLR cameras give the photographer

more scope to influence the quality of the picture. Focusing, aperture and shutter-speed settings can generally all be set in either manual or automatic mode, depending on the camera. A big advantage of this type of camera is that the image that you see in the viewfinder will be the one that you see in the photograph. You can also buy a wide range of lenses to fit these cameras, enabling you to take different types of picture (but remember that you will have to lug your photography kit in addition to your fishing gear).

Users of 35mm cameras have the option of choosing either slide film or print film. Slides can be shown on a projector, and the colour resolution is often extremely good, making them ideal for reproduction in magazines. Prints, on the other hand, are perfect for putting in an album and showing to your friends.

For general use, choose a film with a speed rating of 100 to 400 ASA, 100 ASA being suitable for sunny conditions, and 400ASA being better for conditions in which there is less light.

RIGHT Arranging a good catch of chub for a photograph.

Digital cameras

Digital cameras (which are available as both compact and SLR models) are the most versatile medium currently available for taking photographs. Images are stored on a memory card within the camera, from which they can either be printed or viewed on a computer or television screen. The images can also be edited using computer software and saved to disk.

Accessories

A top-quality protective case is a must for any camera that you purchase. It is also advisable to store the camera-containing camera case in a plastic bag to prevent it from coming into contact with water should a watery mishap befall you while you are fishing.

A tripod or mini-tripod is useful for taking self-portrait shots. Alternatively, you could buy an adaptor with which to convert a bank stick into a camera stand. A good-quality lens cloth is useful for wiping spray from the lens, but note that it is important to ensure that you do not scratch the lens while you are cleaning it.

Taking photographs

A few basic guidelines will help you to produce good results and avoid making the blunders that can destroy a keepsake image, whichever camera you are using. And although observing the following tips may seem a lot of trouble, they offer the only way of obtaining decent pictures time and time again, unlike when simply relying on guesswork and pointing and shooting.

■ Always check your camera before setting out for the day. Have you got enough film? Are the batteries fully charged, and do you have spares?

■ Always take the time to think about what you want to appear in the picture and make sure that it is framed in the viewfinder. Take care not to cut out anglers' heads or other vital parts of the image. (This may seem obvious advice, but I have seen plenty of photographs showing a specimen fish, but without its captor's smiling face.) Another common error is to fail to fill the frame with the subject. Whenever anyone is taking a photograph of a fish, I urge him or her to get up close and fill the frame.

■ Consider the background to the subject matter. If there is a plastic bag or rubbish in the frame, for example, remove it. It is so easy to pose with a fish in the excitement of the moment, and to spoil the end result because the image contains a distracting element.

■ Try to take several shots of the subject, varying the camera angle and setting. If you take half-a-dozen photographs, there will always be one that stands out from the rest.

■ When out by the water, keep your eyes open for any interesting photo opportunities that may present themselves and provide an evocative reminder of your day. Anglers see some lovely sunrises and sunsets, as well as all manner of weather conditions and wildlife. If you are fishing on your own, you will need to use a self-timer facility with which to capture an image of you and your fish. Before posing for the camera, you will need to set up your frame, as follows.

■ Choose, and, if necessary, tidy up, the spot where you intend to hold the fish for the picture.

■ Place the camera on a tripod, or else on a bank stick, using a suitable adaptor.

■ Mark where you are going to kneel.

■ Place an unhooking mat where you

1. Mark where you are going to kneel or stand with a bank stick and focus the camera upon it.

are going to hold the fish.

■ Place a bank stick at the point where you will be and focus the camera on it.

■ Use two further banksticks to mark the outside edges of the frame.

■ Look through the viewfinder and ensure that all three bank sticks are correctly positioned. The top of the central bank stick should be at eye level, and the two outer sticks should be slightly above head height.

■ When you are happy that all is set up correctly and the camera is focused on the right spot, remove the bank sticks.

■ Place the fish on the unhooking mat and cover its head with a wet sack or

2 Focusing on the bankstick ensuring the outer banksticks are out of shot.

4. The final portrait.

weighing sling to keep it subdued.

■ Initiate the auto-timer and then quickly move into position with the fish and pose. Most self-timers will give you about 10 seconds in which to do this, which is usually long enough, as long as the fish behaves and you have time to adopt the right expression.

You could alternatively take a picture of the fish laid out on either an unhooking mat or soft, wet grass. If you do take a picture of a fish without its captor, however, ensure that you include something in the image that provides a sense of proportion.

3 Initiate auto timer

Chapter 7

Angling clubs and organisations

Clubs and organisations, with a diverse range of members and constituions, are widespread throughout the angling world. Yet the many anglers who choose to opt out, who belong to no club or body and have little interest in the wider issues that affect the sport, instead preferring either their own company or

that of a few select companions, are the silent majority. I wish that every angler belonged to a club or organisation, however, because this would undoubtedly boost angling's profile.

Understanding the role that clubs and organisations play within the angling world will help you to make an informed decision about whether joining such a body would suit your needs, or, indeed, those of angling (it being rather selfish and short-sighted only to think about what angling can offer you).

LEFT Anglers enjoy a friendly club match.

RIGHT Two anglers enjoy a chat during a break from fishing.

Angling clubs

Clubs are the social backbone of angling, and there are many associated with each branch of the sport.

Sea-angling clubs, for example, may send out newsletters, organise competitions, outings, social events, boat trips and other such events, as well as casting tuition, and their members will have the opportunity to win trophies for catching specimen fish. They will negotiate with local councils for angling rights on piers or for bait-collecting access to estuaries. A club may also be affiliated with a national body that looks after anglers' interests on a wider scale. Its main function, however, will be as a social link for its members. Large angling clubs may own their own clubhouses, boats and minibuses for club outings.

Freshwater-angling clubs often own, or rent, fishing rights, so that joining such a club will give you access to fresh water at a reasonable price. These waters are often well stocked, but far less heavily fished than commercial day-ticket waters. Such clubs will also organise competitions and perform similar functions to sea-angling clubs. A freshwater-angling club may furthermore hold competitions against other clubs and have a team that fishes within a league.

Joining an angling club is not generally expensive, and may offer you all of the above benefits, along with the opportunity to meet other anglers. And the quickest way to learn about a locality's waters, and which angling methods will succeed on them, is to talk to other club members, who will usually divulge such information freely, as long as you are tactful. Most anglers will keep a little under wraps in order to protect their favourite mark from invasion, but as time goes by, friendships deepen and secrets are revealed. (You may eventually find yourself helping a newcomer to the area; would you tell you all about your favourite mark straightaway?)

In addition to local, grass-roots angling clubs are a large number of single-species clubs or societies, whose members share a passion for a particular species of fish. These clubs' priorities tend to be conserving the

species targeted by their members, supporting their members' rights and pooling experience to help to improve their members' success. If they are national bodies, they may be divided into regional clubs to ensure that local activity occurs under the umbrella of the organisation as a whole. Rather than competitions, these groups typically organise educational or social get-togethers that are often referred to as 'fish-ins'.

There are many such groups in the United Kingdom, including: the Carp Society, the Pike Anglers' Club of Great Britain, the Bass Anglers' Sport Fishing Society, the British Conger Club, the Shark Angling Club of Great Britain, the National Anguilla Club (eel anglers), the Catfish Society, the Barbel Catchers, the Lure Anglers' Society, the Wild Trout Society, the Grayling Society and the National Mullet Club. Many of these groups are affiliated to the sport's national bodies.

National and international angling bodies

Angling's national bodies are, in effect, the governors of the sport, and, as such, are involved in negotiations with governments. The United Kingdom has several such bodies, the major ones being the National Federation of Anglers, the National Federation of Sea Anglers, the Salmon and Trout Association and the Specialist Anglers' Alliance. These organisations represent anglers and try to uphold their rights in disputes with other water-users or local authorities. Legislation relating to angling methods is changed in consultation with these bodies, too. They are staffed primarily by volunteers, and only a handful of their administrators receive a wage.

There are also international angling organisations, such as the International Game Fishing Association, which keep world-record fish data, for example.

Chapter 8

The future

As the world of angling continues to evolve, fashions and fads may come and go, but it seems that little is truly new at a time when many long-forgotten techniques and baits are being rediscovered and hailed as the latest wonder. Methods and tactics for catching fish are continually being refined with the help of modern technology, but whether this is good for angling is open to debate, and, indeed, each revolutionary new angling method or item of tackle has its fans or critics – years ago, the fixed-spool reel was condemned for supposedly taking the skill out of angling, for instance. This progression is natural in any sport, be it angling, golf or tennis (and maybe you remember the wooden clubs and rackets of old). And although all sports are influenced by modern advances, their essence remains the same, and it is the attitudes and spirit of those taking part that is truly important.

So what of the future of angling? A worrying trend appears to be the lack of juniors entering the sport. This is probably partly due to the attractions of the modern world and partly due to parents' reluctance to allow their children to set off on their own to fish in an environment that they regard as being potentially dangerous. Fear of being held liable in the event of an accident, and ever-tighter controls on adults who work with children, are furthermore deterring many older anglers from helping young people to learn to fish. This is such a shame because angling is a great sport for young people, not least because it introduces them to the wonderful world of nature and gets them out into the fresh air and away from the temptations of drugs and crime.

Some people would like to see the sport of angling banned, believing that it is cruel. This debate has raged for years, and it seems that logical argument has little sway over a subject that stimulates such strong feelings. In addition, I have been an angler for most of my life and have seen many positive advances emanating from the sport. Anglers have become far more conservation-minded in recent years,

for instance. Carp and coarse anglers ensure that the fish that they catch are treated with respect and handled carefully to avoid injury. Ointments can be used to treat any marks left on fish by hooks. Unhooking mats ensure that any damage to the fish is minimal, while modern nets are made without knots to avoid removing fishes' scales and mucus. Sea anglers are also returning large numbers of fish to the sea and keeping only the occasional one for the table. And the wholesale slaughter that once comprised bag-weight sea-angling competitions is now being replaced by catch-and-release or best-specimen competitions; points systems are also being introduced to enable inedible or unwanted fish to be returned to the sea.

Anglers are often accused of leaving litter behind them at the end of a day beside the water, an accusation that is often true, but then this is a problem that is common to society in general, and not just to anglers. Many waters have been lost to anglers as a result of littering, and I strongly urge all who fish to take their litter home, as well as that left by others.

A few years ago, I would have said that one of the major threats to angling was pollution. Today, however, this is not so much the case. A greater awareness of environmental issues and the pressures on the planet has resulted in many watercourses being cleaned up, while raw-sewage discharges are becoming a problem of the past as public pressure increasingly opposes the once flagrant polluting of our waters. That having been said, pollution can still wipe out aquatic wildlife in one fell swoop; anglers are often the first to spot a potential problem, and, by reporting it promptly to the relevant authorities, have saved many waterways from destruction.

The world's ever-increasing population has led to the extraction of increasing amounts of water from the world's rivers, often with devastating effects on fish stocks, while incidents of major pollution are magnified by the lack of water available to dilute the pollutants. More positively, however, this demand for water has prompted the construction of hundreds of reservoirs, many of which provide much successful work is now being done to protect fish stocks and boost the reproduction of different species. And it is nature's way that fish stocks naturally follow cycles of fluctuating populations, and that if humankind overfishes one species, another will fill the gap that has been left. Truly wild fish will admittedly become harder to find in fresh water, but commercial fisheries will continue to thrive as we seek to escape the pressures of the modern world. In addition, many fish have no commercial value, but provide good sport for the angler.

The world still has an abundance of beautiful locations for the angler to explore. There are certainly more than enough venues and fish to keep me casting out in hope!

excellent fishing.

The world's oceans are being heavily fished to provide food and fish-based fertilisers. Sadly, political considerations, short-term greed and competition between nations, along with a lack of consideration for the future, all spell continuing grief for those who seek to catch fish from salt water. Without careful management of this trend, stocks of fish are in danger of collapsing, leading to the loss of thousands of commercial fishermen's livelihoods and, of course, the demise of the angler's quarry. By contrast, if the world's oceans were to be correctly managed, perhaps a healthy diversity of fish stocks would survive and provide both sport and food for all. In some countries, the economic value of recreational fishing has been recognised, and areas set aside to preserve stocks.

From my summary of the future thus far, you probably think that I believe it to be bleak. This is not the case, however, perhaps because, as an angler, I am an eternal optimist. We are starting to wake up to the vulnerability of our planet, and

A final message

Those who have never been fishing have little perception of what is involved in the sport, so my message to the non-participant is that fishing is fishing, that is, putting bait on a hook and attempting to catch fish. Although there is far more to angling than that, anglers would do well to remember that this definition is basically true of all branches of the sport. So before you become entrenched in your niche within angling, remember this simple truth, and do not be critical of other anglers just because they fish for a different reason than you. Match anglers who spend their time amassing bags of minnows should not condemn pike anglers who fish with a different agenda, and pike anglers should in turn respect match anglers and try to see their point of view. But if a conflict does arise, seek a compromise that keeps the peace.

I hope that I have given you a good basis for your journey into the fascinating world of angling. When I started writing this book, my friends wondered how I would find enough words to fill the pages. In reality, I have only touched the surface of what is actually a vast subject, and each branch of angling has been the subject of hundreds of books over the years. I realise that much of what I have written will be open to criticism. Right and wrong are often hard to define in angling, when methods, tackle and tactics are constantly changing, as are our moral codes and perceptions. Indeed, I may myself disagree with some of the things that I have written here and currently believe.

Whatever type of angling you opt for, remember to enjoy it. This may sound strange, but, believe me, I have met many anglers over the years who seem to have lost sight of this reason for going fishing. It may be that to enjoy success you will need to make sacrifices, fish at unsociable hours and put a lot of effort into your sport, but this will make your reward all the more enjoyable when it comes. Learn to accept unsuccessful outings philosophically, and remember that a bad day's fishing is often far superior to a good day at work!

I hope that angling brings you a rich network of friends with whom to share your days and nights by the water. As a side effect of fishing, you may find that related hobbies enter your life. Some anglers become driven by the urge to cast vast distances over grass in the sport of tournament casting, for instance, often giving up angling as this sport takes over their lives. Many fly-fishermen take up the art of fly-tying, a pastime that occupies the dark winter nights; as they create their flies, they think of warm summer nights and the places where they will cast their creations. As for me, I collect angling books and search second-hand bookshops for rare editions to grace my library; these books give me glimpses into the world of other anglers, increase my knowledge and stimulate my desire to go on further angling excursions.

Wherever angling takes you, enjoy the journey and remember to smell the flowers on the way!

Tight lines and best fishes – Wayne Thomas.

Index

A

angling clubs and organisations 492–497

angling environments 14–37

angling holidays 446–453

angling photography 482–489

B

bait 122–171

barbel 45, 57, 67, 93, 132, 137, 140, 316

bass 24, 36, 45, 46, 47, 155, 168, 173, 178, 260, 368, 371, 372, 389, 424, 429, 437, 456

 sea 186, 200, 436

beachcasting rods 48

beaches, fishing 35

bite indicators 82–85

boat-fishing 34–35

 safety 471–472

 saltwater 374–399

boat rods 52

boilies 131–135

bread, as bait for freshwater fishing 127–130

bream 24, 26, 45, 85, 93, 132, 137, 140, 233, 241, 329

brooks and streams, fishing in 14–16

C

canals, fishing in 26, 264–271

carp 24, 31, 44, 57, 67, 81, 86, 93, 118, 129, 132, 137, 140, 186, 203, 233, 241, 329, 387, 424, 431, 436, 455, 456

 fishing 75, 103, 136, 143, 243–257

carp rods 45

casting 202–213

 safety 475

catching fish 216–413

centre-pin reels 57

char 28

chub 24, 45, 130, 140, 200, 260, 316

clothing 94–98

coarse fishing 43, 125

cod 168, 178, 424

commercial pools 135

 fishing in 31

D

dace 16, 22, 43, 200

dangerous fish 476–477

disgorgers 89

E

eels 16, 144, 145, 168

 conger 89, 372, 433, 441

estuaries, fishing in 24, 37

F

feeder-fishing 325–330
fish and shellfish as bait
  freshwater 144–146
  saltwater 150–159, 165–171
fixed-spool reels 58
float, types of 77–78
float-fishing 234, 236–239
floating baits 143
float rigs 119
float rods (see match rods)
flounder 24, 45, 368, 371
fly-fishing 183–201, 222, 225–230
fly-fishing rods 55
fly, types of 193–201
food and drink 106
freshwater fishing 14–32
  bait for 122–149
  bait-fishing 222, 230–231
  canal-fishing for pike 264–271
  flies for 193–199
  float-fishing 234, 236–239, 330–331
  fly-fishing 183–201, 222, 225–230
  free-lining 234
  rivers, in 16–25, 314–331
  salmon fishing 302–313
  still water 232–239, 240–257,
    278–301
  trout streams 220–231

G

geographical features 438–441
gravel pits and quarries, fishing in 30
grayling 22, 43
groundbait
  for freshwater fishing 147
  for saltwater fishing 171

H

hook, types of 70–74
  safety 473
hooking a fish 401–413

I

inshore boat-fishing 34

K

knots 108–117

L

landing a fish 401–413
landing nets 90–92
legering 330
leger rods 44
lights 105
light values 433–436

line, types of 64–69
  safety 474
lowland lakes, fishing in 30
lunar cycle, the 427
lure-fishing 172–182, 258–271
lure rods (see spinning rods)
lure, types of 173–180

M

maggots as bait 125–126
marlin 60
match fishing 458
match rods 43
meat baits 140–142
migration 429
mullet 368
  grey 24, 45, 349, 350, 372
multiplier reels 60

O

offshore boat-fishing 35
opportunistic angling 454–457

P

particle baits 136–139
paternoster rig 118
perch 26, 28, 67, 144, 145, 173, 178,
  233, 260, 275
Nile 54, 92, 449, 452

pike 24, 26, 28, 33, 46, 47, 85, 90, 93,
  118, 119, 144, 145, 173, 199, 264,
  274, 275, 424, 431, 438, 456
  fishing 77, 264–271
pike rods (see carp rods)
poles, fishing 42
ponds and pools, fishing in 32
predators, tempting
  with live and dead baits 272–272
  with lures 258–271

Q

quiver-tip rods (see leger rods)

R

reel, types of 56–63
rigs 118–121
rivers, fishing in 16–25, 314–331
  estuaries 24
  lower reaches 24
  middle reaches 22
  upper reaches 21
roach 24, 26, 43, 44, 128, 132, 137,
  138, 200, 316, 329, 402
rocks, fishing around 37
rod, types of 39–55
rod-rests 86–87
running leger rig 118

S

safety 468–479

salmon 21, 22, 29, 45, 47, 90, 173, 183, 199, 316, 373, 410, 429, 441

fishing 302–313

saltwater fishing 33–37

bait 150–171

boat-fishing 374–399, 471–472

flies 200

shark fishing 78, 171, 392–399

shelters 103–104

seasons 33

seats 103

shark 35, 60, 89, 121, 383, 402, 412, 424, 429, 437, 441, 477

fishing 78, 171, 392–399

shelters 103–104

shore fishing 35–38, 332–373

spawning 431

spinning rods 46

still water, fishing in 27–32, 232–239, 240–257, 278–301

commercial pools 31

gravel pits and quarries 30

lowland lakes 30

ponds and pools 32

upland lakes 28

swivel, the 78–79

T

tackle 38–93

carriers 99–102

fly-fishing 191–192

tench 26, 44, 132, 137, 140, 233, 241

tides 33, 428

trout 30, 55, 137, 173, 186, 191, 315, 316

brown 14, 21, 22, 28, 199

catching 220–231, 278–301

rainbow 28, 183, 282, 431

sea 29, 198, 199, 373, 436

tuna 35, 173, 399, 408

U

unhooking mats 93

upland lakes, fishing in 28

W

wading 470

weather 418–427

weight, types of 74–75

worms

for freshwater fishing 123–125

marine 160–164

Credits and acknowledgements

I must give thanks to those who have helped in the making of this book. Over the years, I have enjoyed fishing with many anglers who have given me valuable help and inspiration. My wife, Pauline, has tolerated my many hours in pursuit of fish, and has given me much assistance in proofreading the pages of this book. My son, James, is a willing pupil in the art of fishing, and a joy to introduce to the world of angling. Through his eyes, I am fortunate to be able to relive my own formative angling experiences.

Special thanks to the following, who have given of their time and expertise: Guy Harrop: photographer; Nick Hart: fly-fishing guide and casting instructor; Hugh Parkyn: beachcasting instructor; all at Summerlands Tackle, Westward Ho; Blakewell Fisheries; Stafford Moor Fishery; and Ashley Clarke and Carl Degabrielle, for taking me boat-fishing aboard Glomar Biscay, off Lynmouth in Devon.

All photography by Guy Harrop and Wayne Thomas.